EVERY BUSINESS IS A GROWTH BUSINESS

HOW YOUR COMPANY CAN PROSPER YEAR AFTER YEAR

Ram Charan & Noel M. Tichy

THREE RIVERS PRESS • NEW YORK

We dedicate this book to
the next generation of our families—
21st century growth seekers.

Published by Three Rivers Press, New York, New York.
Member of the Crown Publishing Group.

Random House, Inc. New York, Toronto, London, Sydney, Auckland
www.randomhouse.com

THREE RIVERS PRESS is a registered trademark and the Three Rivers Press colophon is a trademark of Random House, Inc.

Originally published in hardcover by Times Books in 1998.

Printed in the United States of America

Library of Congress Cataloging-in-Publication Data
Charan, Ram.
Every business is a growth business: how your company can prosper year after year / Ram Charan and Noel M. Tichy—1st ed.
1. Organizational change. 2. Leadership. 3. Corporation—Growth. I. Tichy, Noel M. II. Title.
HD58.8.T498   1998   658.4'06—dc21   98-16201

ISBN 0-8129-3305-2

10 9 8 7 6

ACKNOWLEDGMENTS

We owe many people a great deal of gratitude for their support in making this book a reality. Our first thanks go to Charles Burck. As tearchers, we develop and share our insights face-to-face with people. Putting them on paper is a different art, for that we turned to Charles Burck. Charlie is a close listener, with a keen grasp of ideas, and a prose craftsman as well. He organized the thoughts, presentations, dialogues, and related research into a clear and logical flow. His own reporting was informed with an understanding of our principles and practices. He helped us structure our thinking with his questions and sweated the details of getting everything tied together at the end. More than a writer, he was a partner.

Other important partners in writing this book include all the business leaders who gave of their time, their trust, and their ideas. We are very grateful for their participation in this project and hope that they are well represented in the pages of the book.

This book reflects decades of teaching and consulting work by both of us around the world. We have been greatly enriched by these opportunities to stretch our own ideas and thinking. We are grateful to the many executives and MBA students we have had the privilege of working with over the years. For us, there are a few key institutions, such as General Electric, where Noel ran GE's famed leadership development institute, Crotonville, in the mid-1980s, and where Ram has taught for 25 consecutive years. Crotonville provided us with a think tank for shaping ideas on growth and transformation. In addition, the close association formed while helping many CEOs work through their transformations to achieve balanced growth shaped our ideas and teachable points of view.

In doing the research for this book, we were assisted by many business leaders who are mentioned in the book. Others who contributed as much, like Joyce Hergenhan of GE, Mark Greenberg at AlliedSignal, and Tom Momchilov at Reynolds and Reynolds, do not get the public recognition they deserve, and we thank them.

We are grateful to our academic colleagues who provided us with intellectual challenges and ideas that are reflected in this book. Professors Michael Brimm of INSEAD, Andy McGill of the University of Michigan, Larry Selden of Columbia University, Hirotaka Takeuchi of Hitotsubashi University, and Hugo Uyterhoeven of the Harvard Business School deserve special thanks.

Additional colleagues who helped shape this book are Eli Cohen and Chris DeRose, both of whom continue to provide great insights as we work in the field.

Of the team that made this book come together, J. T. Allen was key, staying on top of the research and the details and providing invaluable editing. Working closely with J. T. was Tricia Ricci. We thank them both for burning the midnight oil. Keeping the Michigan team together was Noel's administrative assistant, Launa Artz, who miraculously pulled off yet one more complex project. In Dallas, Texas, the team of Carol Davis and Elizabeth Thayer toiled to make this project a success. Thank you.

Both of us want to give special thanks to Noel's wife, Patricia Stacey, who so graciously gave up precious family time on Sundays and holidays to let us do our thing. She also provided many helpful insights to our frameworks and hypotheses.

We end our acknowledgments with thanks to one of the world's great editors, John Mahaney, who had the belief, the vision, and the perseverance to make this book something we are all proud of.

R.C.
N.M.T.

CONTENTS

P R E F A C E

Every Business Is a Growth Business is based on our combined fifty-plus years of experience in working with and learning from many of the world's best business leaders, people such as Jack Welch of General Electric, Eckhard Pfeiffer of Compaq, Larry Bossidy of AlliedSignal, John Reed of Citicorp, Alex Trotman and Jacques Nasser of Ford, Chad Holliday of DuPont, and many others.

There's one thing we've noticed that's consistent among this group of very different people in very different industries:

> They believe in and act on the idea that there's
> no such thing as a mature business.

Their companies may be in high-growth industries or those in which growth has come to a standstill. But, their companies manage to churn out double-digit growth, year after year, no matter whether the economy is in recession or on a roll. In the early part of the 1990s, for example, no part of AlliedSignal looked like a worse prospect for growth than its aerospace division. Today, while the aerospace industry is still muddled in a no-growth mode, Allied's aerospace business has been growing at a rapid clip for the past several years. How they—and others like them did it—will be explored in depth throughout this book.

Another quality we've seen time and again from our experiences with successful leaders:

> Their growth is profitable, sustainable, and capital efficient.

How often do you see stories in the business press about companies that are growing like mad but not making any money? Empty, profitless growth may even be a worse business sin than those who err by thinking that their company's business is mature. How have the leaders of Compaq—and Dell, as well—grown their businesses and made the investment in the company worth more this year than last? Relentless attention to costs, cycle time, and efficient use of capital, without which growth often ends in disaster. There is no end to the value of productivity as a business tool. It makes you more competitive and generates resources for growth. Our emphasis on the financial realities of growth is, we believe, a unique contribution of this book that you'll find in few other places.

A third quality of successful companies:

> They grow because growth is in the corporate
> mindset, created by the company's leaders.

Growth doesn't happen because managers decide to broaden the product line or spend more money on technology or beef up the salesforce or acquire another business. These and the other familiar tools and techniques for expansion are just that: tools. They are part of the execution of a growth strategy, no more.

The mindset of growth starts with an insatiable curiosity about the world's needs. It doesn't accept the limits of existing products and existing markets; it quests endlessly for new opportunities to expand beyond these artificial boundaries. In a phrase we use, it's about broadening your pond—enlarging the scope of your business activities by defining and meeting the new needs that change is always generating.

As a concept of strategy, broadening the pond is new. But it's what successful growth leaders do intuitively. Like every fundamental business truth, it is both inexorable in its power and logic yet simple once you understand it. As you read about it, you will discover that most of what you regard as "strategic planning" is obsolete.

And last, but not least:

> The mindset of growth starts at the top,
> but it must reach all the way to the bottom.

As Gary Wendt, CEO of GE Capital Services, puts it, "Business development is everybody's responsibility." Leadership—at all levels—is the key. Leaders of growth companies work as hard at transforming the thinking of their organizations as they do at anything else.

Many people think of this as changing the corporate culture, but cultural initiatives rarely produce significant change. What leaders specifically influence is *how people make decisions and work together.* These behaviors are mirrors of the leaders' own decision-making and leadership styles, and they drive culture at the most fundamental level. They become what we call the *genetic code of the organization,* a pervasive set of signals and cues that shape how people think and behave in all areas of their working lives from how they look at opportunities to how well they learn from other people.

By pinpointing for the first time the underlying determinants of culture, the concept of the genetic code lets you precisely engineer the meaningful, lasting changes that will make business development everybody's responsibility.

For those who want to build profitable growth companies, there is no single answer, no cotton candy high, no quick fix. What we are talking about is not easy. It takes a deep commitment to change on the part of leaders grounded in reality, with clear teachable points of view on growth.

In the end, it comes down to the quality of leadership—a major theme of this book. Leaders with the growth mindset and business common sense turn dying enterprises into thriving ones; conversely, when companies go off the rails, it's largely a leadership problem.

The days are gone when managers got rewarded for simply maintaining their enterprises. The bar has been raised: Today, business leaders are judged by their success or failure in achieving sustained, profitable growth. Every leader in your organization must understand that enlarging the pond, improving productivity, and making business development everybody's business are essential. You can't choose among them. Nor can you choose between achieving short-term goals and building for the long term. Staking out now for the company's future positioning—which includes training coming generations of leaders—is as crucial as earning credibility and generating resources through short-term performance.

There's no standing still. What works today probably won't work tomorrow. The most common failure of leadership is not to adapt when strategies have begun to decay or become obsolete, or when operational excellence has begun to decline. And the ultimate test of leaders is their ability to build an organization that continues to adapt and grow after they are gone.

P A R T

Why Every Business Can Be a Growth Business

CHAPTER

*T*hinking Clearly About Growth

*I*n mid-1997, we were talking with a group of Ford Motor Company's top people about how to grow profitably. It was the second day of a six-month senior executive leadership development program launched by CEO Alex Trotman. We had designed a program that would help them to think about new ways to create shareholder value, and to develop leadership skills that they, in turn, could pass on to the rest of the organization. Later stages of the program would reach throughout the company.

Ford has transformed itself heroically over the past decade—cutting costs, raising quality, reducing cycle time, and making good money, especially with its highly profitable trucks and sport utility vehicles. In the segments that count, it is a market leader.

But leader of what? The auto industry is considered mature: it has tough competitors, increasing worldwide overcapacity, and viciously cyclical demand. No company playing the established game can hope to grow profitably and sustainably much faster than the broad economic growth rates in its markets. Trotman knew that the successful present was already history; in the future, he was sure, Ford had to do something different. He was determined to transform his company into one that could grow and make money reliably in the twenty-first century.

Alex Trotman knew he needed more than a game plan. Ford's people were terrific at playing the old game—and that was part of the problem. Whatever the new game might be, it would require a whole new way of defining opportunities. Everybody at Ford would have to learn how to think differently.

The leadership development program was a beginning. Trotman and his executive committee aimed to do nothing less than develop a generation of leaders who could escape from the company's old view of the

3

business. In this first stage, we were working with two dozen "high-potential" executives chosen by top management to team up and develop proposals for everything from lowering fixed costs and finding new growth to exercising corporate citizenship. Trotman was with us for this early morning session, awaiting his turn to work with them as teacher and coach.

Trotman was listening carefully but quietly. Suddenly he began scribbling notes. What had caught his attention was a favorite story of ours—how the late Roberto Goizueta transformed Coca-Cola in the early eighties.

Most people have forgotten just how bad Coca-Cola looked when Goizueta took over. At the time, the company dominated the U.S. soft-drink market, with roughly a 35 percent share[1], and everyone *knew* the market was mature. The game involved fighting for tenths of a percent of market share—at exorbitant cost to the bottom line—or defending each tenth of a percent, since PepsiCo was kicking Coca-Cola's can in marketing. Security analysts and business writers were all but composing its obituary.

Goizueta didn't buy it. But how does one break the mindset of a mature business—the deeply ingrained set of beliefs that circumscribes everyone's thinking and hopes, dulling their minds and imaginations? His company was full of talented people butting their heads against a stone wall—the inexorable logic of squeezing out drops of market share in a zero-sum game.

Goizueta had an insight—a simple but stunningly powerful one that he shared with his senior executives in the 1980s. What, he asked almost casually, was the average per-capita daily consumption of fluids by the world's 4.4 billion people? The answer was: 64 ounces. And what, he asked, is the daily per-capita consumption of Coca-Cola? Answer: Less than 2 ounces.

Finally, he asked: What's our market share of the stomach? Not Coca-Cola's share of the U.S. cola market or the world soft-drink market, but of all the fluids everyone in the world drinks on a given day. Coca-Cola's share was scarcely measurable.

Coca-Cola's people had invested a lot in the idea of PepsiCo as their enemy. But Goizueta led them to see that the enemy was coffee, milk, tea. The enemy was water.

With a few simple questions, Goizueta redefined Coca-Cola's market to be vaster than anybody had imagined. And he changed the psychology of its people. They saw that their company was not a large fish constrained in a small pond, but a small fish in a huge pond. Rather than facing the depressing chore of struggling to not lose more fractions of market share, they could set their sights on winning a larger share of a huge opportunity.

Obvious? Yes—but not until Goizueta pointed it out. It was the beginning of Coca-Cola's transformation from a threatened leader in a mature business to the greatest market value creator ever. (Goizueta's stockholdings at the time of his death were worth over $1 billion, making him the first "hired hand," or nonfounding head of a company, to become a billionaire.)[2] PepsiCo, the comer when Goizueta took over, is no longer in the same league.

After our presentation, the leaders—Ford executives from around the world, from all functions—broke into groups to work on the growth exercises. Gathered at four round tables, six people to a table, they were teaming up for an hour to start developing the new ideas and strategies that they would eventually present to top management as actionable plans.

Trotman started the session by telling the assembled teams: "We have to have quality. We have to have low costs, and we have to get to the market faster. We have to satisfy our customers. But that's not enough.

"We have to become innovative. We have to find new trajectories of profitable growth.

"This is what I want you all to think about: What is Ford's *water?*"

As Trotman moved from table to table, asking questions, listening, engaging in informal dialogue, he was totally immersed in the energy and excitement that filled the room.

That's something we observe every time. When people shift from talking about holding the fort and cutting costs to talking about growth, they come alive.

Once again, a simple question redefined how a company's leaders could and should look at their opportunities and possibilities. In the months that followed, Ford's executive groups met and worked through long weekends, simultaneously developing their leadership skills and a new view of the possible.

First, they took a hard and realistic look at the limits of their traditional business. In terms of a vehicle's lifetime usage and total cost, the company's value added is less than 15 percent. Profit margins are typically less than 4 percent—about the same as the grocery business, but with only a fraction of the inventory turns. Moreover, the cyclicality of the business causes automakers' balance sheets to take a terrible beating during recessions; as earnings tank, they usually have to borrow money. So even though they're big and their products are permanently in demand, returns on investment are mediocre, and the relative valuation of their stocks is among the lowest on the market. Automakers' p/e ratios are typically well under half those of the S&P 500.[3]

Next, the executives stepped outside of the box—away from their customary ways of looking at their businesses and markets—to expand their view of the possible. Over the life of a vehicle, consumers' major expenditures are for financing, maintenance and repair, and all of the other services associated with use and ownership. Such opportunities for lucrative growth amount to the best part of a vehicle's full profit potential. Profit margins are much higher, and capital intensiveness is lower. These after-purchase businesses are dramatically less cyclical than manufacturing.

And so they came up with Ford's water: the lifetime use of the product, including all of those other associated services. Ford's challenge now is to identify the likeliest ports of entry to this richer territory.

It's too soon yet to know what will happen. An enormous amount of hard work and radical change lies ahead, not only for the company's leaders but also for every Ford employee. Formerly, their careers were steeped in a certain inevitability—the limits to growth, the poor returns, cyclical downturns, and underperforming stock. Such long-held ways of thinking die hard. But the leaders have taken the critical first steps away from muddling along in a mature industry and toward coming alive with growth prospects. They are identifying opportunities, developing criteria, and selecting the avenues for profitable growth.

Growth is a hot topic today. Business leaders who have been through the wringers of repetitive downsizing, reengineering, and all the rest, are discovering that they must now focus not only on operational excellence but also on growth. Incremental market-share gains won't secure a future for their companies. There's nowhere else to go now; literally, they either grow or die.

There are five crucial points to the story above. They're what this book is all about, and they set it apart from anything else you'll read or hear about creating growth opportunities for your company. They are the hidden secrets behind many familiar success stories. When you understand them, you will have a *real* understanding of how, say, a GE or a Coca-Cola or a Compaq grows. These crucial points are:

1. **There's no such thing as a mature business**. Get the ideas about mature businesses out of your mind forever. Any company of any size in any industry—no matter how "mature" the industry—can grow, once its leaders learn how to look beyond their traditional definitions of industry and markets.

2. **Not all growth is good**. Growth at all costs, or growth for its own sake, can be a recipe for disaster. Good growth is sustainable, profitable, and capital efficient; don't confuse it with feverish spurts of volume that ravage earnings or steal from the future.

3. **Growth is a mentality created by a company's leadership**. It starts with the spark of a new point of view, and it catches fire when everyone buys into what the leaders are teaching and coaching.

4. **Balanced growth is the key to prosperity in the twenty-first century**. Sustainable growth—growth for the long haul—requires meticulous attention to the basics: cost structure, quality, product development cycle time, productivity, asset utilization, investment of capital, supply chain innovation, customer service satisfaction, and all the other components of operational excellence. Neverending focus on these generates the resources for growth.

5. **Growing is less risky than not growing**. You'll hear people say that growth is about taking risks, but they're wrong. Personal risks, yes; it takes courage to stand up for new ideas. But a sustainable growth strategy, based on tightly defined customer needs, is far less risky than rearranging the furniture while a competitor grows at your expense.

This book challenges you as a leader to develop a clear point of view about growth, and to make it a part of your company's genetic code—a concept we'll elaborate on later in the book.

The lessons and principles are universal. We talk mainly about big, complex corporations because that's where we've gotten most of our experience. But what we've learned is invaluable for companies of all sizes and in all stages: small or large, publicly or privately held; not growing but needing to grow, or growing now but needing ways to sustain growth.

The principles are the same; in general, so are the practices. Even leaders of nonprofits will find the thinking and tools offered here valuable in focusing, energizing, and strengthening their organizations.

We're not giving you yet another potpourri of tactics, strategies, slogans, and convenient examples, nor a theoretical view from 50,000 feet. This book is reality-based; it is a journey to the very roots of the corporate psyche and human behavior. It brings together the best practices and ideas within a new framework forged from our combined fifty years of experience working with companies struggling to change.

Our central theme is common sense, a much-abused term. People tend to dismiss it as too subjective to take seriously. Or, they confuse it with conventional wisdom, which, because it looks to the past, usually is not commonsensical at all. Common sense is very uncommon.

Yet there *is* a business common sense, and it informs the views and actions of all true businesspeople, whether they run giant corporations or trinket stands in the third world. Roberto Goizueta literally urged his people to act with "the common sense of a shopkeeper."

We offer two original, fundamental, and common sense insights into the secret of creating and perpetuating a growth company:

1. Our fresh approach to strategic thinking cuts through the muddle of conventional planning to provide a clear path for identifying market opportunities. We call it *strategy from the outside in*.

2. The distinction between growth companies and also-rans starts with leadership. Growth companies' leaders create operating mechanisms, behaviors, attitudes, and dialogues so deeply ingrained in the corporate psyche that we liken them to a genetic code. For the new growth strategy to work, *changing the genetic code* is essential.

Chapters 4 and 9 explain these insights in detail. For now, here's the short form.

Strategy from the Outside In

Growing is a creative game. It doesn't require a degree or a license. It requires curiosity, imagination, and emotional energy—qualities that exist, and even abound, among the people working in most companies today.

They may not be visible, but enormous amounts of dormant creative potential flower in the companies we see—once the leadership frees them up.

A sustainable growth strategy starts with understanding the difference between what you make and what people need—which often turn out not to be the same thing. Tapping your sources of energy and imagination, you look at your company from the perspective of your once and future customers, and asking endless questions about what's going on in the real world. What's happening in your marketplace? How are needs changing? What's causing the changes? Where are the resulting opportunities?

Having stepped outside of your business, you then work backward to ask such questions as: What needs do we satisfy now? What needs *could* we satisfy now? In the future? What's the gap between them and what we do now, and how do we bridge it? What advantages do we have? What advantages do we need to create? What old competencies do we need to deemphasize?

That's called looking from the outside in. Sound simple and obvious? Then probably your company is doing it already. The fact is, it's human nature to look from the inside out. Astonishingly few companies ever try to see themselves as others see them.

In what we call an inside-out company, people typically look at their business environment through the lens of their internal products and processes. They look at what they make, and try to figure out how they can sell more of it. If there's no way to sell more, they look for something to sell that's visibly in higher demand. These companies and their people are trapped in their own past and experience. Looking from the inside out, they see mainly that they are stuck in industries and core competencies that have limited prospects.

In the outside-in company, the key word is *need*, not *product*. Its people are not focusing on getting half a point of market share; they're totally immersed in the minds of their customers, looking for ways to *expand demand*. Their business plans and value propositions derive from the marketplace, based on knowledge gathered at ground level. Often, the needs they define haven't yet been identified by the customers themselves.

This is real world strategic thinking. It is both imaginative and highly disciplined. And it has never been more important than now. In this era of unparalleled change and opportunity, the profitable growth will go to the companies whose leaders can see the possibilities beyond their traditional served markets. In the remaining chapters of Part I, you'll see how outside-in thinking transforms businesses that are "mature," "commoditized," or otherwise supposedly without growth prospects.

People in outside-in companies think expansively. They are, in a phrase we use regularly, broadening the ponds they fish in. They focus not on how much they're improving, but on what portion of wealth creation they're missing, and how they can enlarge the market itself. They want an ever bigger share of each customer's wallet; they look for ways to offer the customer more (and more profitable) products and retain the customer longer.

The process is circular: growth energizes people. If you are fighting for gains on the right side of the decimal point—the tiny increments that seem to be your only opportunities for growth—it's hard to be imaginative and energetic. In fact, it's hard to feel really good about what you do. To how many people at a cocktail party would you say, "I work for a mature business . . ."?

What energizes people is the broader horizon, the excitement of new challenges and big opportunities. When their leaders offer this excitement, people come alive.

Changing the Genetic Code

Your outside-in strategy will bring a whole new way of looking at your business—a new mindset. But the mindset doesn't flow automatically out of the strategy. You must first set your mind to host certain patterns of thinking and behavior. If you've been focusing on restructuring, cost cutting, trench warfare over market share, and all the rest, you have precisely the *wrong* mindset for enlarging ponds. So do all of your people. You must be ready to articulate a new point of view that you can teach to the others.

We cannot overstate the importance of confronting this issue head-on. People tend to be heavily invested in the past; it has determined their rewards, their career paths, even their identities. Left untouched, old reflexive behaviors will defy any new direction imposed from above.

You could call these embedded behaviors part of a company's *culture*. This term includes all of the well-known intangibles that powerfully shape organizational behavior: basic assumptions, expectations, values, myths, and the like. But how do you get your hands on the levers that change them? For the past decade, companies have launched thousands of cultural change initiatives, most to little avail.

We view culture as a dependent variable, and we use the concept of the genetic code as a way of focusing on the underlying determinant. The concept draws on the "nature versus nurture" debate long argued in the biological and behavioral sciences. Cultural change, promulgated through training, coaching, and workshops, represents a nurture intervention designed to reshape an organization's behaviors. But the genetic code is nature, and—in organizations, at least—it is the more powerful determinant. It shapes corporate culture at the most fundamental level, because it specifically decrees *how people make decisions* and *how they work together.*

The code originates with the organization's leaders—their thinking and behavior send signals and cues that set the pattern for everyone else. In time, these become the organizational genetic code. And this code is all-pervasive. As in a biological organism, the genetic code's signals direct what the body does, no matter how the brain might try to contradict them. They influence how people think and behave in all areas of their working lives, from how they look at opportunities to what kinds of working relationships they form with other people. They determine which ideas fly and which ones sink; who gets promoted and who gets ignored. In the end, they determine whether the corporation succeeds or fails.

So real and lasting change can come only from fundamentally re-engineering the genetic code. Doing so is just as important as devising your growth strategy. In fact, it's part of the strategy, because it determines what the strategy will be and whether it will work.

The Critical Role of the Leader

Changing the genetic code is a major challenge for an organization's leaders. The old code embodies the thinking of past leadership, and its inertia is amazingly powerful. The new code has to be consciously created by leaders who aim to transform their organizations. This will require either new leaders, such as Larry Bossidy at AlliedSignal, Eckhard Pfeiffer at Compaq, and Dave Holmes at Reynolds and Reynolds— or strong leaders who can fundamentally change the definition of the organizations, as Jack Welch did recently in defining GE as a global service company.

When Alex Trotman launched his plan for transforming Ford, it was no accident that he focused on leadership. His goal was to create, at all levels, leaders who could change the embedded beliefs and spread the new ones throughout the entire organization. Jacques Nasser, president of Ford Automotive Operations, took charge of training the top 200 leaders in his organization to think differently about growth and about creating shareholder value—and to train, in turn, the 5,000 managers below them. In 1998, Ford's top 1,000 leaders were made responsible for teaching the same ideas and values to all 53,000[4] of the company's salaried employees.

Noel Tichy wrote, in his book *The Leadership Engine:*[5] "Winning companies win because they have good leaders who nurture the development of other leaders at all levels of the organization." Good leaders possess *a teachable point of view*, which includes:

1. **Ideas** based on clear knowledge of what it takes to win in the marketplace and how the organization should operate.

2. **Values** that support the business ideas and that everyone in the organization understands and lives up to.

3. **Emotional energy** that drives the leaders themselves and is actively communicated to create positive emotional energy in others.

4. **Edge**, the leader's ability to face reality and to champion tough decisions about products, investments, and people.

In growth companies, the leaders' teachable points of view revolve around grasping opportunity and creating value. These become the genetic code of the organization, once they are shared and deeply ingrained among the critical mass of leaders at all levels.

Leaders aiming to transform their companies into growth engines may have to start by changing their own points of view. Alex Trotman had to shed some long-held beliefs about growth. Those beliefs were born of hard experience in an industry where expansion inevitably led to overproduction, cyclical collapses, and huge financial losses and layoffs. To his immense credit, he was able to look beyond the conventional wisdom of his industry and see creative new possibilities for growth.

A lot of people don't have that kind of vision. Often, a company's top leaders and designated successors are so trapped in the old genetic code that new leaders have to be imported—leaders whose fresh insights and perspectives will make change possible.

Some organizations have found great potential leaders in unexpected places. Jack Welch at GE, Roberto Goizueta at Coca-Cola, and Eckhard Pfeiffer at Compaq were rogue genes in terms of their companies' old genetic codes. Welch was in the plastics business, away from the mainstream; Goizueta was a Cuban immigrant who rose through the technical side of a company historically headed by marketers; and Pfeiffer came from Compaq's European operations.

Developing Your Own Teachable Point of View

Growth company leaders are people like you. They face and struggle with the same challenges and opportunities, and they put their careers on the line to transform their organizations. We can't repeat this often enough: *They are leaders at all levels.* Like Goizueta, they have teachable points of view—earned wisdom that they can impart so that others can develop their own teachable points of view.

They may not use the genetic code metaphor (though more and more are starting to do so), but they intuitively understand its usefulness. Through their teachable points of view, they transform the genetic code into a replica of their own mental architecture.

You'll notice that, whenever possible, we try to avoid talking about what "companies" do. We talk about what leaders do, and what people do. This is no small distinction. Organizations don't do things, people do. We always admired the old British practice of referring to companies as "they," not "it" (as in "Glaxo have raised their earnings . . ."), for this seemed to us to implicitly recognize the distinction. Alas, in recent years, the British seem to have adopted American anthropomorphism; Glaxo, Grand Met, and all the rest are now "its," like GM or IBM. We would have preferred the other way around.

In fact, we think that the common practice of personifying the organization is positively dangerous. It feeds into the victim mentality: "It's not me, it's the system." We've never heard Andy Grove or Jack Welch or Eckhard Pfeiffer talk about being victims of the system. Real leaders, at any level in an organization, control their own destiny. They use their teachable points of view to change the system, i.e., the genetic code.

After you read this book, we want you to come away from it a leader able to develop your own teachable point of view. This means learning from the experience of others, taking ownership of it, and using it to help others to lead. We want you to have clearly articulated ideas that you can communicate to people in your own company and in outside companies. Your customers, suppliers, and shareholders—and their proxies, the securities analysts—need to hear your point of view. So do the people you want to hire. A persuasive and realistic growth story is the key to attracting and energizing the best employees.

The ideas, principles, and practices explained here run the gamut from identifying marketplace needs to developing incentive systems. All are field-tested; other executives and managers are using them to build powerful growth companies. (Your closest competitor may be among those already using them.) They're flexible—you can adapt them to your own requirements. And as you come to understand them, you will doubtless invent some of your own.

Some are new, others are familiar. It's the viewpoint that's radical—the framework that links them and synchronizes them to energize people, change their focus, and realign their thinking and behavior. Used together, they give you the power to do things you've never done before.

You'll see some unfamiliar words and phrases. People applying any new management concept such as reengineering develop a specific language to pinpoint what's different and to give immediacy to ideas. For example, growth companies focus their thinking about growing the market with such phrases as "broadening the pond" or "getting a bigger share of the customer's wallet." (Conversely, if they talk about a "mature" market, it's with a derisive curl of the lip.) We've borrowed some of the language of growth from companies where it's in common use; other vocabulary we have created ourselves.

We hope that as you read this book you will say repeatedly: "Aha! That's simple. That's obvious." The simple is not always simple, and the obvious is not obvious until it hits you. Any good idea can be stated plainly. But simplicity, like common sense, gets short shrift in the organizational world. Too often, an insight or truth is veiled in so much complexity that nobody can see it. A convoluted presentation is sometimes deliberate; people are afraid that, in being simple, they will seem simpleminded.

Aim for simplicity and clarity in your own efforts to lead change, but be aware that understanding complexity and making it simple is hard work. You'll be most successful in getting new ideas across to your associates if you can peel away the outer layers and serve up the clear truth in the center. Making things simple is one of the great strengths of a true leader. As AlliedSignal CEO Larry Bossidy puts it: "Complexity is not the sign of an intellectual gift. Making things simple is."[6]

One final note: People don't live happily ever after unless they keep working at it. New problems arise, systems and approaches that worked in the past pump out red ink, and suddenly yesterday's king of the hill is today's dinosaur.

In 1981, when Coca-Cola was awakening to infinite possibilities, PepsiCo was the company to beat. For four decades, PepsiCo led the FORTUNE 500 in top-line growth, setting an unequaled record.[7] But PepsiCo lost its way in recent years, and CEO Roger Enrico is struggling to get it back on track. In later chapters, we'll give examples of companies that got into trouble when leaders who had done the right thing for years took their hands off the steering wheel.

Frankly, there's no guarantee that the companies we hold up as shining examples today will continue to ascend. Just as no market is permanent, no strategy is immune to becoming obsolete or irrelevant. Any company's genetic code has to encourage continual questioning of the status quo, constant challenges to existing assumptions.

And no strategy will succeed without good execution. Chapter Six describes how Eckhardt Pfeiffer transformed Compaq from a failing company into one of the most powerful players in its industry. His strategy was undeniably brilliant. Yet in March of 1999, Pfeiffer was forced out after Compaq's earnings plunged—because his strategic ambitions had gotten ahead of the company's ability to execute.

You can start to challenge your own assumptions right now. Are you proud of your dominant market share? If so, wipe the smile off your face and rethink your opportunities. Change your organization's point of view. What is the bigger pond of which your share is minuscule? AT&T, for example, has nearly 50 percent of the American long-distance telephone market[9], but is that its pond? Or is its pond the global market for voice, data, and video transmission and other related services? Chase is the biggest U.S. bank measured by assets[10], and a merged NationsBank and Bank of America would be the biggest in terms of deposits[11], but what does that mean? Are banks fishing in the banking industry, or is their pond the global market for financial services?

The ultimate secret of sustainable growth is the secret of life itself—permanent change and constant adaptation to the ever-changing external environment. Don't forget it for a moment.

The change begins in these pages. This book gives you the power to look from the outside in, and expand your horizons, opportunities, and capabilities. You are holding in your hands the ideas, tools, and techniques for making your company grow profitably. This is the most exciting transformation you can imagine. Unlike cost-cutting, which is most often defensive, growth is energizing. As you grow, your people will grow—and they are the ultimate competitive advantage.

There's No Such Thing as a Mature Business

> *"Your bias as a leader can't be for stability, predictability, for policy conformance. The passion of leadership has to be to grow a business. You just have to wake up every day thinking about how you are going to grow it."*
>
> Dan Burnham, CEO, AlliedSignal Aerospace[1]

> *"Growing your way to success is a lot more fun than cutting your way to success."*
>
> Tom Dunham, Vice President, GE Medical Systems[2]

> *"When the headhunter came to me, I wasn't interested in leaving. My father had worked for the company, my wife worked for it, and I'd spent my whole career there. But we were cutting back; it wasn't what it used to be. So I went to look at Reynolds and Reynolds. I spent a day talking to people. The difference was like night and day; I saw it immediately. They were growth-oriented. There was freedom. Everybody was rooting for everybody else. Nobody was trying to stab anybody in the back.*

> *"I got home and said to my wife, 'These people seem to have a whole different outlook on life. And I want to be part of it.'"*
>
> Pete Granson, Senior Vice President, The Reynolds and Reynolds Company[3]

What distinguishes companies that grow from companies that can't grow? It's not the businesses they're in—there are losers in growth industries or markets, and winners in declining ones. It's not the tactics they use. More than anything, it's a state of mind.

Whether they're high-tech entrepreneurs or the leaders of old-line industrial corporations, the leaders of growing companies wake up every morning thinking about growth. They are men and women with imagination and curiosity. They ceaselessly look for opportunities; when they spot them, they define the risk, develop the new skills needed to exploit them, and abandon earlier opportunities that are no longer relevant.

They are creators and builders of wealth. They don't sit around congratulating themselves when their business is number one in its market; instead, they look for ways to build share in markets far bigger than the ones they now serve. Great growth leaders want to grow the whole market—and grab 100 percent of the growth for themselves, if they can.

They're after a bigger share of the value creation; they look for ways to capture more—as we put it—of the consumer's total wallet. They deliberately plan how to retain customers longer and more profitably.

But they seek only *profitable, capital efficient* growth. When they acquire, it's to leverage their ability to add value, not for the sake of size alone. When they talk about creating shareholder value, they truly aim to increase return on investment. Their yardstick for success is the approval of the financial markets, as reflected in a rising price/earnings ratio for their stock.

Growth is in their mental architecture. It's how they're wired.

And it's their teachable point of view. These leaders energize their people with the same restless ambition, teaching them to build and look for new opportunities. In the daily dialogues everywhere in their companies, the loudest decibels are about growing.

Do You Work for a Growth Company?

Is growth the passion of your company's leadership? Are the daily dialogues about change and opportunity?

Or are you frustrated because you can't find a way to grow your business profitably? Are you wrestling with how to create shareholder value while margins are declining, and have you realized that cost cutting alone won't take you there? Do you catch yourself saying, "My business is mature?" You're not alone.

Every great or once-great corporation started as a growth company. Yet growth eludes many companies today. For every profitably growing Procter & Gamble or Compaq or GE, there's a faltering Kmart, a shrunken Apple, a disappearing Westinghouse. As Morgan Stanley chief economist Stephen Roach observed, "Corporate America has gotten very good at focusing on operational effectiveness, but in doing that, it has dropped the ball on sustainable growth."[4]

For too many corporate leaders, growth is not a natural state of mind. Again and again, we hear the lamentations of CEOs and other leaders of companies that have stopped growing. Here are some recurring themes drawn from our conversations with them:

"We have gone through three writeoffs since I became CEO— we seem to be doing it every other year, and it has eaten the fabric of the company. We had to buckle down and reduce costs, conserve cash, and rationalize capacity. But while our people are very good in cost cutting now—they're good people to save a company—I wonder whether they know how to grow. I worry that most of my leaders down the line don't have the mindset and skills to spot opportunities, or the imagination and willingness to take risks. I know they don't have the tools, and I'm pretty sure some of them don't have the skills. They are essentially inwardly focused."

"We know that we must grow. We talk about the desirability of growth all the time. But our business is mature. Any growth is going to come through expensive competition for market share. Margins are already declining. Acquiring is uneconomical and downright dilutive—the prices are sky-high these days. Most alliances do not work. Going to emerging countries is risky; our people don't know how to build businesses there. We're totally frustrated; we just don't know what to do."

"We designed incentive systems to reward people for growing the bottom line—no matter how they got it. But we never factored in top-line growth. Now we have only a few people left who are oriented toward top-line growth. The balance is missing; how can we restore it?"

"In the late eighties, we learned the concept of core competencies—focusing on the things you do well, sticking to your knitting, all that. It saved a lot of overdiversified companies, ours included, from going over the cliff. Frankly, we were in businesses we should never have been in—businesses we didn't understand, and where we had no competitive advantage. But that was then. Now it's

clear we're living in a world of discontinuities, where whole industries are changing and becoming unrecognizable—even disappearing. Nobody can visualize all of the opportunities out there."

"If the limit of our psychology is to look only at those opportunities that intersect with our existing core competencies, we are going to miss the boat. What new core competencies do we need? How can we get them, master them, and transition into a new competitive space?"

"The senior executive group told me recently they want more. They're asking me to grow the top line as well as the bottom line. But demand isn't growing. The competition is global, and it is intense. I have done a really good job during my 30 years here, and my business unit has been very profitable under my leadership. But I don't know how to do this, and I don't think it is reasonable of them to ask me to do it. I told them that maybe it's time for them to replace me."

The Era of Unequaled Opportunities

Growth shouldn't be so difficult. Things were different a couple of decades ago, when fashionable thinkers were explaining why an age of shrinking possibilities lay ahead. Today, a global economy is taking shape. It is so unlike anything in the past that people increasingly call it "the new economy," and it promises opportunities unequaled in all of human history. World trade is growing at more than four times the rate of world gross domestic product (GDP).[5] Expectations are rising everywhere; human creativity is flowering in every field. Emerging economies are industrializing, and everyone is joining the digital revolution of boundless information and seamless electronic commerce. The ideas, technologies, and capital to satisfy new needs flow freely.

The new economy will have setbacks and crises, just like the old one. But the evidence strongly suggests that, over the longer term, we are in an extraordinary era of growth akin to those that were catalyzed by the steam engine, electricity, the internal combustion engine, telephony, and airplanes. Changing circumstances and new technologies changed the world profoundly in the past. None of these produced trouble-free economies, of course, but they all created opportunities previously undreamed of. Microprocessors are among such technologies, and only now are they beginning to achieve their full potential for transformation. Economic historian Paul David, of Stanford University, judges that, in terms of its impact on society, computer technology today is about where electricity was in 1900—roughly halfway to its peak.[6]

Growth eras have some characteristics in common. They produce huge discontinuities, create new industries and destroy old ones, and accelerate global economic growth in the process. The combination of the personal computer (PC), packaged consumer software, the Internet, deregulation, and globalization is creating the mother of all discontinuities.

Change brings opportunity to those who can grasp it, and the discontinuities of the new economy offer unlimited opportunities. Because the growth is based increasingly on knowledge, not on hardware, it offers unprecedented ease of entry—especially through the Internet. No company, however big, has more than a minuscule share of the endlessly evolving growth markets. Any company, no matter how small, can reach out to catch the attention of a liberated global consumer—an Italian entrepreneur, a newly escalated middle-class Mexican family, or a software designer living in a hut in Bangalore, India.

Resisting the Tide

Why aren't people in companies everywhere excited about the possibilities? Too many businesspeople have difficulty seeing the opportunities for growth that are all around them. They may lack the imagination or the creativity to envision what could be, as opposed to what already is. Their gazes are turned inward; their energies are consumed with doing business as usual. Some may be so ecstatic or complacent about being number one in their market that they can't think about anything else.

Or, they may be frightened. Change can be emotionally wrenching—even terrifying. When leaders present their organizations with the prospect of radical change, the first reactions they're likely to notice (if they're paying attention) are fear and anger, perhaps cloaked as skepticism, and stubborn resistance to the new. People worry about losing power, about having to unlearn all the things they've learned before, about facing new uncertainties. They must deal with feelings of deep loss as the old ways and the familiar products begin to disappear.

A certain amount of fear can be useful—if it's the kind of fear that mobilizes people to action. Resistance tends to melt in a crisis; change may be frightening, but the alternative is worse. In the absence of crisis, leaders can cultivate a healthy fear about what could happen if change imposed from outside were to overtake the organization. As Intel Chairman Andy Grove says, "Only the paranoid survive."

When people are finally freed from the devil they know, it's a whole new world. When we're not scared, or when we're driven by healthy paranoia rather than paralytic gloom, there's nothing more exciting than change and growth. Growth is humanity's energizer, the source of all progress. As individuals, we look for new ways to expand our capacities. As parents, we take joy in our children's growth. As societies, we seek to expand wealth, however defined, so that all may share in it.

In organizations, we thrive personally as our enterprise thrives. When new ideas and challenges become routine, we look for more that's new—wider horizons, bigger stakes, new tests of courage and imagination, a higher bar to challenge our vaulting skills.

If Your Business Is Not Growing, You're Dying

If your business isn't growing, your people are denied the joy of growth in their work. In this central part of their lives, they are quietly dying. The best will get out when they can, and the business will lose the very talents it needs to live and grow.

What should scare people is the prospect of *not* changing. A company that can't grow is an accident waiting to happen. The strength of the economy has made almost everybody look good during much of the nineties. But so did the inflation of the seventies, with its illusory revenue and profit gains. When the reckoning came, it was brutal. As this book went to press, companies in scores of industries were struggling to learn the new rules of a game that has been changed dramatically by deflation and disinflation.[7]

The global economy can steam into an iceberg at any time, and the next downturn will batter companies that do not have sustainable, profitable growth. Many won't be around for the subsequent expansion. The survivors will be the companies, at home and abroad, whose leaders understand the secrets of growing profitably.

These are the facts of life that face you today if your business has no top-line growth prospects:

1. **Your markets are at risk**. No matter how good you are, your marketplace is not safe anymore. Powerful, growth-hungry companies—companies you may not even identify as competitors today—are moving in on it. When they arrive, they will meet your customers' needs better than you can. Do nothing until they attack, and you'll be starting too late to catch up.

2. **Your market valuation is at risk**. Investors—whether a public company's stockholders or a private company's bankers—won't settle for only cost-cutting gains; they'll want to see increased earnings from growth as well. Research by our colleague Larry Selden, a professor at Columbia University, shows that revenue growth and return on assets correlate more closely than any other variables with stock price performance.[8]

3. **Your human capital is at risk.** If you aren't growing, you cannot attract and keep the people you need—the ones with confidence, enthusiasm, ambition, imagination, and ideas. They're looking for companies with expanding horizons. We hear stories almost daily about slow-growing companies that have lost out to someone else in recruiting new talent.

Who Dropped the Ball, and Why

To understand why so many business leaders lack the will and skill to grow their companies, we need to briefly review the recent history of corporate upheavals.

The great post-World War II expansion era, in which growth came easily and naturally for almost everybody, trailed off in the sixties and ended with a whimper amid the oil shocks and inflation of the seventies. In the zero-sum mindset that followed, growth became a game played by financial engineers, who put together conglomerates and other portfolio companies of diversified businesses. It was paper growth; the numbers men did not have the operating knowledge needed to manage and truly grow businesses they didn't understand. In the eighties, when new foreign competition arose—first from the Japanese, who utilized cheap financing and brilliant operating skills, and then from other Asian nations—entire American industries, such as autos, found themselves in deep trouble.

Downsizing and restructuring were necessary remedies during three decades or more of accumulated management myopia and incompetence. Business leaders finally got down to the nuts and bolts of running their companies: developing and strengthening core businesses, lifting quality and productivity, and squeezing out waste and layers of excess managers. Focusing on their known strengths and markets, they created lean, flexible, competitive organizations. Companies that successfully executed process reengineering, total quality, team building, and the like, dramatically improved the quality of their organization's daily operations and decision making.

The companies that are ahead today are those whose leaders were simultaneously lifting productivity and looking for growth opportunities. From the time Jack Welch took charge of GE in 1981, he was changing the mix of businesses, sharpening the focus, redeploying assets, and driving uncompromisingly for speed and higher productivity. But he was also consciously creating the foundations for growth.

Such leaders are the exceptions. The great wave of slashing and squeezing was the creative destruction of capitalism at its best and worst. Far too often, downsizing was done badly and unimaginatively. Obsessed with the bottom line, the downsizers gave growth short shrift. Even Emerson Electric's Chuck Knight, who set records for earnings per share growth, confessed in the mid-nineties that he had focused too long on cost reductions and not enough on top-line growth.[9]

Repetitive shrinking squeezes the life out of companies. Managers who must, above all else, make their numbers or fill their quotas rob the future to feed the present. Along with all excess baggage, out go the people with ideas, imagination, and expansive vision. The survivors are those who know how not to make waves—people whose skills and mindsets are suited only to milling away ever-finer layers of cost.

The survivors are usually exhausted, scared, and cynical. Just as bad management destroys shareholder equity, recurrent downsizing ravages *emotional equity*™, a term that sums up the alignment of employees with their company and its goals—the psychic energy, the trust, the willingness to follow the leaders eagerly and give 110 percent to the effort.

The leaders themselves are typically in no shape to lead a growth charge anyway. They have spent the recent past—maybe their prime career years—cutting costs and downsizing. They, and most of their subordinates, are stuck in old ways of thinking. They've learned to build on what they have—their core competencies—rather than reach out for anything new. Change seems too risky; often, they've lost touch with the consumer channels and other pipelines to the marketplace that would show them the change that's going on all around them. Even when new ideas rise from the bottom up, these leaders haven't built any process for weighing and selecting them.

The "Mature Market" Trap

Trouble starts with the way business leaders think about their business prospects. Consider the term mature market. AlliedSignal CEO Larry Bossidy has a short rejoinder for any executive who uses it: "There's no such thing as a mature market. We need mature executives who can find ways to grow!"[10]

No market, Bossidy points out, is fully penetrated. "The auto industry has been fully penetrated for 25 years," he says. "You have the SUV [sport utility vehicle] coming out five years and sweeping this country and now Europe and even Asia. Home Depot went into the fully penetrated building supply market; it's now a $14 billion company. Circuit City went into a fully penetrated appliance business, and now it's the leader."[11]

AlliedSignal was in three "mature" and highly cyclical industries when Bossidy took over in 1991: (1) aerospace, (2) plastics and chemicals, (3) automotive components. It's still in the same basic industries, but as of 1997, the company could count nearly two-thirds of its businesses as growth businesses, versus 13 percent in 1990.[12]

The aerospace business was beyond mature; it was contracting. Yet Dan Burnham, whom Bossidy put in charge of the division, found new, unconventional ways to define the customer needs and segment the market. He broadened the pond, redefining the business by stepping outside the familiar territory where others in aerospace were trapped. Even before the market recovered, he put the Aerospace division on a new growth trajectory. From 1993 to 1997, sales rose 42 percent, to $6.4 billion, and income rose 130 percent, to $515 million.[13] (We'll give the details in Chapter 10.)

"Growth is a mindset," says Bossidy. "It's an ability. When I hear people say, 'I can't grow my market,' I say, 'You know, it's you, not the market.'"[14]

Seeking Success in Segments

An important secret of growing in a mature industry is that any market has pockets or segments of growth potential—if you know how to look for them. Customers' needs are always changing, and new ones arising; the first company to identify them can prosper.

When Lou Gerstner became head of American Express's credit card business two decades ago, some of his direct reports told him the business was mature and his prices were too high. Gerstner proved them wrong by segmenting; he created the Corporate Card, the Gold Card, and the Platinum Card. Each met a specific need that no established card was serving. Combined with superior use of information technology, the segmenting yielded average annual revenue growth of 19 percent for the credit card division over the next dozen years.[15]

Retailing looked like a mature market to the Sears Roebucks and JC Penneys of that era—but not to Sam Walton, who built Wal-Mart by meeting the needs of a huge segment overlooked by the big guys: small-town people who wanted low-priced merchandise. Casual footwear was considered mature during the eighties. Indeed, Wolverine Worldwide Company, which virtually owned the market via its ubiquitous Hush Puppies, couldn't find much growth, and today is an insignificant player. But even as Wolverine was shrinking, Nike CEO Phil Knight was extracting average annual growth of over 19 percent[16] from this mature market by creating new market segments based on specialized types of athletic shoes. (Later in the book, we'll look more closely at Wal-Mart and Nike, to see how they did it.)

"All Kinds of Alternatives"

Leaders of growth companies understand that they have to look beyond their familiar served markets. GE Capital, General Electric's most powerful growth machine, has grown over 20 percent a year for more than 15 years, at the same time racking up an almost unbroken string of profit increases.[17] The secret? Its leaders look everywhere for opportunities. CEO Gary Wendt doesn't think of his company as being in a specific industry. "If you define yourself as a maker of men's business clothing and focus only on that, you'll fail," he says. "But if you say, 'I am in the business of providing garments to people in the world,' all of a sudden you have all kinds of alternatives to look at."[18]

Simple, once you get the idea. But so many leaders of powerful companies don't get it. Great companies still falter or go down the tubes because they define their markets as the equivalent of men's business clothing, rather than garments for the world.

Experience may be a wonderful teacher, but it often teaches the wrong things. Leaders can become captives of their own experience. Their knowledge of the industries they've grown in, and the conventional wisdom of those industries, has been reinforced by their dealings with peers, trade associations, and even the media and security analysts.

For example, think about how banks are universally compared to each other. They're ranked by the public and in the minds of their own people by their size, measured in assets. But that criterion has become irrelevant in a world where discontinuities are completely reshaping boundaries in financial services. There's no such thing as a banking industry anymore. Instead, there's a consumer financial services industry, of which banks altogether have a tiny fraction of the market, and nonbank companies like GE Capital Services are getting the growth.

Bankers who can't expand their minds beyond the traditional definition of banking will find their lunch being eaten by new competitors. Citicorp CEO John Reed put it succinctly when he met the press to announce Citi's proposed merger with Travelers Group Inc.: "The customer doesn't want to shop from place to place and be sold time and again."[19] Reed long before had rejected the old size criterion; his goal is profitable growth that will improve shareholder value, and his yardstick for success is return on investment. (See Chapter 5 for more on the nuts and bolts of how he achieved it in one of his core businesses.)

Reed aims to reach a billion consumers, using a brand as global as Coca-Cola. Such a company would enjoy an advantage unmatched by any consumer company: relationships with, and information about, one billion customers.

Capitalizing on Opportunities

Larry Bossidy's remark is actually a restatement of an old idea. "There is no such thing as a growth industry," wrote Theodore Levitt, the Harvard marketing guru, in the *Harvard Business Review* more than thirty years ago. "There are only companies organized and operated to create and capitalize on growth opportunities."[20]

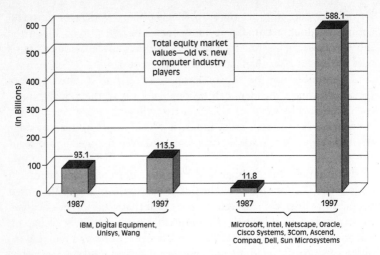

Figure 2.1   Grabbing the Growth: The microprocessor provided immense opportunities for creating wealth. But early players in the industry missed out over the past decade, as younger companies seized most of the opportunities. *Source:* Charan Associates

The microprocessor has been the engine of the twentieth century's greatest growth business, but the benefits did not accrue automatically to all the players in the computer industry. The winners and losers are distinguished by who capitalized on opportunities and who didn't. Figure 2.1 illustrates this point.

The ten companies on the right recognized and seized the opportunities. The four on the left had all of the necessary resources and core competencies, but they missed the boat.

The Perils of Success

When its leaders aren't constantly open to new opportunities, a company is permanently at risk. Even a growing industry may become "mature" for existing players if new ones are changing the rules of the game. New competition comes from all directions, including some you thought you had covered. Customers develop new needs, different from the ones you're so good at meeting. As Bill Gates says, "Success is a lousy teacher. It seduces smart people into thinking they can't lose. And it's an unreliable guide to the future."[21]

One need only look at the power shifts in the computer industry to see the recurring pattern. IBM created the commercial computer industry and defined it for decades. Then upstarts redefined it. One of those new kids was Digital Equipment Corporation (DEC), which, in 1960, introduced the minicomputer and met the need for cheaper and smaller machines. Soon, a minicomputer industry, dominated by DEC and carved at IBM's expense, was challenging the previously monolithic mainframe industry.

But Ken Olsen, Digital's brilliant founder, didn't understand what Theodore Levitt had said either. Along came small desktop computers, suitable for home use as well as business. Olsen contemptuously dismissed them as "toys."[22] By the time he found out otherwise, the computer industry had been redefined again by upstarts like Compaq and Dell. It was a moment of poignant irony when Olsen's successors agreed, in 1998, to be acquired by Compaq—the company that, more than any other, changed the rules of the industry by leveraging the potential of the PC.

Bill Gates was another upstart. While hardware makers tried to retain customers with proprietary systems and designs, Gates expanded the market with user-friendly operating systems that any manufacturer could license cheaply. Microsoft focused not on product but on needs. Instead of trying to defend what it already did, it continually reinvented itself in light of what people might want and could use. As a result, Microsoft did more than any other company to grow the industry.

Gates learned a history lesson along the way. Even so, Microsoft—driven by a vision, beating the stuffing out of all its competition, and dominating its field—came close to losing its leadership in the hottest growth area of computerdom. In two short years, a new market force, the Internet, burst onto the scene. The Net's explosive growth and almost unimaginable potential for usefulness created a whole new set of needs—for new kinds of software and for new thinking on the part of suppliers.

Gates missed the significance of the Internet at first. But unlike the CEOs of IBM and DEC, and other brilliant executives who could not see beyond their core competencies, he had his eyes trained on the marketplace and his mind attuned to change—as well as history's lessons. In a remarkable 1995 statement, he admitted: "We said back then, 'Don't DEC and IBM know they're in deep trouble?' Now here we are, staring at the same kind of situation."[23]

Gates made the Net his top priority; within a year, he was going after it with every resource he owned or could buy. After introducing his own Web browser, he launched into providing "content," most notably through MSNBC, a joint venture of NBC and the Microsoft Network, with its TV-like programming. He invested $1 billion in a cable operator, Comcast, and bought WebTV. He began building a position in electronic commerce, developing sites for travel, car buying, real estate, investment, and arts and entertainment. In April 1998 Microsoft joined with Sony Corp. to develop high-speed communication standards for linking home PCs and digital television equipment. The collaboration permanently broke the boundaries between consumer electronics and PC manufacturers, introducing a new game with new segmentation and new opportunities for growth.

All the activity had a slightly frenzied look, especially since Microsoft's core Windows operating system was simultaneously coming under attack from Sun Microsystem's Java technology. Java can link many different types of computers on a network, using web browsers that don't rely on Windows, and it's widely regarded as the most serious threat, to date, to Microsoft's dominance of computer operating systems. Perhaps more ominously for Microsoft, its aggressively expansionist tactics put it in the middle of a major antitrust brouhaha. Prodded by angry existing and potential customers—banks and newspapers are among those who see threats to their own businesses—the Justice Department filed suit, arguing that the company uses Windows to dominate sales of other Microsoft products. As a score of state attorney generals joined the fray, Gates himself became a political target, compared with John D. Rockefeller[24] and coming under suspicion even from consumers who had previously regarded him positively.[25]

But then, change is inherently messy. In the first stages, it's often hard to tell whether the change leader is a visionary or a fool. What's certain is that a leader who doesn't change will eventually be a loser.

P.S.: Gates is investing some of Microsoft's enormous earnings in the distant future; he's hiring star scientists from academia to do basic as well as applied research in centers Microsoft is building around the world. "The future of computing is the computer that talks, listens, sees,

and learns," he told FORTUNE late in 1997. "That is what is being created at Microsoft Research."[26]

The Limits of Core Competency

One thing that hamstrung the IBMs and the DECs was their devotion to
their existing skills and capacities—their perceived core competencies.

The concept of core competencies is useful—to a point. Focusing on
competencies was a powerful antidote to the promiscuous expansion engineered by portfolio managers laboring under the delusion that they
could run any business by plugging in numbers and economic models.
The concept helped companies to pinpoint their strengths, and many
underperforming conglomerate and multi-industry companies were
saved from going over the bankruptcy cliff.

But today, the concept needs serious rethinking. Its drawback—fatal
for many companies—is that it promotes inside-out thinking. Far too
often, executives define their organization's core competencies too narrowly. IBM perceived its core competencies through the lens of the
mainframe computer; DEC channeled its skills and technologies into
building minicomputers. Had each company been able to assess its core
competencies from the outside in, it could have spotted ways to meet or
even define new consumer needs—needs that required still cheaper and
more flexible machines and systems.

Most companies have competencies they haven't recognized as de-
serving that label—competencies they can use to widen their markets.
Under the leadership of founder Rod Canion, Compaq's people understood their core competencies as the skills needed to produce high-end
PCs. Eckhard Pfeiffer, who replaced Canion as CEO when Compaq
was in deep trouble (see Chapter 6), saw that Compaq's true core competency was technological leadership—a competency that would play
successfully across the board in the computer industry.

Many more examples are probed throughout this book. Some of
the most striking scenarios involve manufacturing companies—like
GE Medical Systems (Chapter 7), AlliedSignal (Chapter 10), and
Reynolds and Reynolds (Chapter 11)—whose leaders discovered that
their core competencies included knowhow and management systems
they could use to develop fast-growing and highly profitable service
businesses.

Sometimes, leaders must abandon core competencies that have previously defined their businesses. It's likely to happen when their companies reach what Intel Chairman Andy Grove calls "strategic inflection points"—the moments when massive, discontinuous change occurs, and all bets are off.

Intel's core competencies, for a decade and a half, were the skills and technologies it used to build ever-more-efficient memory chips. But, by 1984, the Japanese were killing Grove's company with high-quality, low-cost products. In endless meetings, Grove and his senior managers debated the options: build a new plant to meet the Japanese head-on; look for a new technology the Japanese couldn't match; focus on special-purpose memories. None seemed to hold much promise. "During that time, we worked hard without a clear notion of how things were ever going to get better," Grove wrote in his book *Only the Paranoid Survive*. "We had lost our bearings. We were wandering in the valley of death."[27]

In 1985, Grove and cofounder Gordon Moore made a radical decision to scrap the business they'd built and concentrate on microprocessors, the chips that do the actual calculating in a computer. It was a tough and painful decision. As Grove recounts, "Intel equaled memories in all of our minds. How could we give up our identity?"[28] But discussing the company's quandary one afternoon with Moore, who was then Intel's CEO, "I asked, 'If we got kicked out and the board brought in a new CEO, what do you think he would do?' Gordon answered without hesitation, 'He would get us out of memories.' I stared at him, numb, then said, 'Why shouldn't you I and walk out the door, come back in, and do it ourselves?' "[29]

Essentially, Grove and Moore looked at themselves from the outside in. Reflecting on the high turnover of CEOs these days, Grove speculated that the replacements are not necessarily better managers or leaders, but they have the crucial advantage of being unencumbered by emotional attachments to past success (or to existing core competencies). "If existing management wants to keep their jobs when the basics of the business are undergoing profound change," he wrote, "they must adapt an outsider's intellectual objectivity."[30]

What made the shift possible were strengths Intel possessed that might not even appear in any by-the-book inventory of core competencies. Microprocessors were only a sideline at that point; they were based on a technology developed in the corner of an old production plant. But Grove saw that Intel's core competencies were deeper and more systemic than the specific skills and technologies that had built the memory chip business.

One was a mode of dialogue deeply imbedded in Intel's psyche. In struggling to achieve its early successes, Grove writes, Intel's people had become good at solving problems and focusing on tangible results. "And from all the early bickering, we developed a style of ferociously arguing with each other while remaining friends," says Grove. (Constructive confrontation is what he calls it.)[31] This strength enabled the organization to confront the challenge and adapt itself to the new realities.

Another strength was the outside-in thinking of people down the line. Intel's salespeople and financial analysts had seen the changes in the fundamentals of the business before senior management did, and were already acting on the new information. While the leaders were still trying to figure out how they could fight an unwinnable war in memory chips, Grove wrote, "Men and women lower in the organization, unbeknownst to us, got us ready to execute the strategic turn that saved our necks and gave us a great future. Over time, more and more of our production resources were directed to the emerging microprocessor business, not as a result of any specific strategic direction by senior management but as a result of daily decisions by middle managers."[32]

It took Intel's leaders a year to realize that they had reached what Grove calls a strategic inflection point, and another year to implement the decision. A third year passed before Intel returned to profitability. But, says Grove, "Had we not changed our business strategy, we would have been relegated to an immensely tough economic existence and, for sure, a relatively insignificant role in our industry."[33]

In short, the traditional definition of core competence is incomplete. A true list of a company's core competencies must come from a thorough inventory of its intellectual capital—the sum of its accumulated technologies, experience, skills, and management processes. Such a list is dynamic, not static. It must be constantly redefined in light of the company's changing knowledge base and the fluid external environment. A company charting a quantum growth trajectory will almost always need to develop or add new core competencies and de-emphasize or drop old ones, no matter how important they once may have been.

A company that is not constantly revitalizing its core competencies will wither away. If you doubt it, just compare the FORTUNE 500 lists for, say, 1958 and 1998.[34]

The Dangers of Unbalanced Growth

Not all growth is good growth. "The curse of all curses is the revenue line," Roberto Goizueta once told a FORTUNE writer.[35] Coca-Cola's revenue growth has been anything but shabby, but Goizueta's point was that creating value for shareholders comes first—and to do that, *the growth must be profitable and capital efficient.*

Far too often, people think of growth as a silver bullet that will, in and of itself, cure a bottom-line problem. They pour resources into a new venture without first doing the hard work of insuring productivity and profitability. It's the *Field of Dreams* approach: Grow it, and the money will come. But unless there is a competitive advantage, the money will only go.

We say that the only growth worth having is sustainable, balanced, top-line and bottom-line growth. Olympic revenue goals must be accompanied by: continuing cost and productivity improvement; restructuring, as required; and intelligent reinvestment of capital.

The consequences of unbalanced growth are most obvious among rising entrepreneurial rockets, where everybody, from the CEO on down, is caught up in the frenzy of success. For example, in 1993, Dell Computer seemed to be on a launching pad. In just two years, sales had soared from less than $550 million to $2 billion. But poor production planning left it without notebook computers, then the fastest-growing segment of the PC market, and security analysts were questioning its accounting and currency trading practices. In the first half of the year, its stock fell from $49 to $16. "Growth had been pursued to the exclusion of all else, but no one knew how the numbers really added up," said FORTUNE magazine.[36]

Michael Dell got to the heart of the problem in his talks with FORTUNE. "One of the things that is confusing and intoxicating when you are growing a business is that you really have little way of determining what the problems are," he said. "You had different parts of the company believing they were making their plan, but when you rolled up the results of the company, you had a big problem. It was symptomatic of not understanding the relationship between costs and revenues and profits within the different lines of business."[37]

Dell brought his company back from its near-death experience by drawing executives from companies such as Motorola, Hewlett-Packard, and Apple Computer to bolster his management. And he learned a valuable lesson. It was, he said "to change the orientation of the company away from growth, growth, growth, to liquidity, profitability, and growth, which has become a real mantra for the company."[38]

Entrepreneurs aren't the only people who overdose on growth. The story of the Coca-Cola and PepsiCo rivalry affords a classic example of the difference between balanced and unbalanced top-line growth. In philosophy and strategy over the previous two decades, PepsiCo had been the hotshot, and Coca-Cola was the Cool Hand Luke. For most of those years, the contest looked like a close one. Both companies created a lot of value for shareholders. Then PepsiCo's mistakes caught up with it.

PepsiCo's leaders made revenue gains their main goal. Their superb marketing campaigns to capture share in the U.S. soft-drink market included the Pepsi Challenge, which put Coca-Cola on the defensive in the early eighties, and the pioneering use of celebrities such as Michael Jackson and Madonna. They spent lavishly, invested in bottling operations, and acquired and built food businesses, including Frito-Lay, Kentucky Fried Chicken [KFC], Pizza Hut, and Taco Bell.

PepsiCo expected to keep the growth rolling on and on.[39] To achieve the growth, managers were fired up with a gung ho growth spirit and given a great deal of latitude, including the power to spend. The spirit was perhaps best captured in the apocryphal race driver's advice, repeated often to his troops by Chris Sinclair, former head of international operations: "Press the accelerator to the floor and keep turning left."[40] PepsiCo executives became much-sought by headhunters for clients who wanted to bring some of that drive and energy to their own operations.

Goizueta, meantime, had defined Coca-Cola's growth opportunities clearly with his legendary share-of-the-stomach metaphor. But he always focused on return on investment. Coca-Cola dropped its diversification efforts and focused singlemindedly on building its brand and its distribution. While PepsiCo spent heavily on razzle-dazzle marketing, Coca-Cola built a powerful, multi-channel distribution infrastructure—a new core competency that PepsiCo couldn't match. Coca-Cola partly spun off its capital-intensive bottling operations, dramatically increasing its returns on investment. The stake it retained in major "anchor bottlers" gave it a critical measure of control. Coca-Cola gave the anchor bottlers financial and managerial help, and used them to expand its network around the world. So successful was Coca-Cola's expansion overseas that, by the mid-nineties, some 70 percent of its revenues and 80 percent of its profits came from abroad—precisely the opposite of PepsiCo's percentages.[41] By 1997, Coca-Cola widened its global market share lead over PepsiCo to almost thirty points.[42]

Distribution was a key part of Goizueta's philosophy, as revealed tellingly in an early incident during his leadership. In 1985, troubled that the company's stock price didn't reflect the possibilities he was starting to capture, he flew a group of securities analysts down to Atlanta, put them on a bus to nearby Rome, Georgia, and had them driven around to schools, libraries, and other public buildings. Imagine what will happen, he said, when there's a Coke machine in each of these—as there soon would be. The "Journey to Rome," as it was called at Coca-Cola, made its point to the analysts; shortly after their excursion, Coca-Cola's stock price began to rise.

Today, the U.S. cola market is still considered mature. But Goizueta's successor, M. Douglas Ivester, is still confident that Coca-Cola can increase its share of the stomach at home by making it easier for people to find its products—for example, by putting more vending machines in every site from apartment and office complexes to tanning salons and amusement parks. He expects to lift Coca-Cola's share of the $54 billion carbonated soft-drink market[43] from 43 percent to 50 percent by 2000.[44]

At PepsiCo, the "curse of all curses"—the revenue line—hit with a vengeance in the mid-nineties. Earnings and stock price got hammered. PepsiCo's soft drinks were losing share in the U.S. market. In Latin America, it lost two major bottlers: one in Venezuela, to Coca-Cola, and the other, in Argentina, to ill-conceived and poorly executed expansion plans. Its restaurant chains, locked in deadly and costly market-share battles, were eating up capital. Because it was fixated on revenue growth, Pepsi lost control of the basics.

While it lasted, PepsiCo's run of growth was remarkable. The company has enormous power and resources. Frito-Lay, its snack food division, is a consistently profitable growth machine. Having routed a hugely expensive challenge by Anheuser-Busch, Frito-Lay looks virtually untouchable in its markets. Roger Enrico, PepsiCo's CEO since 1996, is a brilliant marketer and, perhaps more important, a leader who knows how to create leaders. By spinning off the restaurants in 1997, he restructured his company into a manageable enterprise.[45]

If anybody can put PepsiCo back on track, it's Enrico. But as we will see in the next chapter, the financial markets—the ultimate and most ruthless judges of a company's prospects for the future—are waiting for more evidence before they again put PepsiCo in the same league with Coca-Cola.

The curse of the revenue line doesn't always take years to surface. In many of today's fast-moving markets, growth can get out of balance with frightening speed. A case in point is Nokia Corp., the Finnish maker of telecommunications equipment. As *Business Week* put it, "How Nokia stumbled—and recovered—could be a case study in how precisely electronics companies must manage all aspects of their business to survive in the Digital Age."[46]

Nokia has been one of Europe's stellar success stories in the nineties. When Jorma Ollila was named CEO in 1992, Nokia was a faltering high-tech conglomerate that was unfocused and losing money. The former CFO, and an economist by training, Ollila was only 41 years old. But he swiftly replaced top management with a new and equally young team, and he sold off the weakest businesses.

Ollila focused Nokia's strategy and resources on mobile phones. The Nordic countries had the world's highest usage, thanks to a pan-Nordic mobile phone standard adopted in the early 1980s. The company was a low-cost producer with highly efficient research and development—it spent about 7 percent of sales on R&D, just under half as much as rival Ericsson[47]—and was good at developing features customers liked. Ollila saw that the global market was expanding rapidly because of deregulation, and he drove into it full throttle, growing mobile phone sales by as much as 100 percent a year.[48]

By 1995, Nokia's revenues had more than doubled, to $8.4 billion.[49] After Motorola, it was the second largest mobile phone producer in the world.[50] Then came serious problems. In just two years, the cellular phone business had "gone from an industry of predictable product cycles and operating margins as high as 16 percent to steep price cuts, single-digit operating margins, and the kind of turmoil familiar to makers of personal computers and camcorders." A chip shortage slowed production, inventories piled up, and productivity fell. Meantime, falling prices in the increasingly competitive marketplace were eroding margins. In the United States, Nokia misjudged demand: it had too many digital phones and too few analog ones. At the end of the year, the company warned that profits were under pressure, and its stock dropped 36 percent within a week.[51]

Three years of stunning success had left the company's young managers (average age of its employees: 31 years) overconfident—even arrogant. Many a company in similar straits has lost its edge forever. But Ollila acted swiftly. According to *Business Week*, "He formed 'commando teams' to slash inventories, speeding up turnover of raw materials and finished goods. He let regional managers renegotiate contracts and strong-arm suppliers. Chip vendors were told to cut delivery times from 12 weeks to 8." Nokia also overhauled its management information system, installing new software to give purchasing managers more control over inventories. In six months, the magazine reported, the teams cut raw material inventories from 80 to 40 days' worth, and tripled the turn rate.[52]

By the end of 1997, Nokia was back on track, gaining market share against archrival Motorola. Revenues were $9.8 billion; profits were $1.1 billion[53], and productivity was again rising. The pipeline was full of new products, such as high-margin Internet telephony equipment, and components for the fast-growing data communications market.

In 1997, with the company's stock back around its former high, we reviewed the Nokia journey with Jorma Ollila himself. He was able to share a powerful story about what it takes to get balanced growth in a company such as his. The experience, he said, had been an important opportunity to learn painful but valuable lessons about how to compete in the future.

As we talked with him, it was clear he had formed a teachable point of view about balanced growth. One lesson was that operational excellence is critical; without it, a company can die. Another was that a workable set of corporate values must include humility, healthy paranoia, and a strong belief in energizing people by stretching them, and then sticking with them through tough times. (Ollila didn't fire any of his senior people, though some spent time in the penalty box.) Finally, he learned how to teach his team what *edge* is all about: making the tough decisions about cost, savings, and investment.

Virtually Infinite Opportunities

Any company can grow, no matter what its size. Was GE too big to grow when it hit $27 billion in 1981? In the years since, its sales have roughly quadrupled.[54] Its market value in 1981, $13 billion, has grown to more than $272 billion.[55] Coca-Cola was no pygmy when Goizueta took charge. Now three times the size it was then (its sales were $18.9 billion in 1997), the company is still growing at 7.5 percent a year, and profits are growing at 20 percent annually.[56] Its market value reached $191 billion in May 1998,[57] up from $4 billion in 1981.[58]

In his last annual report letter to shareholders, Goizueta wrote: ". . . truly, *we are just getting started*. I say that because never before have we had the capability we have today for taking advantage of the virtually infinite opportunities before us." His successor, M. Douglas Ivester, feels the same way.

Can a company that's dead in the water be brought to life? Compaq, a brilliant success during the eighties, was being eaten alive by competitors in the early nineties. Eckhard Pfeiffer, who took over as CEO in 1991, turned the company around. He methodically but aggressively expanded its marketplace, first from portable computers to PCs, and then to complete computing systems. Over the next four years, revenues almost quintupled, to $24.5 billion.[59]

Four points sum up the history lesson:

1. No company is too big to grow.

2. No industry is 100 percent mature; there are always markets that are not fully penetrated.

3. No market is safe, because there's always someone who can come along and redefine it.

4. No company is too successful to fail.

Leaders at all levels must learn these lessons and act accordingly. If they don't, their companies will fall behind, get acquired, or disappear.

The Inertia of the Genetic Code

We said at the outset that growth is, above all, a state of mind. When Alex Trotman set out to reshape Ford for the future, he didn't just say that Ford needed a new strategy. He also said, in effect, "We've got to think differently. We must wrestle with our business thought process, and change our old ways of thinking from top to bottom. We've got to change the genetic code of our company."

It's not enough for a company's leadership to see the new possibilities. Down in the organization, a deeply rooted set of attitudes and reflexes will defy efforts to create and execute a growth strategy. This is the genetic code at work, and it influences just about every decision people make. Nothing much will happen until the leaders fundamentally change the genetic code—and keep reinforcing it with a teachable point of view.

Let's take a look at a company that can't get its growth engine started. A fairly typical product of the downsizing era, it's a composite of scores of firms we've worked in. Maybe you work for it.

It's lean and restructured. Clearheaded executives, after covering the walls with flipcharts at numerous offsite meetings, pinpointed the core competencies and pruned away everything else. Everybody's hunkered down and working hard. But the CEO has recently enunciated the obvious truth: This game has no future—you can't shrink forever. He may be getting his marching orders from the financial community, which these days is looking for balanced growth. Feeling the heat, he announces ambitious targets for top-line growth, earnings, and return on equity. To his people, he says, "Stretch goals, guys. It's time to grow! Time to strategize a big assault on the marketplace. Reallocate resources. Win new customers. Reorganize. Go out there and kick butt."

Then comes the handwringing from the business unit managers. How can we grow when our industry is mature? How can we grow when our competitors are just as lean and efficient as we are? How can we grow when everybody's scared to take risks? Boss, nobody here has any *ideas!*

They may win some incremental gains. But in a fiercely competitive game for which others are constantly rewriting the rules, there will be no quantum leaps. Nowhere to be found is the plan that will keep them expanding profitably for years to come—because this company's leaders have not altered the genetic code.

That strategy that looks so good on paper? It's not going to work, because the people know only how to look inward—all of their experiences, all of the imperatives that come from the existing genetic code, focus their efforts on the internal needs and workings of the company.

To win new customers, they have to look at their company from the outside in—from the customer's point of view, from the perspective of the fast-changing marketplace. And that's a major shift, callings for a new mindset and new skills. It can't be imposed by fiat or by a new incentive structure alone.

Reallocate resources? The leaders might as well be using their computers to do addition and subtraction. They will be making the mistake that former GM chairman Roger Smith made a decade ago, when he spent $40 billion for new equipment and technological knowhow[60] but failed to change his company's genetic code, with its bureaucratic mindset. The money vanished into a black hole, GM's market share continued to shrink, and Smith was retired unceremoniously, an emblem of massive corporate failure to adapt. GM's market share slide, continuing to the present, is almost as great as the gains by all Japanese automakers.[61]

A new organizational structure? The leadership may need to change the one it has, but moving boxes on charts isn't, by itself, the answer. A superior value proposition? Brilliant channel management? Fine, but can people translate these advantages into growth day after day, year after year?

The genetic code of this company is sending the same instructions that it has been sending ever since the first round of downsizing. And they're precisely the wrong ones for a company with new ambitions:

Make those numbers.

Don't take risks.

Watch your back.

By contrast, the genetic code of a company that's growing sends a completely different set of signals:

Widen your horizons.

Unleash your imagination.

Go for it.

In such a company, the dialogues and working relationships are 180 degrees different. The mental architecture of profitable growth rules at all levels. People are learning where the sources of growth lie. They are curious about new markets, new needs, new technologies, and they talk about them with one another. They're comfortable with ambiguity, and able to make the subjective judgments needed to deal with the unknown.

Everybody understands the company's strategy, which is clear and simple, and they communicate in the language of expansion and opportunity.

Information about opportunities travels through the organization like lightning; people are charged up by it, energized with the possibilities. Growth is in their genes.

Which of these companies do you work for? Hint: Do you wake up in the morning looking forward to your business day, and return home energized by the possibilities for tomorrow? Or do you enter your office with dread and leave with your emotional energy drained by struggle to keep your head above water?

If the latter, what can you do to change things for the better? If the answer is, "Nothing," shouldn't you leave?

Creating the genetic code of profitable growth is a big job, but strong leaders with a teachable point of view can get change rolling quickly. And as you start to grow, you will find that the changes bring new vigor to the battle for the bottom line. By itself, this battle is nothing more than bloodletting, a zero-sum game that focuses people inward. With top-line growth, it becomes energizing.

Growth is a mindset—great business leaders have demonstrated it time and again. In this era of virtually unlimited opportunity, no business is mature; no markets are fully penetrated. The road to change starts with a grasp of basic business thinking—the common sense underlying strong financial performance. It is surprisingly uncommon, and it's the subject of the next chapter.

CHAPTER 3

Common Sense and Capital
THE BUSINESS THINKING UNDERLYING TOP-LINE GROWTH AND BOTTOM-LINE RESULTS

We've said before that there's good growth and bad growth. Good growth is profitable and sustainable; it's responsible growth. Bad growth—growth for its own sake—is profitless, wasteful of capital, and even reckless. It has been the undoing of many business leaders obsessed with the drive for size.

It's amazingly easy to tell the difference between good growth and bad growth. Good growth is profitable and capital efficient, and it more than repays the money invested in it. Whether your business is growing fast or slowly, whether it's big or small, there is just one criterion, one simple fact you need to determine: What's the return on my investment?

As a leader, you can summarize your job in one sentence: Take the investment we have today and make it worth more tomorrow. For anybody running a business of any size or type, in any country or culture, the criterion is the same. A shopkeeper in India will ask: "Did I earn more on my borrowed money than I will pay to the lender tonight?" The CEO of a publicly held company will (or should) ask: "Are we creating shareholder value?"

Same question—and the answer means the same thing. If *yes,* the business is successful; if *no,* it isn't. But the Indian shopkeeper is more keenly aware of the difference. If the answer is *no,* there's no cash to take home. His family will go to bed hungry.

Return on investment is a common sense universal business criterion passed on from generation to generation. A third-world shopkeeper intuitively understands it. Communist and socialist economies collapsed because they ignored it. In market economies, stock prices decline when managers don't understand it. Asia's economic crisis resulted partly from investments made without realistic regard to returns.

Amazingly, many sophisticated executives don't think enough about return on investment. They get enmeshed in the details of running big, complex corporations, or they become enchanted with the high-altitude conceptualizing that characterizes the so-called strategic approach. Cruising in the stratosphere, they lose sight of this simple principle.

The classic example of a CEO who produced lots of growth but failed to create long-term returns was the late Harold Geneen. A frustrated accountant who had attended a Harvard advanced management course, he got himself named head of ITT in 1959. By 1978, he had built the erstwhile $500 million-a-year international telephone company into a sprawling conglomerate with more than $19 billion in sales.[1]

Geneen ran his empire with a spider web of elaborate financial controls, and he terrorized Wall Street as a raider. He was undeniably a brilliant financial engineer. But he was clueless about how to operate or grow businesses. After the acquisition binge petered out, ITT ran downhill rapidly.

Compare ITT's record with that of GE, whose leader did understand business and the simple truth of return on investment. Between 1978, when both companies had roughly the same revenues, and 1994, ITT's market value grew from about $3 billion to just over $10 billion. GE's market value rose from just under $11 billion to $87.5 billion.[2] Ultimately, ITT's performance was so disappointing to investors that Geneen's handpicked successor, Rand Araskog, could only preside over its dismemberment. In 1997, he sold off the last of its businesses, and Geneen's ITT ceased to exist.[3]

The Secret of Business Acumen

No matter what business you're in, your shareholders—whether public or private—want to see both growth *and* real return on investment. It's that simple.

You can calculate return on investment (ROI) any number of ways, and the financially gifted can argue for hours about their relative merits.

You've doubtless heard the acronyms for ROI's sometimes mysterious relatives—ROA, (return on assets) ROE (return on equity), EVA® (economic value added),[4] MVA (market value added) and more. These are useful measurements, but keep your eye on ROI itself.

It's not high finance, it's not technical nuance. We are talking about nothing more or less than simple business acumen. The essence of it is the thought, the *idea*—not numbers, not equations. The uneducated but successful shopkeepers in the world outnumber the highly trained senior executives, and these shopkeepers are successful because they intuitively understand ROI in stark naked terms. Among the executives, this understanding separates the successes from the wanna-bes.

Stick with this fundamental measure of success and master it. No MBA is required—and any business school that fails to teach it should refund your tuition.

You will also want to know how your company's return on investment compares with those of other companies that are competing with you for capital. The better and more consistent your return, the more people are willing to pay for your stock. The simple yardstick for this comparison is the price/earnings ratio of your stock. The ratio of share price to fundamental earnings per share will tell you all you need to know about whether shareholders regard you kindly or unkindly. If your company is privately held, your bankers have (or should have) already calculated an imputed price/earnings ratio for you.

The price/earnings ratio is something anybody in your company can understand, from the CEO down to the mailroom clerk. Any leader with the skill to cut through complexity to the big ideas can make it clear. And everybody *should* understand what it means; understanding it helps align their energies with the company's creation of wealth, which is the ultimate guarantee of their own economic well-being. We'll return to the price/earnings ratio shortly, when we explain how the capital markets make their judgments and why you need to pay attention to those judgments.

But first we'll look more closely at the basics behind ROI as they are understood and practiced throughout the world, and have been for thousands of years. We'll see the common sense of business, starting at the ground level. This is how Ram Charan learned it, at the age of 11 in an $8' \times 8'$ stall, when he had to take over the family shoe business after his elder brother who ran it became ill.

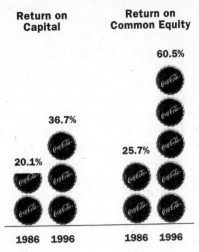

Figure 3.1   Coca-Cola, 1996. *Source:* Coca-Cola 1996 Annual Report.

Note carefully: Common sense is very uncommon in business. When you've got thousands of suppliers, hundreds of plants, five layers of marketing and twenty or more business units, it's hard to keep the simple principles in mind.

When he was CEO of Coca-Cola, the late Roberto Goizueta understood the problem better than most. Here's how he put it: "Although our business is large and geographically diverse, we strive to operate with the drive, resourcefulness and common sense of a successful kiosk owner or shopkeeper."[5]

Goizueta always watched his return on investment, emphasizing it in conversations, speeches, and publications. Figure 3.1 is a typical example, prominent in Coca-Cola's 1996 annual report.

The Message from Masaya

Here's our favorite example of the common sense of business. In 1969, Ram was teaching in Nicaragua at INCAE [Institucíon Central Americana de Empresas Administrucíon], a school for MBAs that Harvard had set up years before at President John F. Kennedy's request. On the second day, Ram took his students out of the classroom to learn some basics of business. They traveled eight miles outside of Managua to a market named Masaya, a warren of 8′ × 12′ stalls where some 100 merchants and peasants (almost all women) sold everything from pineapples to shirts and necklaces.

They approached a woman selling clothing, and, through an interpreter, Ram asked her how she got the money to pay for her merchandise. She borrowed from the "sharks," she replied—moneylenders who charge 2.5 percent interest a month. One of the students did some quick mental arithmetic and announced that this amounted to a 30 percent annual rate. "No," she replied, "it's more like 34 percent." (In fact, it's 34.5 percent, based on those monthly payments.) Then he asked how much money she made. "*Poquito, marjen*[sic] about 5 percent," she replied. That was a painfully thin profit margin, given how much her money cost. So, Ram asked, how could she make a living that way? "Idiota," she muttered—clearly thinking, "Who is this well-dressed man who knows so little about business?" Propping her right elbow on her left hand, she cut through the air with several sweeping circular motions. She meant rotation of stock—rotation of inventory.

The equivalent in corporate lingo is asset turns—what assets are required per dollar of sales. It's calculated by dividing net sales by average total assets, which includes plant, people, equipment, and working capital (accounts receivable plus inventories, minus accounts payable).

We call it **velocity.** The higher the velocity, the more revenues you get per dollar of assets—or, conversely, the fewer assets you need to produce a dollar of sales. For example, a velocity of 2 means that a business is generating two dollars of sales for every dollar of assets. A velocity of 10 means a business is producing annual sales equal to ten times its assets.

Ram drew out the point on the spot: "She knows that her return on investment has to be greater than her cost of capital. And with thin margins, she must make her living on velocity. *Return on investment is margin multiplied by velocity.* No business anywhere is exempt from this principle."

At the end of a business day, all the complexity comes down to that: business acumen. The people who came to the bazaar with Ram learned it in less than an hour.

The Universal Business Rule

This fundamental truth of business success can be stated as a simple formula—the universal business rule of thumb:

$$R = M \times V$$

Return = Margin × Velocity

where R is ROI, M is profit margin, V is velocity.

For the Managua vendor, here's how the formula works. Her profit margin, M, is 5 percent. If she turns her inventory (which is virtually all of her "average total assets") over four times a year her velocity, V, will be 4, and her annual return 20 percent. Because her borrowed money costs almost 35 percent, she wouldn't last long in business (or perhaps in this world, if the sharks caught up with her). If her velocity is 8 inventory turns per year, she's just above breakeven (R = 40 percent). At 10 turns, she's earning more than 50 percent on her investment—or better than 15 points after her cost of capital—and eating well.

Now let's restate the equation in more detail:

$$R = M \times V$$

$$R = \frac{\text{INCOME}}{\text{SALES}} \times \frac{\text{SALES}}{\text{ASSETS}}$$

This is still not complicated. Profit margin (M) is income divided by sales. Velocity (V) is sales divided by assets.

"Hmmm," you may be saying, "isn't it even simpler if you factor out the sales and define R as income over assets?" Technically, yes—and that's what most people do, because it is algebraically correct. But in so doing, they miss the details that provide the meaning in this whole thought and decision process. You have to pay separate attention to margins and velocity. Each is its own concept, with its own components and relationships among components.

Successful business leaders think about each of the components of margins and velocity, and how they interact with each other—everything from the products, sales mix, and customers to the manufacturing techniques, configuration of assets, and working capital requirements. In these details, creativity, judgment, and business savvy pay off.

These are the basics, and you ignore them at your own peril. We saw in Chapter 1 some examples of what happens to companies whose leaders slighted them because they were caught up in growth fever.

People at all levels need to understand them. Successful business leaders not only grasp the basics, but also have the ability to cut through the mumbo-jumbo and teach them in the simple, universal language of business.

If a company is at A and wants to go to B, which way should it go? The classic route is through the top left quadrant, but it's usually a mistake. This is the *Field of Dreams* approach: Grow and the money will come. It can be a recipe for disaster. Companies at point A usually have their basics wrong, and they need to fix those basics before they charge off in search of top-line growth. If you map your route through the lower right quadrant, you will win. (See Figure 3.2.)

The universal business rule demands that leaders think about each of the components of profit margins and velocity, and how they interact

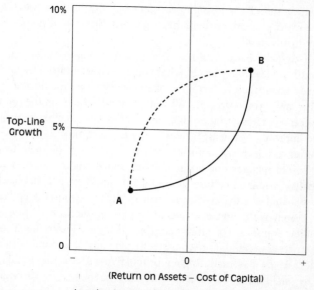

In going from A to B—in most cases—the thick line is a better route than the dotted line.

Figure 3.2 Growth versus Cost of Capital.

with each other. Although there are many components, these will most often be the key ones:

M (MARGIN):	V (VELOCITY):
► Annual productivity improvements.	► Faster inventory turnover.
► Faster time to market.	► Lower capital investment per dollar of sales.
► New products and services.	► Reduced working capital.
► Creative segmentation and resegmentation of markets.	► Additional sales from the same assets, via products of higher value.

No matter how complex his or her organization is, a person with high business acumen routinely looks to these simple criteria.

Profit Margins

The margin side of the formula has gotten a lot of focus in recent years, and we won't plow all of the familiar ground. But several points should be kept firmly in mind.

In fixing the basics, start with the margin requirements and work backward. Always ask yourself what you can do to improve them. What do you do better than your competitors now? What do you do worse now, and how might you correct it? What might you do better in the future?

Everybody talks about productivity, for example, and most everybody tries to improve it—at least fitfully. But winning companies are relentless in making productivity improvement a regular part of their business goals. Toyota remains one of the all-time champions at this game. With its highly disciplined culture of continuous improvement, it ceaselessly reduces manufacturing costs, rationalizes capacity, shortens cycle time, works closely with suppliers—including those in the United States—and streamlines logistics. For more than three decades, Toyota has increased productivity faster and more consistently than any of its competitors.

Jack Welch has made higher productivity a crusade at GE since the late eighties. Most recently he has intensified it through the Six Sigma drive for quality, launched in late 1995.[6] The Six Sigma methodology, pioneered by Motorola, includes defining, measuring, analyzing, improving, and controlling processes of all sorts. Calling it "the centerpiece of our dreams and aspirations" in his 1997 annual report letter to share owners, Welch wrote that "it is transforming everything we do." With senior executive compensation now heavily weighted toward success in the program, he added, "Six Sigma is quickly becoming part of the genetic code of our future leadership."

Even in its second year, Six Sigma is showing strong results. The company attributes its 1997 total cost productivity (sales in relation to costs) of 4.2 percent largely to Six Sigma. By contrast, the 2.9 percent number for the previous year was mainly the result of higher volume. Savings amounted to more than $300 million in operating income, and the company was expecting more than twice as much in the coming year.

That translates directly into an impressive expansion of margins. Noting that GE's operating margins had hovered around the 10 percent level for decades, Welch wrote: "With Six Sigma embedding itself deeper into Company operations, GE in 1997 went through the 'impossible' 15 percent level—approaching 16 percent—and we are optimistic about the upside."

Importantly, Six Sigma helps both GE and its *customers* achieve better business results. Noted Welch: "These projects usually focus on improving our customers' productivity and reducing their capital outlays, while increasing the quality, speed and efficiency of our operations." The program, he concluded, proves his long-standing belief in GE's "infinite capacity to improve everything."[7]

Companies who have learned the productivity lesson build annual improvements into the targets managers are expected to meet every year. Those who haven't learned the lesson are doomed to recurring bouts of frenzied cost cutting, and restructuring writeoffs that erode profit margins and gradually destroy the fabric of the company.

Similarly, you must constantly be generating new products and services that capture a share of the consumer's mind and wallet. At 3M, it was a long-standing discipline that 25 percent of revenues had to come from products less than five years old. In 1993 the goal was raised to 30 percent from products less than four years old.[8] A Compaq or a Dell could not survive without perpetual innovation and the ability to get the new products to market faster than the competition. The shorter cycle time allows more flexibility in defining and meeting the new needs that arise almost daily. Such companies can be proactive in pacing and timing their new product introductions—they don't have to lose time catching up with change.[9]

Segmenting and resegmenting means slicing up markets differently in light of changing needs, and pinpointing the market slices in which you can find growth opportunities. Segmenting is a powerful methodology for generating growth ideas and for changing the rules of the game to your own advantage. We'll explain it fully in Chapter 4.

By improving margins, you generate the money that will underwrite your growth. Each component, by itself and in combination with the others, will improve margins if it is proven to be better than the competition. And not just today's competition; it is not likely to be standing still. Keep your eye on *where the puck is going to be*—what will the competition be doing tomorrow—and set your goals accordingly.

The battle never ends.

Velocity

Velocity is the most underappreciated component of return on investment. For too many business leaders, it's not even on the radar screen. Companies tend to focus almost entirely on improving margins (and, within margins, on the direct labor costs that are generally less than 10 percent of total costs)[10]. The fundamental business truth that the vendor at Masaya understood intuitively has escaped them completely.

If you're in an inherently low-margin business and you don't have enough velocity, your business will die. It may be a long, slow death. The margins of U.S. automakers, for example, are about 3—in good times. The manufacturers will continue to struggle for a long time, but with the same margins as retailing, and only a fraction of the velocity, this industry has a dim future.

Even if your margins are high, you still need to think about velocity. For one thing, margins have a nasty way of shrinking as new competitors join the fray—say, via the Internet. For another, higher velocity can make almost any business more rewarding to its stockholders.

Fortunes have been built by those who grasped the importance of velocity, and lost by those who didn't. Compare, for example, Wal-Mart and Sears, Roebuck & Company. In the mid-1970s, Sears was the colossus of American retailing, but its chairman, Arthur Wood, was glum about the future. He told students at Northwestern's Kellogg School of Management: "There is no growth in retailing."

Sam Walton wasn't there to hear this oracular wisdom. The legendary founder of Wal-Mart was too busy opening stores and growing revenues at 32 percent a year—earning, by the way, a return on equity of 28 percent after taxes.[11]

Walton, with no MBA and driving a beat-up truck, had the business common sense of a shopkeeper—which in fact he was, having learned the business running five-and-dime variety stores in Missouri and Arkansas. To the end, he ran Wal-Mart as if he were running a small-town store.

Walton's common sense began with his grasp of velocity. He grew Wal-Mart by offering value. Many people ascribe Wal-Mart's pricing edge to its tough negotiating with suppliers, but the real story is the speed built into its operations. It's a major reason why, even today, the company adds $11 billion of new sales each year[12] in a market that doesn't grow very much.

The system Walton set up captures information at the checkout counter and instantly translates it to suppliers. Given these data, they can optimize their production schedules, lower their costs, and increase their inventory turns—which in turn allows Wal-Mart to pay a lower price for the merchandise, stock less inventory, and log less wasted time.

Almost mirroring Japanese automakers, Wal-Mart's system embodies the concept of the extended enterprise. Besides what Wal-Mart owns or controls, the system includes the suppliers and the logistical people, each of whom must pay the same attention to margins, productivity, and cycle times in order to keep pace. As a result, Wal-Mart's velocity today is still markedly higher than that of Sears.

"Oh well," you say, "that was a different time, and Walton was one-of-a-kind. Revolutions like his don't come along very often. There are no Waltons out there in today's marketplace."

Sure there are. Look at how Michael Dell turned the PC industry on its head in 1996 and 1997, changing the rules of the game and forcing his competitors to play catch-up. As *Business Week* put it: "How has the computer maker managed to defy the naysayers and turn a classically low-margin mail-order operation into a high-profit, high-service business that's the envy of the industry? In a word: speed."[13]

Dell, who pioneered mail-order sales to business customers, had long been building computers to order—his people would look at their screens, call up the various configurations, price the product on the spot, and send the order to manufacturing with a push of a button. In 1996, he ratcheted up the speed by organizing suppliers and shippers into a seamless extended enterprise. By mid-1997, when a customer called or e-mailed Dell, the computer would be boxed and on a delivery truck within 36 hours.[14]

Not incidentally, Dell added sales via the Internet. By the end of 1997, Net orders were accounting for some $3 million in sales per day. For several days during the Christmas season, the intake was up to $6 million.[15]

On the velocity side of the equation, you can raise return on investment by increasing sales relative to assets, or by reducing assets relative to sales. Building to order facilitates both methods:

1. It minimizes the cash tied up in inventory. Dell carries hardly any finished goods and only some 7 days' worth of parts[16]. It relies on close working relationships with suppliers to keep components coming to its plants as needed.

2. High velocity minimizes the risk to margins from obsolescent inventory. With electronics and computer component prices dropping sometimes weekly, the fresher the inventory, the lower its cost. As Michael Dell told *Business Week,* this translates into a 6 percent profit advantage over competitors on components alone.

3. Payments come in quickly when a computer is built to order. Because Dell's customers pay by credit card, the cash is typically in hand in less than 24 hours—versus about 16 days for Gateway 2000, his big mail-order competitor, and some 35 days for Compaq, which sells through dealers.[17]

All of these results combine to hold down working capital, and any time a company reduces working capital, it frees up cash—tax-free cash—for better purposes. At Dell, in fact, working capital is *negative:* Because Dell gets paid almost instantly and pays its suppliers on the customary thirty-day basis, it has the use of that money for three to four weeks.[18]

Result: Dell has been able to keep costs 12 percent below Compaq.[19] In 1996, sales soared 47 percent, to $7.8 billion[20]—just under three times the growth rate of the industry.[21] Despite a profit margin of around 7 percent, earnings almost doubled, to $518 million.[22] In two years, Dell's market share grew from 3.1 percent to 5.9 percent,[23] catapulting the company past Hewlett-Packard, Packard Bell-NEC, and Apple to number three in the PC business after Compaq and IBM.[24] In sales of desktops to medium and large corporations, Dell was number two at the end of 1997.[25]

In 1997, when sales reached some $12.3 billion,[26] Dell's return on investment was a stunning 216 percent, almost 2.5 times that of Compaq.[27]

Increasing velocity also yields some extremely valuable benefits. Reduced inventories save money in plant space and warehousing—the old just-in-time bonus. They improve margins. And customers are happier. Building to order customizes the product for them, and they get it quicker.

In switching to build-to-order, Michael Dell changed the rules of the game for everyone. Retailers such as CompUSA began vying to offer their customers more choice in configuring computers, and manufacturers—led by Compaq—were scrambling in 1997 to find alternative ways to achieve similar or better velocities.

Raising velocity can produce more sales per dollar of assets or the same volume of sales with fewer assets. But neither of these outcomes is a goal; you don't approach the proposition saying, "If I just cut assets, or increase my sales per assets, my ratio will improve." The goal is to identify the tools you can use to increase velocity itself.

The specifics of raising velocity vary from business to business. Retailing requires one set of tools; manufacturing, another; knowledge-based businesses like software, yet another. In manufacturing, for example, a central component is the use of rigorous demand-flow technologies and systems. *Demand flow* manufacturing reverses the mass-production paradigm of the past, in which batch sizes were driven by the need to run machinery at its optimum rate. Instead, as the name implies, production flow is pegged to demand. Ideally, it produces a batch size of one.

Here's how demand flow manufacturing raises velocity: Orders are translated swiftly into products via a streamlined, reliable process in which supplier, manufacturer, and customer are seamlessly linked. The small batch size and shorter cycle time increase the manufacturer's flexibility, so that he can produce to the specific demand of the customers without carrying finished goods inventories. Because this increases the customer's velocity as well, it also increases customer satisfaction. As an example, take Lear Corporation, which supplies interiors to the auto industry. Working closely with its customers, the company has built a worldwide network of ninety just-in-time assembly plants,[28] most of which are dedicated to a single customer. Over the past decade annual inventory turns at Lear's plants have increased from just under 6 to 30.[29]

Fast delivery and fast payments have cut the company's working capital requirements drastically—in 1995, it even achieved negative working capital of $69 million.[30] Lear essentially financed its operations on the float between money coming in from customers and money paid out to suppliers. This performance has helped Lear rack up one of the strongest financial performances in its industry. Higher velocity has also helped Lear to expand strategically. The cash freed up, along with Lear's rising stock price—the two are related, as we shall see—provided the financial muscle for broadening its pond.

Through a string of acquisitions in what we call adjacent segments, Lear has transformed itself from a domestic seating manufacturer into a fully integrated global supplier of complete interiors for the auto industry. It has been able to pay the acquisition premium by applying its demand flow tools to the companies it acquired. We'll talk more about adjacent segments in the next chapter.

Many companies working to raise velocity focus on a goal of reducing working capital. That's the approach at American Standard Company, a $6 billion-a-year maker of air conditioning, plumbing, and automotive products.[31] American Standard was heading for disaster in the early nineties, swamped in debt and junk bonds after a 1988 leveraged buyout. CEO Emmanuel Kampouris responded by articulating a goal of achieving zero working capital, and he adopted demand-flow technology as the centerpiece. By the end of 1996, six of his twenty-two divisions were operating with zero or negative working capital. For the company as a whole, working capital accounted for under 5 cents of every sales dollar, down from 16 cents in 1989.[32] As a result, his company has some $40 million in annual cash that it wouldn't have had at the old rate. And lower operating costs have lifted operating earnings by a third, or some $200 million, since 1990.[33]

Do the financial markets care about this gritty stuff? You bet. Along with inventory turns, the working capital numbers are among the yearly accomplishments Kampouris cites proudly at the top of his letter in the annual report. In 1996, two pages of that report were devoted to explaining to stockholders exactly how demand-flow technology is making them richer. "The core competence of our Company is Demand Flow Manufacturing (DFM)," wrote Kampouris in his

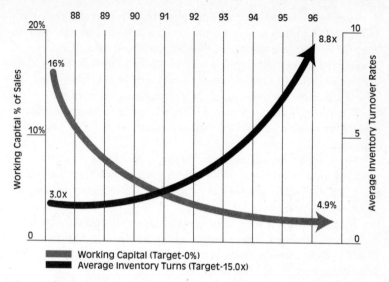

Figure 3.3 Higher velocity has nearly tripled American Standard's inventory turns, and has reduced working capital needs by $640 million annually. (Source: American Standard Annual Report, 1996.)

annual letter. "DFM is a flexible, formulated process that systematically aligns workflow production resources—people, machines, materials and space allocation—in the most efficient manner . . . . [It] is the defining culture of our company." (See Figure 3.3.)

Jack Welch is another leader who thinks investors are interested in the nuts-and-bolts subject of working capital. When he explains what he calls "The New GE" to securities analysts these days, working capital turnover is one of the things he stresses. In the 1980s, he will point out, GE's working capital turned over 3.5 times a year. By the early 1990s, the figure had risen to 4.5 times and by 1997 was pushing toward 8.[34]

Velocity, Growth, and the Capital Markets

Velocity is not some bit of technical arcana. It is not a manufacturing thing or a marketing thing or a financial thing. It's a business thing. Just about any business can benefit from it. Here's how:

Imagine a business in which most players have a 5 percent profit margin (typical for many industries) and generate annual sales equivalent to four times their assets—that is, their velocity is 4. Assume the cost of funding the assets is 20 percent a year. Using the formula $R = M \times V$, we see that the return is 20 percent. The companies in this industry are just covering the cost of their capital—they are not creating any value.

What happens if one company's leaders manage to increase velocity from 4 to 8? They've doubled their return on assets to 40 percent (a 5 percent margin times 8 turns).

How? First, the company uses less cash to finance its operations. Let's say its sales are $100 million. With a velocity of 8, its cash needs are $12.5 million. Its competitors must spend $25 million to achieve the same sales volume.

Ford is among the companies now starting to use demand-flow tools to improve velocity and net margins, which frees up tax-free cash. One result is more customer satisfaction: with shorter cycle times, orders from dealers are being filled faster.

Reducing fixed investment also increases margins over time in capital-intensive companies. The reason: Depreciation charges are lowered. For example, at Ford, automotive operations President Jacques Nasser has cut the annual capital investment from $8 billion to $7 billion (while increasing sales). Over a five-year depreciation cycle, this cumulative $5 billion cut will reduce depreciation by $700 million at the end of the period. On projected automotive sales of $120 billion, this will yield a 0.6 percent improvement in net margins—adding roughly 36 cents to earnings per share, after taxes, and potentially more than $3.50 per share to the stock's value.[35]

The concept of velocity applies to service companies, as well, where it is determined by dividing revenue by total capital employed. Leaders who want to raise it ask such questions as: Where is the capital employed? How productively is it employed? How can it be more productively employed—can we, for example, leverage it through outsourcing or an alliance?

Can you think of ways to increase your velocity? If you can, your capital will work harder for you. In some cases, higher velocity can also boost your margins. The cash you free up will make your whole business stronger and will help you grow your top line. You'll have more money for acquisitions, R&D, capital investment, marketing, and promotion.

And if you apply the same skills to acquisitions with much lower velocity, the savings will reduce the cost of acquiring them.

Finally, velocity will help raise the price/earnings ratio of your stock. The combination of higher returns and profitable growth is what the markets look for. The higher the return on investment, and the higher the rate of sustainable growth you can achieve with that investment, the greater the value investors will assign to your stock.

The Price/Earnings Scorecard

What numbers do you look at when you measure your company's success? The answers we get to this question vary from company to company, from industry to industry, with circumstances, and over time.

Some people focus on total profit; others seek cash generation, growth in cash generation, or return on investment. Still others look to profit margins, revenues, growth in revenues, market share, market value—the list goes on and on. There are also nonfinancial indicators: new product introductions, "competitive advantage" (however defined), customer satisfaction measures, and the like. But only one number will tell you what you need to know if you've got your eye on the future: Your price/earnings (p/e) ratio. Your p/e ratio reflects how much credence investors give your future earnings prospects—what they think of the quality and composition of those earnings.

The price/earnings ratio of your stock is the fundamental earnings per share divided into the price. (As noted before, privately held companies have imputed p/e ratios, which their bankers or investment bankers calculate.) It is as simple as the scoreboard in a basketball game—visible, real-time, and unequivocal, a score even a child can keep track of. All of the other numbers we hear are important. But they're secondary information, like the basketball team's won–lost record for the season, or tallies of rebounds, assists, and the like. The p/e ratio is the score on the board, the one investors in the bleachers and boxes watch.

Note carefully: We are talking here about *fundamental* p/e ratios— what financial experts call *underlying p/e ratios*. Some investors are chary of price/earnings ratios because transient factors can drive them out of whack. Markets will get carried away from time to time, overvaluing a stock when it's fashionably hot (was Netscape ever worth a price equal to 130 times earnings?) or savaging it when there's been an earnings disappointment or writeoff. A company's managers may jack up its p/e ratio for a time with accounting tricks or extraordinary gains.

Securities analysts and investment bankers strip these distortions out when they calculate an underlying p/e ratio. So does the passage of time: Investors look at a p/e ratio's trend. Over a period of years—typically, three—and in comparison with the broad market indexes such as the S&P 500 and/or peer group performance, the underlying p/e ratio shows through the spikes and dips. It emerges as the financial markets digest and assimilate the underlying realities—as they almost invariably do.

Like the investment bankers and analysts, you have to look at your p/e ratio with a cold, clear eye on its fundamental components.

The essence of the p/e ratio is capital-efficient and profitable growth— a combination of R = M × V and top-line growth. The higher and more sustainable it is, the stronger your stock is. The stronger your stock, the greater your ability to make acquisitions, reinvest in growth, and attract better people, whom you can then reward with stock options.

The p/e ratio separates the many business leaders who talk about shareholder value from the leaders who walk their talk. Take, for example, Coca-Cola and PepsiCo. As we saw in Chapter 1, PepsiCo set an all-time record among FORTUNE 500 companies for top-line growth over four decades. From the mid-eighties to the mid-nineties, its annual average rate of 13 percent was three points higher than Coca-Cola's.[36]

But remember: Investors look for growth *and* return on investment. Coca-Cola's return on total capital rose from 18.3 percent in 1987 to 48.5 percent in 1997,[37] while PepsiCo's was barely changed at 18 percent.[38] The capital markets were onto PepsiCo's shortcomings relative to Coca-Cola long before PepsiCo got conspicuously into trouble. PepsiCo's p/e ratio rose from roughly 16 to 29; Coca-Cola's climbed from 18 to just over 42.[39]

PepsiCo's financial people, top management, and directors were as sophisticated as any in the business world. But in all of their analysis and calculation, they missed the message from the markets, which was contained in the p/e ratio.

The message is loud and clear, across businesses and industries of all types. The price/earnings ratio is the closest thing you have to a crystal ball. It contains what no other single number can: the collective intelligence of the capital markets, focused on the expectations of future performance. The p/e ratio tells you what people who have a dispassionate view of your company think of its future ability to make money. It reveals how much of their money they are willing to bet on your success in the quarters and years to come. Here are the key points to remember:

1. A high p/e ratio means that the capital markets believe your company has some substantive advantage—it achieves consistently superior performance by doing some things uniquely well. They see that you have built a track record for delivering high revenue and earnings growth reliably and predictably over time—through expansions and downturns, in the face of changing markets and new competition. The growth has been based on fundamental operating performance, not accounting games, acquisitions, asset sales, or other one-time boosts.

2. More importantly, the premium price embodied in your high p/e ratio reflects the markets' expectation that your company will continue to deliver this performance. Investors believe your company can adapt to change. They expect that it will maintain its particular advantage and thrive in the future, no matter how dramatically your markets shift, or how hostile the business environment turns. They're willing to pay a premium price for this reliability.

The markets watch every quarter's results not because they're short-sighted but because they are looking for evidence that you still have an advantage. They will also look for interim indicators that may provide a basis for estimating the coming quarter's results—for example, the computer industry's book-to-bill ratio, which compares new orders with shipments. But it's the consistent quarterly evidence that lights up the scoreboard.

Business leaders have to understand what this central piece of the scoreboard is, and be extremely clear about explaining it. They must deliver that understanding to investors—through their proxies, the securities analysts—every quarter, without fail.

Your Opponents

Who else is on the scoreboard? What team are you playing against? The comparison can have enormous implications. Companies with high p/e ratios effectively pay less for acquisitions, since their stock is worth more.

Conversely, those with low p/e ratios are more vulnerable to being acquired. And their leaders' jobs are less secure—boards of directors are not as patient as they used to be with CEOs who don't deliver strong returns to the owners. Wall Street calls leaders who sustain high p/e ratios "overachievers." Companies with low p/e ratios are labeled "undermanaged."

Comparisons are easiest for companies listed on the New York Stock Exchange (NYSE). You're familiar with the Standard & Poor's 500 (S&P 500), a broad composite of 500 NYSE stocks that serves as a proxy for the performance of the market as a whole. The S&P 500 has its own p/e ratio. The number will vary over time, based on the state of the economy, the state of the market, and investors' expectations. But what's constant is the significance of any company's p/e ratio when compared to the composite. Higher is good, lower is bad. It's that simple.

The S&P 500 is not necessarily the only opposing team in this game. You also need to look at the p/e ratio for your peer group, whether it's an industry or a selected group of companies that are comparable in other ways. (You can usually identify a peer group in reports by security analysts.) If your own ratio is higher than the ratio of the S&P 500, but your peer group's ratio is even higher, you're still likely to be heading for trouble.

Perhaps your peer group's ratio is lower than that of the S&P 500. The markets have made a judgment about the quality of the market space your company occupies—for example, it may be deemed "mature." Does that mean you're in the wrong business? On the contrary. You're going to grow anyway, because you are learning that there's no such thing as a mature market. As you grow, investors will notice.

How the Markets Judge You

To create a higher p/e ratio, you have to show the financial markets that you are earning a solid return on investors' money and growing profitably—and that the investors can count on you to keep up the good work in the future. Here's how the markets make their judgments:

The Components of the P/E Ratio

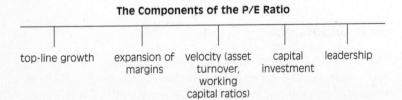

| top-line growth | expansion of margins | velocity (asset turnover, working capital ratios) | capital investment | leadership |

Top-Line Growth: If you've read this far, you don't need any further explanation. The days are gone when the markets would settle for earnings gains from cost-cutting alone.

Expansion of Margins and Velocity: This is return on investment—$R = M \times V$. (Few investors or security analysts as yet use the term "velocity," though Michael Dell's frequent references to his velocity are making the term more prominent. But they do look for the performance measures that reflect it—i.e., asset turnover and working capital ratios.) As noted earlier in the chapter, leaders with business acumen constantly work to improve each of the components of margin and velocity.

Capital Investment: The markets look for disciplined, productive reinvestment of capital. After all, who would want to trust you with their money if you can't invest your own corporate capital wisely? Take the advice of Warren Buffett, one of the world's most celebrated stock pickers. Buffett doesn't interfere in the operating management of any company in which he holds an influential stake, but he demands to know one thing: How does the company reinvest its capital? Buffett's criterion is simple. If the company can't show a minimum of a $1 increase in market value for every $1 invested, management is not doing its job. Would Warren Buffett want your stock in his portfolio?

The Leadership Factor: The role of strong leadership in creating a growth company is a major theme of this book. Good leadership is what ensures the quality and continuity of growth.

If you don't think the stock markets really pay attention to leadership, look at what happens to a floundering company when an acknowledged business leader takes command—when Lou Gerstner is named head of IBM, Larry Bossidy of AlliedSignal, or John Trani of Stanley Works. Conversely, watch how the markets punish leaders who don't deliver on their promises. Kodak's stock rose sharply in 1993 when George Fisher, formerly of Motorola, came in as CEO.[40] With his background, he seemed just the man to turn around the stumbling maker of film and photographic equipment. Four years later, it was clear that he had neither gotten costs under control nor come up with a sustainable growth strategy. The lid blew off when Kodak announced dismal third-quarter earnings in 1997, and the punishment was merciless. Its shares, which had a high of almost 100, dropped to less than 60.[41]

Or take the rise and fall of "Chain Saw Al" Dunlap, made CEO of Sunbeam Corp. in 1996. Sunbeam's stock rose from about $15 to a peak of more than $50. But by mid-1998, it had become clear that the notorious turnaround artist knew only how to slash and burn, not how to build. By the time the board dismissed him, the stock was back down to around $15.[42]

Even without such dramatic and visible change, the markets see the importance of strong leadership—and they also see its results over time. The markets know that shifting into a growth mode is a tough order if you've been focused only on cost cutting. They're looking for signs that you understand the difference between the old way and the new. The old way was dealing with the known, the controllable, the quantifiable, the safe, the inward-looking, the predictable. The new way requires leaders who are outward-looking, bold, willing to take risks, able to live with ambiguity and change. Investors want to see leadership in depth, leaders at all levels who can reliably deliver results.

The sources and quality of earnings-per-share (eps) growth have a major impact on price/earnings ratios. If a company is getting good eps growth but not growing its top line, the markets know the eps growth can't last long. Another company with similar earnings improvement, but also with top-line growth, will get a substantially higher p/e ratio.

Your p/e ratio tells you whether the people who've entrusted their money to you believe you are creating profitable, capital-efficient growth. It is the ultimate reality check on how good a job you're doing as a leader.

> *The basic truth of business is that return on investment must be greater than the cost of capital. Return on investment is simply profit margin multiplied by velocity. That's just business common sense, the universal rule of business—but common sense is very uncommon. The companies whose leaders understand it are the ones that investors reward with standout price/earnings ratios.*

P A R T   II

Broadening the Pond

Strategy from the Outside In

When we ask a group of executives to talk about ways to grow, the session's first round quickly produces a flip-pad full of possibilities. A typical list would include the following: create more products; spend more money on technology; strengthen the sales force; execute more intensively; reduce cost and price; gain market share; take more risks; develop new distribution channels; globalize; acquire; break the rules; develop alliances; improve packaging and/or advertising; reinvent or revolutionize our industry.

Such grab bags certainly include useful options along with the challenging—if woolly—exhortations. (Just which rules do you want to break, and how?) But they're not *why* companies grow. You can spend uncountable hours thinking about the possibilities and never develop a workable growth strategy. In fact, most of the possibilities are not strategies at all. Conventional thinking about growth—and a lot of what's billed as unconventional thinking—tends to be a muddle of tactics and intellectually seductive but usually vague concepts masquerading as strategies.

For example, volumes have been written about Nike's fabulous growth. The focus is mostly on its attention-getting tactics and its power at image making—the big-name endorsements, the extravagant promotions and hard-hitting ads, the sponsorships of teams and events, the antiestablishment persona and attitude, the great merchandising machine—or on the passion of founder Phil Knight and his rule-breaking "continuous reinvention" of his entrepreneurially minded business.

Now try to figure out what all this means for your own business. Even if you could get a Michael Jordan equivalent to tout your wares, or create a rule-breaking culture in your company, so what? The same is true for the message you get from the gurus of serendipity and inspiration, out-of-the-box thinking, and all that. Yes, these are important in generating ideas and unleashing imagination. But they're only a part of the thinking architecture.

The problem is that most corporate leaders seeking growth look at their business from the inside out. That's why they're trapped in the fight for share of a traditionally defined market.

Those who build growth companies, whether they're entrepreneurs or executives of multibillion-dollar corporations, don't worry about share. *They redefine the market, they grow it—and they want all of the growth.* Once they know they've got the basics right (Chapter 3), they follow four simple rules that are the framework for any growth plan or strategy:

1. Look at your business from the outside in.

2. Enlarge the pond you fish in—look beyond your industry's boundaries and existing markets to the customer's total needs.

3. Find market segments that are growing—or create them.

4. Build new core competencies to capitalize on your new opportunities.

Everything else is a subset.

We'll reveal the real lessons from Nike—among others—shortly. For now, let's look at what the four rules mean.

Look at Your Business from the Outside In

This rule is part of the common sense that a good businessperson possesses intuitively. *And yet, few executives heed it.* Many very good businesspeople design new growth games that look great on paper but fail because the designers haven't looked in from the outside. For all that's been preached and written about "knowing the customer," these executives still are not anticipating their customers' changing needs—needs the customers themselves may not yet perceive.

They are thinking about their customers from the inside out. Too often, the question is still: "How can I get my customers to buy more of what I sell now?" It's the wrong question. As Peter Drucker wrote, "We have concentrated these past years on improving traditional information, which is almost exclusively information about what goes on inside an organization . . . Increasingly, a winning strategy will require information about events and conditions outside the institution: noncustomers, technologies other than those currently used by the company and its present competitors, markets not currently served, and so on."[1]

What does looking from the outside in mean, in practice? It's literally thinking outside the box. Consider this basic schematic:

Your company | Your customers | The final users

$\longrightarrow$

That's business, right? Your company produces something, then you sell it to your customers, who sell it to the final users. You start with what you have—assets, an organization, a core competence, a brand, distribution—and try to build on it. You ask, "How can I sell more?"

This is the inside-out view, and it's traditional. Looking from the inside out, people see the future through the lens of present products and distribution channels, and business-as-usual operational and technical thinking. They say: "I'm in this industry. Where is this industry now and how can I make more money out of it?" To take just one example, this was IBM's view when it looked at the world through the lens of a mainframe manufacturer.

Now turn the sequence around:

The final users | Your customers | Your company

New competitors

$\longrightarrow$

This forces a different set of questions. You are looking at the drivers of change—often radical change. You are looking at *needs*. What do people out there in the real world need? How are their needs changing? What new competitors are anticipating and meeting those needs? From this standpoint, what you make and sell is subject to a new set of questions, too.

Mega question: Do the changes mean that what you're producing today is on its way to being obsolete, or becoming a subset of some new need? The answer is probably yes, and probably sooner than you imagine. So other questions follow: What's a different way of doing it? How can you meet the needs before anyone else? Create new needs?

Growth starts with looking at your company from the perspective of your present *and* future customers. What's happening in your marketplace? How are needs changing? What's causing the changes? Where are your resulting opportunities? Then work backward from there. What is required? What do we have? What's the gap and how do we fill it?

What are you really looking for? Simply this: profitable revenue streams; sustainable revenue streams tied to growth. All of the questions boil down to these three:

1. How can I identify or create needs?

2. How can I meet them?

3. How fast can I meet them?

Your Value Proposition

Defining a clear value proposition is especially important for leaders of industrial and/or OEMs (original equipment manufacturers). Too often they focus on sales to the intermediary between themselves and the final customers; they haggle over price and struggle for market share in their existing ponds. Instead, think about how your products and services fit into your customers' complex of needs. What is the combined value of the fit between the customers' processes and your product? How can it help the customers get a competitive advantage in their marketplaces? With some imagination, you may be able to help your customers improve their own margins and velocity and expand their own ponds. That's an irresistible value proposition. To cite just one example, it's a value proposition that Jack Welch is pushing heavily these days at GE.

The more rigorous, fresh, unbiased, and robust your understanding of your customers' needs, the more secure your future is. Look from the outside in. Reach into your customers' thoughts, see their needs, and work backward. That's the fundamental lesson. The rest is execution.

Cutting the Risks

Charting growth from the outside in is critical to reducing business risk. Does that seem counterintuitive? After all, focusing inwardly, on such things as cost and process improvement, is deterministic and certain. The results are easy to foresee; feedback is quick and direct. An ambitious growth plan, by contrast, means dealing with unknowns, making subjective judgments, and betting your capital on the strength of those judgments. It's creative, often intuitive. Outcomes are uncertain.

Many companies have seemingly done well thinking from the inside out. 3M achieved legendary success as an innovator by giving its people room to develop their ideas for new products in quasi-entrepreneurial fashion. For years, it ranked among the leaders on FORTUNE's list of most-admired companies.[2]

But during the first half of the nineties, 3M grew its top line less than 4 percent[3] despite the brilliance of its entrepreneurial technologists. There wasn't enough feedback from the marketplace—missing were the insight into the customer's mind, and the intuitive observations about needs that could have translated inventiveness into powerful growth. Only recently has new leadership got the company back on track with outside-in growth initiatives.

Simple fact: Outside in is *less* risky. We've seen again and again that the greatest source of risk in a business is failure to understand the needs of the customer or end user. If people don't look from the outside in, external change will overtake them, no matter how much energy they lavish on their businesses.

It's common today to hear someone say that so-and-so is deficient as a leader because he or she won't take bold risks. That's precisely wrong. Soul-stirring as it may be to talk about betting the farm, good businesspeople don't take unnecessary risks. Instead, they quantify the risks and find ways to reduce them. And there's no more important step than working backward from the customers' needs, defining them tightly, and subjecting them to disciplined analysis and testing.

The Sources of Growth

We identify nine basic souces of growth. All are potential opportunities for creating new growth trajectories.

1. Natural growth, where the market for what you make is strong and expanding.

2. Gaining market share through low cost—high productivity growth, rapid cycle times, high asset turnover.

3. Proprietary or patented technology.

4. Highly-developed distribution channels that you've built over time.

5. Opening new markets for your existing products—for example, globalization.

6. Gaining power in the marketplace via acquisitions, alliances, vertical integration.

7. Expanding your pond.

8. Resegmenting your markets.

9. Moving into adjacent segments.

The first six are familiar: If you haven't tried them, you can read about them in other books and in countless articles in the business press. They have been used with varying degrees of success—the variation depends largely on how successful the leaders using them have been in looking at their businesses from the outside in.

The last three are not part of the standard repertory. In fact, they are ways of thinking, more than anything else. They represent the distillation of outside-in thinking, and they are the ones we focus on.

Enlarge the Pond You Fish In

Looking from the outside in, successful growth companies' leaders think expansively. They ask, "Are there any related marketplaces that we can serve?" They are, in the phrase we use regularly, seeking to enlarge or broaden the ponds they fish in.

It's not an entirely new idea. Many businesspeople around the world have long understood it and prospered from it. But broadening the pond has not become a part of the genetic codes of most companies. Now it must. In this era of unparalleled opportunities, where growth has become paramount, it is mandatory for corporate leaders to open their eyes to what is possible.

Broadening the pond forces outside in thinking. The central idea behind it is usually stunningly simple—once it's articulated. In Chapter 1, we noted Roberto Goizueta's "share of stomach" concept as a classic example of broadening a pond. He defined Coca-Cola's pond not as cola, not as soft drinks, but as all of the fluid humans consume. Once Ford Motor Company's leaders got the idea, they broadened their pond from the market for vehicles to the lifetime needs of vehicle owners.

During the eighties, Taco Bell CEO John Martin also talked about share of stomach in redefining the fast-food chain's pond. When he took over, Taco Bell's people thought of themselves as being in the Mexican fast-food business. Martin first redefined the pond as the quick-service restaurant business, meaning that Taco Bell's competition was hamburgers, chicken, pizza, and all of the other fast-food varieties. To grow in this larger pond, Taco Bell created a new value proposition by overhauling everything from kitchen design to management structure so it could deliver food cheaper and faster than any of its competitors.

Later, Martin redefined the pond yet again, from quick-service restaurants to "the business of feeding people." As one of his executives told Harvard Business School professors Leonard Schlesinger and James Heskett, "That takes the Taco Bell universe from an $80 billion universe to an $800 billion universe." The company staked out its territory in that universe with thousands of new "points of access," such as stalls and kiosks in airports, malls, convenience stores, and high school and college cafeterias. The pond-broadenings helped raise Taco Bell's sales from less than $1 billion in 1984 to nearly $4 billion in 1993. Net profits over the period rose from $59 million to $253 million.[4]

Broadening the pond is the antithesis of going for market share. The goal, in fact, is to put your current market share in its proper perspective by restating it as your share of your potential market. If you now have, say, 40 percent of a $10 billion market, you need to look for the much larger pond of which your share is perhaps 4 percent. That's literally what Jack Welch tells his business unit leaders at GE: Redefine your market to one in which your current share is no more than 10 percent. The buzz phrase he uses is "10X"—meaning, expand your pond tenfold—and it's on the mind of every business unit head. It punctures any arrogance that may have come with success; it unlocks creativity and releases energy.

Companies that create sustainable growth trajectories are always looking to broaden or enlarge the ponds they fish in. They may be aiming to enlarge their own ponds by annexing territory currently held by nontraditional competitors. Or, they may be enlarging the total pond, creating new demands that add to the sum total of business activity. Either approach can be a source of sustainable growth.

Great growth companies are very serious pond-broadeners: They grow the whole market. Leaders like Henry Ford, Thomas Watson Sr., Sam Walton, Konesuki Matsushita, Ingvar Komprad (Ikea), Fred Smith (Federal Express), Steve Jobs, and Bill Gates built world-changing companies because they enlarged the total ponds, creating demand not only for their own products and services but for those of many other companies as well. In effect, they created entire new industries.

Leaders of this caliber are never content to broaden their ponds just once. They do it over and over again. Gates did it most recently by staking out the Internet. Eckhard Pfeiffer has broadened Compaq's pond three times so far—roughly, once every twenty-four months.

You don't have to be Henry Ford or Bill Gates. You don't have to redefine an industry or invent an entirely new one (though it doesn't hurt to think about that possibility). What's important is that you think expansively. Learn everything you can about your customers' needs, including those that the customers haven't yet identified. Develop insights into those needs. From those insights, you can extract what we call *mega-ideas*—market-stretching concepts that burst the bonds of supposedly mature industries. The minivan was a mega-idea; so were Nike's concept of athletic footwear, FedEx, CNN, Microsoft's low-cost consumer PC operating system, Barry Diller's TV home shopping network, online merchandising . . . and the list goes on.

A cautionary note: Some leaders define a pond, expand it into a lake, and then see an ocean. But an ocean will sink a boat that isn't seaworthy. It takes discipline to know how far and fast *not* to push.

Find Market Segments That Are Growing—or Create Them

Sustainable, profitable growth starts with breaking markets down into segments. If you look at the broad aggregate of demand, you may see a "mature" business. But any market is the sum of many segments, and each segment fulfills a need. Learning to identify those segments is the first step in getting out of the "served market" trap—the blinder that keeps you focused on your current business and ignorant of opportunities within and around it. Eliminate "served market" from your business vocabulary.

Segmenting means simply slicing up a marketplace differently, in light of needs that are constantly changing. The causes of changes are endless—demographics, new forms of distribution, technology such as the microprocessor or consumer software, shifting tastes, economic cycles, government regulation or deregulation, the confluence and convergence of industries in new fields such as the Internet, and many others.

When you break your market down into segments, you've got a powerful methodology for generating growth ideas. Which needs are changing? Which ones are growing or declining? How do you tap into the new and growing needs?

You can resegment a market by value proposition, consumer motivation and buying behavior, price points, technology, line extensions, distribution channels, and the like. You can expand into existing segments, or you can resegment the market, creating new ones based on new needs. Segmentation is a tool you can use as modestly or ambitiously as you want. You can use it to make incremental gains or to map out a whole new range of possibilities.

Whatever market you serve, there's more than one way to segment it. Rarely do two competitors define a segment precisely the same way. Tip: In defining your markets, avoid the data your industry association gathers. Typically they are based not on needs but the physical products sold, many of them no longer relevant as market segments. And the data tend to be whatever is easiest to compile.

Enlarging the pond and resegmenting are the hidden keys to truly understanding a lot of familiar success stories. For example, the most useful lesson from Nike is how the company has continuously enlarged its pond through segmentation. In the context of Nike's troubles during 1997 and 1998, it's worth noting that Phil Knight discovered his strategy only after he was blindsided in the mid-eighties by Reebok. Even great leaders make blunders; their greatness comes, in part, from their continuing ability to change course when they need to.

The story of that corporate crisis is familiar enough: Nike rose to phenomenal success by designing high-quality running shoes for serious athletes, manufacturing them in Asia, and underselling competitors like Adidas. The company branched out into making shoes for basketball, tennis, and football. When jogging and fitness boomed, Nike moved its products out into the broad consumer marketplace. By 1984, when revenues passed $900 million,[5] Nike had an estimated one-third of the U.S.

athletic footwear market.[6] Then along came Reebok, with stylish shoes for the so-called athleisure market. Sales of Nike's sturdy, clunky-looking footware slumped; in three years, Nike's market share fell by almost half.[7]

The problem wasn't only style. Reebok had begun to segment the consumer marketplace, designing specific shoes for women's aerobics. Responding to the crisis, Knight decreed a dual goal for Nike: sharpen its focus as a sports company and, at the same time, zero in on specific market segments.

As Knight described it in a 1992 *Harvard Business Review* article, his discovery of segmentation was an accident. "I can't say we had a really smart strategy going forward," he admitted. "We had a strategy, and when it didn't work, we went back and regrouped until finally we hit on something. What we hit on was the Air Jordan basketball shoe. *Its success showed us that slicing things up into digestible chunks was the wave of the future.* [Emphasis added.] We created a whole new segment within Nike, focused on basketball."[8]

A technical and stylistic innovation, the shoe used the air-cushion technology Nike had developed originally for running shoes. Named after and promoted by Chicago Bulls star Michael Jordan, it became wildly successful—for about two years. Then sales collapsed as the fad cooled and Jordan himself was sidelined with injuries.

Analyzing the disappointment, Knight produced a classic pond-broadening paradigm. "We started asking ourselves, are we trying to stretch Air Jordan too far? Is Air Jordan 70 percent of basketball? Or is it 25 percent of basketball?"[9] In other words, what was the total basketball shoe market, and how else could it be sliced and diced?

Defining a new segment means defining a consumer need that nobody else has thought of or addressed before. The answer for Nike was two new segments based on shoes for different styles of playing basketball: Force, for the aggressive style exemplified by Charles Barkley; and Flight, for the quick, high-flying style of Scottie Pippen. Force and Flight took off, and, by 1992, Knight was able to say: "We actually have three distinct segments, each with its own brand—or sub-brand, really. Each has great athletes representing it, a complete product line, shoes and clothes that are tied together. Instead of one big glop, we have the number one, the number two, and the number four brands of basketball shoes."[10]

Thus did the tool of segmentation transform Nike. As sales and market share rebounded, the company went on to create similar segments in tennis—the Challenge Court collection, promoted around the rebellious personalities of John McEnroe and Andre Agassi, and the Supreme Court collection for the conservative majority of players. Ever since, Nike has grown by developing new segments and moving into adjacent ones. It sliced up the fitness marketplace into many segments, large and small, from cross-training shoes to aquatic footwear—capturing nearly half of the U.S. athletic footwear market and expanding around the world. It began selling apparel and accessories, and opened retail stores. From 1995 through 1997, Nike sales grew at an annual average rate of 39 percent, and profits at a 41 percent rate.[11]

Phil Knight's ambitious plan to double Nike's revenues to $12 billion by 2001[12] floats on an ocean-sized pond. Just about anything that can be associated with sports and fitness is included, from bras to hockey sticks and even services, such as managing athletes' careers. For example, the so-called Alpha sportswear line, scheduled for introduction in mid-to-late 1998, even includes watches. "We are in the sports business, not the shoe business," chief strategist Mike Parker told *Time* magazine.[13] So defined, the pond amounts to something in the neighborhood of perhaps $100 billion, of which Nike's share is under 10 percent.[14]

First, however, Knight has to clean up Nike's problems. While he was planning the vast expansion of his pond, the company was blindsided once again by rivals with better insights into changing tastes, including Adidas CEO Robert Louis-Dreyfus. "Nike is reassessing everything, from the way it sells to retailers to the number of times the famous swoosh appears on products and in advertising," said *Time*. Comparing the company to a teenager made awkward by a growth spurt, *Time* added: "It will try to act smaller by developing categories such as golf, soccer and women's as separate business units . . . 'What we have to do is re-energize ourselves, starting with the product,'" says Knight.[15] The lesson: Segmentation is not once and for all; it's a dynamic, ongoing state of mind.

Adjacent Segments

The most accessible and powerful kind of segmentation targets an adjacent segment—the segment next to the present one—where you can sell an additional product or service. It's one way to leverage your existing skills and resources into new business.

You can create new adjacent segments, as Phil Knight did with basketball shoes, as Lee Iacocca did with the minivan, and as Lou Gerstner did with Amex's Corporate Cards. In the late eighties, Toyota (Lexus), Nissan (Infiniti), and Honda (Acura) created a new market segment. They moved in on Mercedes-Benz and BMW with competitive cars priced about one-third lower—and with a superior service network. The value proposition was solid enough to win over potential and current Mercedes and BMW customers, despite the power of their nameplates. Yet the Japanese also expanded this profitable segment as a whole.

Or, you can expand your markets by moving into segments already occupied by others, bringing your particular strengths to bear more effectively than competitors. GE Capital, for example, plays this game with great success (Chapter 8). It's part of how Eckhard Pfeiffer brought Compaq back from near-death (Chapter 6).

Former GE Medical Systems CEO John Trani calls adjacent segments "near neighbors." GE Medical has most recently moved into the service neighborhood; it not only maintains customers' machinery but also trains their people and even provides help in designing management processes. Any near neighbor to the machines is an opportunity, because the company's eye is on the total wallet in medical equipment and related services. The goal Trani enunciated is simple, and it still holds: "We want every dollar."[16]

Indeed, service is a hotbed of adjacency these days; there are vast opportunities for capturing more of the customer's wallet. Manufacturers have a trove of untapped core competencies to offer in meeting customers' needs for maintenance, support, upgrading, systems management, and all of the other functions associated with ownership of a product over the long haul. Some even sell the management processes they've developed for improving operations and raising productivity.

Such growth is both profitable and sustainable. Capital investment tends to be lower, profit margins are higher, and earnings are more predictable. Once you're established with your customers, it's harder for them to switch suppliers—few competitors should be able to match your expertise and experience base.

As John Trani puts it: "Your installed base equals credibility, equals leverage the others don't have. And what happens to the other guy? He gets weaker. The competitive intensity goes down, the further you move from the product. When that happens, you have everything."

Services are what Ford has its eye on in targeting the lifetime use of its vehicles as its larger pond. AlliedSignal (Chapter 10) is making hay in services. Reynolds and Reynolds CEO Dave Holmes essentially re-defined his company by moving into ever larger adjacent service segments (Chapter 11).

No pond looks bigger to Jack Welch than services. In his 1996 annual report, he wrote: "Services is so great an opportunity for the Company that our vision for the next century is a GE that is 'a global service company that also sells high-quality products.'" From the time he made it a top priority in 1995 through the end of 1997, service revenues grew from $7.5 billion to $9.7 billion,[17] and Welch's goal is to almost double that before 2001. The push is strongest at four of its businesses: (1) aircraft engines, (2) power systems, (3) medical systems, and (4) transportation systems (locomotives). Some 40 percent of these business's revenues in 1997 came from services, versus 33 percent in 1991.[18]

Creating the Framework

Once you start looking from the outside in, how do you translate what you see into a plan? You start by identifying the combinations of existing and new customers you can reach, and the existing and/or new needs you can meet for those customers.

The 2 × 2 in Figure 4.1 is your basic outside-in strategic tool. The moment you look at it, your whole framework for planning changes. You're focusing on needs, not on products.

With the 2 × 2, you define and choose your universe of potentially profitable revenue streams as:

Customers—existing and new.

Needs—existing and new.

Any path you pick lies in one of the four quadrants:

A. Existing customers with existing needs.

B. New customers with existing needs.

C. New customers with new needs.

D. Existing customers with new needs.

A need is an end need. Somebody may already be supplying it, but it usually can be satisfied by more than one product. Could that product be yours? Or can you create a new need?

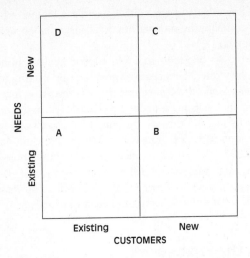

Figure 4.1

Make the 2 × 2 a part of your daily life. Pick up a piece of paper any-where—in a hotel room or on an airplane—and fool around with it. It's a brain builder. The more you use it, the more ideas you'll find.

Later in the chapter, we'll study the quadrants in detail. But first, let's think a moment about how to define needs—especially those that may not seem at first glance related to your core competencies.

Defining Needs

Needs are always changing; new ones keep arising. But what is a need? What do people in your marketplace want? Once you've got a need pinned down, satisfying it becomes strikingly simple. But until then it's usually not obvious, even to the customer.

Invention is the often mother of necessity. Before they saw one, how many people thought they needed a minivan? Who yearned for a mutual funds portfolio? Capital equipment leasing? Cross-training shoes? Computer purchases via the Internet? Outside-in thinking brings such new products and services to market; outside-in thinking is about looking for unmet needs.

New technologies often create new needs, but far more important is understanding the nature of needs and using imagination to meet them. Indeed, technologists may be the last persons to see the potential. Ken Olsen developed the minicomputer and founded Digital Equipment Corporation. Yet, in 1986, "the most successful entrepreneur of all time," as FORTUNE magazine once called him,[19] could not conceive that people would want to use computers at home. Even as he spoke, Bill Gates, Rod Canion of Compaq, and others were betting differently. From the perspective of a minicomputer builder, the PC was a problem, not an opportunity. Looking from the inside out, Olsen missed the future.

The technologists themselves must learn how to look for needs—in effect, they have to kick the tires in the customers' parking lots. Greg Summe of AlliedSignal (Chapter 10) looked at his aerospace division's intensively engineered avionics equipment and asked: "But what does the customer really want?" He got his engineers to start asking that question too, and he offered them a new business model. Think about our business as being like the consumer electronics industry, he said, where producers entice customers with countless small but profitable product variations—things that make the products more useful or appealing. Spend time with your customers to find out what sort of enhancements and embellishments appeal to them. Very quickly, his pipeline filled with hot-selling new products.

No matter what business you're in, you have to separate your perspective on the marketplace from your attachment to what you already do. Leaders who can't make this tough call are found moaning about being stuck in mature industries. Remember Arthur Wood, the Sears Roebuck chairman we mentioned in Chapter 3, who saw no growth left in retailing? Wood was right—about his company. He wasn't looking for needs; he was pushing Sears Roebuck's existing value proposition at customers who were looking for a better one. There was plenty of growth for people like Sam Walton.[20]

But no one has a monopoly on spotting new needs, and no company is immune to losing touch with the total needs of its customers. Next time you're in a mall that has a Wal-Mart, see whether there's a Target store in the same mall or nearby. Target, the biggest division of Dayton-Hudson,[21] has become a small but painful thorn in the king of retailing's side.

Target used to be a fairly successful "commodity retailer," slightly more pricey than competitors like Kmart, and it tallied up solid earnings and growth records by surfing the wave of general discount retailing during the seventies and eighties. As Wal-Mart made that game tougher, though, Target's CEO, Bob Ulrich, took a look at his environment from the outside in.

He spotted an opening in Wal-Mart's strategy. Some of its customers wanted to move upscale—they wanted merchandise with the same value proposition, but just a cut above. Wal-Mart wasn't meeting their needs. Target could, because its historical position was just right: a cut above the big discounters. There was Ulrich's opportunity: aim squarely at the more affluent shoppers in the Wal-Mart crowd, and meet their needs with stores that are a touch classier in the shopping experience—in their merchandise, their appearance, and the quality of the personnel—but offer the same deep discounting that had made Wal-Mart so successful. Very simple, very obvious—once Ulrich thought about it.

Target today bills itself as the "upscale discount store." Can Ulrich keep winning away Wal-Mart's customers? Maybe, maybe not. In his favor: Wal-Mart's potent genetic code so far lacks the flexibility to make the same shift. Vendors and securities analysts sing Target's praises: "It's the discount store of tomorrow," says one supplier. Target continues to expand—it's now focusing on the Northeast. It accounted for 74 percent of Dayton-Hudson's 1997 revenues (up from 45 percent when Ulrich started[22]); 71 percent of operating profits,[23] and much of the increase in Dayton-Hudson's p/e ratio, from the low teens in the early nineties to over 20 in 1997.[24] In 1994, Ulrich was rewarded for resegmenting Wal-Mart's market (and executing brilliantly) by being named CEO of the parent company.

Needs versus Industries

Most people think of themselves as being in a particular industry, and they define the industry traditionally: aerospace, banking, retailing, semiconductors, software, utilities. Most often the industry is the denominator of their goals.

That's the wrong denominator today. In this age of deregulation and the Internet, of manufacturers segueing into services and selling their expertise, players in different industries are realigning. Industries are crossing each other's traditional boundaries and reshaping the game for everyone.

Look at what's happening in telecommunications, entertainment, cable, the media, and software, to take five of the most conspicuous and turbulent examples. Call it convergence or call it confluence; it's a massive reshaping of traditional industry lines based on the information revolution and on disintermediation—the reconfiguring and bypassing of middlemen and established distribution channels.

These five traditionally defined industries are cutting into each other's old territories. They are forming consortiums and alliances. The results: tremendous instability—and tremendous growth.

Inside out thinking is deadly in this kind of situation. In 1995, AT&T's $50 billion long-distance division had about half of the $70 billion-a-year U.S. market for voice and data phone transmission. But its managers were the products of an archaic genetic code. Fixated on defending their traditional business against competitors such as MCI and Sprint, they focused heavily on quarterly tallies of customers saved and lost.

Since then, the landscape has changed radically. Deregulation allows AT&T to compete for local service as well (although as of early 1998 it was not yet making much of the opportunity). At the same time, competition is coming fast from all directions—from new players like World-Com, all but unknown until it challenged British Telecom and GTE for possession of MCI, and from others that will emerge in the deregulated global marketplace. They're after the local telephony market as well—and more.

Competition is also coming from the Internet and from cable-TV operators. Electric utilities are getting into the game, too—their channels to homes can carry communications.

Internet access companies are becoming content providers. Traditional entertainment companies are looking to the Internet as the prime-time TV audience continues to fall off. More and more people are spending their evenings online.

Still other players can and will come out of left field. For example, some software companies sell voice-translation programs that allow people to make long-distance calls anywhere in the world, via their computers and the Internet. The only piece of this business the phone companies get is the payment for the local call that hooks the user up to one of the Internet access providers. These upstarts are so small that their combined annual revenues add up to a fraction of AT&T's *monthly* cash flow.[25] The Internet telephony they offer is still cumbersome. But they're improving, and they aim to develop customers among businesses with intranets. They are making new rules by meeting customers' needs, and their success is creating new pressures on traditional pricing structures.[26]

What's the industry properly called now? Not telephony. Local and global information conveyance and production is an accurate description. Or, more broadly, *electronic commerce*. It will obsolete lots of old industry definitions and boundaries.

What would you be doing today, if you were running AT&T? Faced with the need to raise revenues in an environment of declining prices, the company wants to go after a much larger set of customer needs, including video, multimedia, and online services. That market is potentially at least ten times larger than the long-distance voice and data market. The long-distance division, now standing on its own, has redefined its pond as a total communications market of some $700 billion a year, of which its share is less than 10 percent. AT&T itself is simultaneously jacking up capital spending and cutting costs.

Change has been slow—speed is not a part of the company's genetic code. But CEO Mike Armstrong has made a great start in wrestling with some of the key questions, such as the size and definition of the total customer wallet and the need to use capital efficiently in this extremely capital intensive industry. He will also need more new genes in leadership positions. His bold plan to acquire TCI, the second-largest cable TV company, brings a powerful new one in the form of its CEO, John Malone.

Think about the current status of banking, insurance, investment banking, and any subsidiary businesses where information technology leads inevitably to disintermediation. Whose position is stable? Who knows where they're going to be in five years—or less? The megamerger of Citicorp and Travelers that stunned just about everybody when it was proposed in April 1998 was a clear signal that the move to convergence in financial services is underway.

How stable is *your* "industry?" What companies, perhaps unknown to you, have the power to redefine it? What opportunities, outside of your industry, might you seize if you have enough imagination and focus?

If you're currently saying that your company has a 60 percent share of your industry's market, you're looking from the inside out. You have a much smaller share of a much bigger pond—one that's possibly being redefined even as you speak. If you don't redefine your pond to be broader, others will redefine their pond to include you.

You have to enlarge your list of questions:

- ▶ What discontinuities are on the horizon?
- ▶ What's the new definition of the industry going to be?
- ▶ What is the size and composition of the total customer wallet?
- ▶ What is the new segmentation scheme of customer needs?
- ▶ What growth trajectory can we create, with what bundles of products and services, through what distribution channels?
- ▶ How fast can we move?
- ▶ What alliances and acquisitions do we need?

Capitalizing on Change

Change is a constant, and for those who accept it and embrace it, it is a friend. As Gary Wendt of GE Capital puts it, "You always look where there's change. Change is what creates opportunity."[27] Even if you can't find any scenario that leads to radical reshaping of your industry, bet that it will change to some degree. There will always be discontinuities—breaks or gaps in the expected sequence of events. The first player to see a discontinuity can create a new market. Either you or your competitors will redefine it by spotting new needs and meeting them. Every growth story in this book begins with leaders who capitalized on change.

Let's sum up the groundwork that precedes a strategy:

1. Look outside for discontinuities.
2. Define the needs that the discontinuities create.
3. Identify the competencies required to meet the needs—which ones you have, which ones you need to acquire, which ones you need to discard.

Only by taking these steps can you outline the goals and strategy that will put you on a new growth trajectory.

Also hold on to the truths that are as old as business itself. The language may change—people are always putting old wine in new semantic bottles—but the principles do not. Successful entrepreneurs are guided by business common sense. Take your cues from the environment, and work backward to your strengths.

Be clear about those strengths, by the way; you probably have more than you think. As we saw in Chapter 2, many leaders cripple their companies with overly narrow definitions of core competencies.

The essential game is not one of rote or numbers. It's creative and intuitive, based on ideas, observations, and perceptions. It doesn't require degrees, licenses, or $50,000 sessions with seminar gurus.

The ability to play the game is in the leader's thought architecture, in his or her capacity for creative ideas. Whether he or she runs a cigar store, manages a business unit, or heads a global behemoth, the ideas generated are intuitive and visceral.

The leader doesn't make them final until they've been subjected to rigorous analysis. He or she weighs them according to how differentiated and robust the strategies behind them are, and—equally or even more important—how the organization can achieve an edge in executing them. But the initial ideas come from the gut.

Take the familiar story of Chrysler's minivan. It came from the guts of Lee Iacocca and his collaborator Hal Sperlich, not from a market research bureaucracy. (And don't forget the blunder that Henry Ford II made in refusing to listen to Iacocca, who then took the idea to Chrysler.) Gifted with a powerful curiosity about emerging needs in his supposedly mature marketplace, they saw a discontinuity—a small but significant number of people were using commercial delivery vans for domestic hauling. He also saw that station wagon sales were flat or declining. What did it all mean?

Iacocca and Sperlich found that baby boomers with growing families couldn't stuff all the kids, dogs, and 4′ × 8′ sheets of plywood into station wagons. Some of the more adventurous boomers were using light trucks. And they wondered: How many would buy a light truck built more or less to passenger-car standards? Even they couldn't foresee the scope of the revolution that would come from his simple insight.

Let's stick with the auto industry a moment longer. As a "mature" industry, it offers useful lessons for others in similarly perceived businesses. When the Japanese defined their new luxury segment, they created a major discontinuity for Mercedes-Benz. Mercedes's strengths included its brand image, based on its own and its suppliers' superb engineering, and its customer loyalty, handed down like a legacy from generation to generation. But its weaknesses had begun to show through: higher costs (its own and its suppliers'), long product-development cycle times, an unhealthy dominance of engineering over marketing, a service network in decline relative to the Japanese, and an increasingly stodgy image. During the early nineties, Mercedes's U.S. sales fell from 100,000 units to under 60,000.[28]

Under Helmut Werner, made CEO in 1993, Mercedes's leaders aggressively wrung out costs and cut cycle time. But there was no way they could hope to beat the Japanese solely on this battlefield. Going a step beyond, they broadened their range with a series of successful new segments, such as the C-class, priced competitively with the Japanese; the high-margin SLK sports car, the American-built M-Class sport–utility vehicle; and the radical Smart, the forthcoming city car produced in collaboration with Swatch founder Nicholas Hayek.[29] They sharpened their styling distinction with a unique slabsided and aggressive look. Mercedes has regained its power in the marketplace. In the United States, for example, Mercedes's sales rose to more than 100,000 in 1997, while Infiniti sales were falling.[30]

Target CEO Bob Ulrich, like Lee Iacocca, saw something happening that didn't square with the conventional understanding—in this case, the notion that retailing was increasingly bifurcating into a two-tier industry, rock-bottom and upscale. A sharp observer of the marketplace, Ulrich saw that Wal-Mart wasn't meeting the needs of its own customers who were getting ahead and moving up. The competency was there: Target's strength was in merchandising efficiently to younger, better-educated, more affluent middle-class Americans. By going after dissatisfied Wal-Mart customers, Ulrich sharpened his stores' differentiation from the Kmarts and Wal-Marts. He built them with wider aisles, cleaner signage, and high levels of customer service, and placed them as close as possible to Wal-Mart stores. The Wal-Mart defectors would have no trouble finding a Target, and Ulrich saved a lot of time and money figuring out advantageous sites.

Defining a Growth Trajectory

Look at the companies with consistently high growth rates and you'll see one thing they have in common: a sustainable growth path based on a well-defined set of needs. This is a lot different from having a platform, or even a strategy. We call it a *growth trajectory*.

A growth trajectory defines an expansive set of possibilities. It is not an incremental step (though it may include many increments). It requires shifting perspective and widening horizons.

▶ FedEx created a growth trajectory when it began overnight delivery of components to companies that need to fill orders fast without carrying high inventories. In so doing, FedEx took itself well beyond overnight package delivery and into floating, fast-track warehousing.

▶ When Bill Gates concluded that the future of his business lay with the Internet and not just with producing software, he put Microsoft on a new growth trajectory.

▶ Eckhard Pfeiffer (Chapter 6) put Compaq onto new trajectories three times in six years—first with the total PC market, then the client-server market, and, most recently, with the total enterprise market over the lifetime of computer ownership.

▶ John Trani (Chapter 7) put GE Medical Systems onto new trajectories twice, first with globalization, and, later, by moving into services.

▶ Each of GE Capital's twenty-eight businesses (Chapter 8) started as a new growth trajectory.

▶ Dave Holmes (Chapter 11) defined a new trajectory for Reynolds and Reynolds when he expanded his pond from selling forms and computer systems to helping his customers become more profitable, adding to his offerings everything from database marketing to managerial expertise.

An early challenge for a company's leadership is to define a growth trajectory so that everybody in the company can understand it, from the directors to the front-line employees. Any new trajectory will have at its core a *central idea*. Not just a slogan, a central idea is a clear, robust, and purposeful statement that summarizes strategy and goals. It can usually be stated in less than five sentences; it creates a picture that everyone can visualize.

Some of the biggest central ideas in business history were created with just a few words. Alfred Sloan's central idea for General Motors, "A car for every purse and every purpose," defined the strategy that created the world's biggest company. Roberto Goizueta painted a vibrant picture in asking, "What is our share of the consumer's stomach?" He would elaborate on the picture, asking his people to visualize more people drinking more Coke, more often, every day, and would conclude by saying, "Thus our opportunities are virtually infinite."

Great central ideas have staying power. They are not mere slogans; they create a pithy but true picture of customer needs. Almost two decades later, the infinity sign got a page of its own in Coca-Cola's 1996 annual report, and Goizueta's successor, M. Douglas Ivester, is still pointing out how little of the stomach Coca-Cola occupies.

Customers and Needs: Working with the 2 × 2

As vital as gut instinct, imagination, and creativity are in spotting new growth opportunities, a rigorous analytical framework is equally important. Carefully categorizing and segmenting needs in relation to your own position and strengths will take you a long way toward shaping your strategy.

The categorization starts with the 2 × 2 we introduced on page 79. It's the basic tool for mapping out your marketplace in light of your existing and potential customer bases, and their existing and potential needs.

Make everyone a part of your brainstorming, including front-line people, customers, and even people unrelated to your business. Dialogues are the sparkplug for ideas; diversity within dialogues is the fuel.

Using the 2 × 2, look at your potential pond as the sum of many segments, one or more of which you now occupy. Each segment is a need, one that you either meet now (existing) or one you could meet (new).

The categorizations aren't always neat. Some segments may include both existing and new needs, as well as existing and new customers—cross-training shoes or sport utility vehicles, for example. Some of the needs may be ones that other companies now meet, but which you could meet better; some may be new for the customers themselves. In working the 2 × 2, don't spend a lot of time trying to develop a highly precise taxonomy; define your moves according to the predominant areas they take you into. The question to keep before you always is, What other customer needs can you serve?

Quadrant A, the needs and customers you serve now. Many if not most companies are focused here. It's where you'll find the corporate leaders who are looking inward—at core competence and competitor analysis; at cost cutting, reengineering, and redesign of the organization.

True, people can grow in this quadrant even if the total pond is not growing—by skillful resegmentation, or through consistent superior

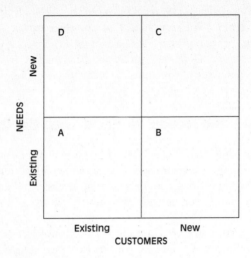

Figure 4.1

execution and attention to costs. Some are even able to grow the market, as Gillette did with endless razor innovations. But too often, this quadrant is a prison for people who have given up on growth because they're in mature markets. They tend to court market share through ruinous price wars. They're playing in a zero-sum game.

Quadrant B, new customers and existing needs. Some companies attack this quadrant by repositioning their products to meet a new group of customers. For example, Michael Dell first built his business by selling computers directly to companies, then broadened his pond by expanding into the consumer market.

More often, geographic expansion is the most common route into Quadrant B—stretching your sales territory to include a new set of customers. For many companies these days, geographical expansion means going global. But not always: There's lots of geography in the United States. Coca-Cola has been global for decades. Today, 70 percent of its revenues comes from abroad;[31] Coca-Cola has 50 percent of the world market,[32] and there's no close second in sight. In 1996, Coca-Cola once again began training its sights on the domestic marketplace, a land of existing customers with existing needs. Figure 4.2 shows how Goizueta demonstrated the opportunities in the mid-1990s to executives who had been thinking of the domestic market as "mature."

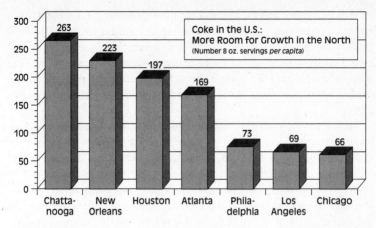

Figure 4.2   Consumption in every one of these markets is less than the national average.

Meeting new needs is what the top quadrants on the 2 × 2 are all about. You find here the best growth trajectories and the biggest ponds—or lakes, or oceans. As you look at the total needs, you can see that Quadrant A (where you are now) is typically a subset of Quadrants C and D. Your existing market is just a fraction of it.

These quadrants are also where the mega-ideas blossom—the needs that are new for the customers themselves. Great businesses are born in these quadrants—indeed, entire industries, from automobiles to computer hardware and software. Creating truly new needs is a win–win game. It grows the market for everybody.

Don't get hung up in thinking that a new need is created only by something radically different—an invention like the steam engine, the light bulb, the semiconductor, or even the microwave or VCR. People have created countless billions of dollars' worth of new needs with ideas that simply redefine existing needs with line extensions, related products or services, new channels, or sharper marketing. The common denominator is knowing how to identify needs.

Quadrant D. The combination of existing customers and new needs usually allows the quickest breakout from the mature market. Once you know all you can about your existing customers, you have the basic information you require to develop ideas about their total needs. Companies at the cutting edge of technology, such as Intel and Microsoft, exist to define and meet new needs for their customers, but innovators in far more mundane businesses find big opportunities, too. The Polaroid camera and Sony Walkman created new needs. Nike created new perceived needs with its variations of athletic footwear. Equipment leasing was a new need for GE Capital's customers. The minivan met a new need for Chrysler's customers (as well as Ford's and GM's and even Mercedes-Benz's).

It works for even the humblest products. What market could be more mundane, more easily understood, or more clearly circumscribed than bathroom fixtures? Yet, at American Standard, they're asking: What share of the bathroom wallet are we getting, and how can we get more? What about shower enclosures? What about installation? Owens-Corning has sold thermal insulation and roofing materials for years. In the mid-nineties, it added acoustical insulation and windows (through acquisition). These days, Owens-Corning is defining itself as a supplier of integrated home building materials systems—an umbrella that spreads over everything it makes for the home and allows some space for expanding into additional materials and services.

Some companies thrive on new-need microsegments—tiny but profitable product line extensions or additions. Rubbermaid is a player here, as well as in Quadrant A. It gets an ever-larger share of existing customers' wallets by meeting their endless need for greater convenience. When municipalities began requiring recycling, for example, homeowners responded at first by reserving three or more garbage cans (or boxes or baskets) for recyclables. Rubbermaid, looking from the outside in, designed a convenient and distinctive product specifically intended for recyclables. Result: A new need, and a small but rewarding expansion of Rubbermaid's pond.

We visited a top executive in his splendid mansion, and do you know what he was most eager to show us? His new Rubbermaid recycling bins. Beaming with pleasure, he said: "Those Rubbermaid guys really know what they're doing."

Manufacturers who expand into providing services for their customers are typically moving into Quadrant D. We will show you numerous examples in the pages ahead, starting with GE Power Systems just a few paragraphs later in this chapter.

Quadrant C. Moving into quadrant C brings higher risks. Dealing with new customers and new needs requires extremely careful selection of the leaders, and meticulous execution. But companies that do it right can reap huge rewards. Motorola, for example, launched its cellular phone business, worth $12 billion a year now,[33] with a huge bet on an unproven need in a market it had never served. Conner Peripherals, a maker of hard drives for personal computers, got its start by selling not to IBM and other existing customers but to new companies like Compaq. Companies often move here when they build or acquire new competencies to develop adjacent segments. Hewlett-Packard has shown again and again how to play this game. To its initial business—instruments for measuring—it added printers, computers, fax machines, multipurpose machines, personal digital assistants, and more. In this journey, HP continued to broaden and deepen its set of core competencies, acquiring new ones and shedding old ones.

Sometimes in fact, the leap from quadrant A to quadrant C can be easier than sliding into quadrant D. You might not think so; after all, your existing customers know you, and you know them. But that may be exactly the problem. Neither your customers nor your sales staff may be able to handle the shift, especially if you're promoting a new technology. Quadrant C is where you'll usually find the new players in the marketplace—players who may be small and unknown but are setting the new rules.

As Joseph Bower and Clayton Christensen of the Harvard Business School pointed out several years ago, leading companies often lose their leadership when technologies change, precisely because they stay close to customers who are deeply invested—both financially and in terms of experience—in existing technologies.[34] A so-called disruptive technology—even one with potential superiority—may have no appeal, particularly if early versions can't match or exceed the performance of the highly developed older technology. It's ironic that the customers who really need the new technology may be the most resistant to it. And their problem can quickly become your problem.

In the early eighties, Seagate Technology was the main supplier of 5.25-inch hard disk drives to IBM and other PC makers. Along came a disruptive technology, the 3.5-inch drive. Seagate's engineers were on the case, produced successful prototypes without spending much money, and proudly turned them over to senior management. Surprise! Nobody wanted them. A key reason: Seagate's principal customers wanted drives with more capacity than the existing drives for their next-generation products, and the little 3.5-inch drives couldn't even match the existing ones. Ignoring the likelihood of refinements that would almost certainly increase the 3.5-inch drive's capacity, Seagate shelved the project.

The engineers who had developed the new drive left Seagate and formed Conner Peripherals. Conner initially marketed its drives to makers of portable computers and small desktop units. Its customers included Compaq, which had never bought anything from Seagate. Conner, meantime, jacked up the capacity of its drives by 50 percent a year. By 1988, the 3.5-inch drive had all the capacity needed for a mainstream desktop unit, and Conner began selling to IBM and the clones. Seagate dusted off its own shelved 3.5-inch drive, but it was too late. Conner and Quantum Corporation, another upstart in 3.5-inch drives, had developed too much scale and experience for Seagate to compete.[35]

Mapping the Markets

The 2×2 is a powerful tool for outlining the broad dimensions of a growth strategy. It also sets the stage for applying the finer tools of market analysis in order to focus on segmentation, including market research, customer feedback, and other sources of information.

The 2×2 can be the basis for detailed market mapping. This methodology, familiar to many marketers of consumer goods, systematically analyzes a company's marketplace by customers, industries, and geography. Growth rates and competitive standing in every identifiable segment are revealed, and the company can focus on areas where it can best compete.

Industrial and other business-to-business companies tend not to use market mapping. They deal with much smaller customer bases, and their operations more often tend to be inside-out: R&D and engineers design a product, and the sales and marketing people go out and try to sell it.

But you can apply market mapping to almost any business, especially if you've gone in with the framework of the customers–needs 2×2. Use them correctly and these tools can drive change throughout your entire organization.

For example, Praxair Corporation has used market mapping to define growth trajectories previously unthinkable in its industry. Spun off from Union Carbide Corporation in the early nineties, Praxair mainly makes or processes industrial gases such as oxygen, carbon dioxide, hydrogen, helium, and various specialty gases. Although Praxair is a leading player in the Americas,[36] it's number three globally,[37] in an inherently slow-growth business. Demand is pretty much defined by the rate of GDP growth in customers' countries.

Looking for ways to break out of his mature business, CEO Bill Lichtenberger in 1995 challenged his thirty top leaders to come up with both a new growth strategy and a process for getting the company's other managers to develop growth mindsets. The team came up with a proposal to bring in Sunil Mattoo, a former McKinsey marketing and strategic planning expert who had been director of marketing at AlliedSignal Corp.

Mattoo and his team used market mapping to teach Praxair's leaders how to look from the outside in, probing their customers' minds and using the information to design new value propositions. Cross-functional groups of executives from all regions identified 8 major segments with more than 70 subsegments, ranging from steel, chemicals, refining, electronics, and electronic assembly to helium balloons, and developed business plans for each new opportunity.

The businesses generated through market mapping have helped put Praxair on a new growth trajectory. Lichtenberger now aims for long-term annual revenue increases averaging 10 percent and earnings per share growth of 15 percent,[38] both well above the industry norms. Meantime, Praxair's leaders are using the same tools and approaches to link all processes in the company; the goal is to focus all innovations on key areas that yield good returns.

"You excel by creating a cycle in which you're continuously creating demand, always one step ahead of customers and always coming in with new ideas from them," says Mattoo. "That may sound simple, but to do it you have to tie together R&D, sales, marketing, far-flung global regions, and the central support functions."[39] In short, the process that began with identifying ways to broaden Praxair's pond has also become an instrument of organizational and personal development.

How One Company Enlarged Its Pond

When a company's leaders really step outside of their existing businesses to look for new needs, the results can be dramatic. In 1994, GE Power Systems had half of the approximately $20 billion world market for large power generation equipment, a sterling reputation, strong relationships with the CEOs of major utilities—and a business that was suddenly stymied. (See Figure 4.3.)

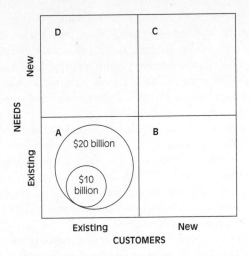

Figure 4.3 In 1994, GE Power Systems had half of the approximately $20 billion world market for large power generation equipment—but the market wasn't growing. (Circles are not necessarily to scale.)

The U.S. utility industry, the company's historical core growth base, was in a mental gridlock. Worried that deregulation would prohibit them from passing capital investment costs on to their customers, the utilities were looking for overseas acquisitions rather than investing in new equipment. What little new equipment they bought, they bought on price. Says CEO Bob Nardelli, "We clearly needed to look at new opportunities in order to grow the business in a rapidly changing environment."[40] In the three years that followed, GE Power Systems completely turned around its old approach to doing business. Its leaders:

▶ Looked at their business from the outside in, abandoning their traditional view from the inside out.

▶ Repeatedly enlarged their pond.

▶ Identified an almost endless string of adjacent segments with strong growth prospects.

By the end of 1997, instead of having half of a stagnant equipment market, the company had a much smaller but fast-growing share of a far bigger market for equipment and related services—a market vibrant with growth opportunities.

Bob Nardelli was brought in from GE Transportation Systems, where he'd led the globalization of the business and the development of a joint venture with Harris Corp. He arrived at Power Systems in May 1995 to lead a group of people who were masters of selling in a mature industry with long cycles. Like the old IBM mainframe salespeople, they were big-ticket salesmen—"elephant hunters" is Jack Welch's affectionate phrase for them-who focused on technology for large power plants and built relationships patiently over long periods of time.

And they were extremely proud of their 50 percent market share. "There was a level of comfort, of intellectual arrogance, that a 50 percent share was pretty good," acknowledges Frank Blake, vice president, business development.[41] The typical attitude, he says, was "'Realistically, how much more share do you think we can get? Do you really want to rent market share, in the form of getting it through price?'"

Nardelli, however, brought a teachable point of view with a broader perspective—one that would very quickly alter GE Power Systems' genetic code. He saw turbines as a subset of a larger pond. Power Systems had just broadened its pond with the acquisition, in 1994, of Nuovo Pignone, an Italian manufacturer of compressors, pumps, and small gas turbines that complemented Power Systems' product offerings. That move not only strengthened its European presence, but also opened up a new market segment in the oil and gas industry, where Nuovo Pignone's products were widely sold for use in pipeline applications. Further, says Nardelli, the acquisition "supplemented a major initiative to put our best people in the poles—the Asian pole, the American pole, the European pole—so that we were closer to customers and we actually made a customer call instead of a customer trip."

As shown in Figure 4.4, the acquisition broadened the GE Power Systems pond to some $25–30 billion. Still, it was mainly an equipment business. In 1996, Jack Welch launched his services initiative throughout GE, asking each of his business leaders to think about their units as "world class service companies that also manufacture world class products." Responding, Nardelli and his leadership team took a step back, as he puts it, "to realize the value of the GE franchise in our installed base— 11,000 units worldwide. We then challenged the organization to quantify the revenue we were generating off each and every unit."

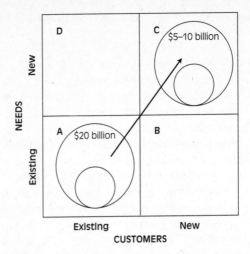

Figure 4.4 The acquisition of Italy's Nuovo Pignone broadened Power Systems' pond to $25–$30 billion, including $4 billion of complementary business in new markets.

The answer was: Very little. As in many other industries, says Nardelli, "We had neglected the parts and service business; yes, if you called, we would service your needs, but we were primarily in a reactive mode."

Service could plainly be a much larger pond than equipment, but it would require a major change in mindset throughout the marketing and sales organizations. To get people looking at the larger pond, the leaders transformed their annual review methodology—the so-called S-1 process in which GE business units lay out their three-year strategies for Welch. At Power Systems, this was traditionally an inside-out exercise conducted by two or three people who looked at the prospects for existing markets and products. They drew a far broader group of people into the process, notably including those who had the closest contact with customers, and taught them to learn what *customers* saw as their most important needs.

The new process became a key mechanism for pond-broadening. "We took the S-1 process from a strategic review about efficiency to a market-back view," says Nardelli. "We said: 'Let's look market-back; let's take one of our best utilities. They have revenues of $10 billion a year.

They make $2 billion in profits. That leaves $8 billion. What percent of our sales is their cost? Every dollar they spend of the $8 billion should be a revenue opportunity for us.'"

The market-back view identified a surprising amount of potential business, including a strong desire for the energy provider to outsource maintenance, and a significant need for other high-tech services that add value to the customer's business. "We introduced inspection services and remote monitoring and diagnostics," says Nardelli. "We began focusing on long-term service contracts for operating and maintaining entire facilities." The goal, he adds, was to fundamentally transform customer relationships. "We needed to move beyond the one-at-a-time transactional 'deal' mentality and approach customers with a much larger porftolio of services and products, and to engage them in a deeper contractual relationship."

Adding it all up, GE Power Systems in 1996 was able to identify a pond of some $43–$48 billion—the total of power-plant equipment and service expenditures worldwide (see Figure 4.5). This business has fatter profit margins and is significantly less capital intensive.

The next step was putting talent and money to better use. As Jack Welch advises his business leaders *resources should be allocated on the*

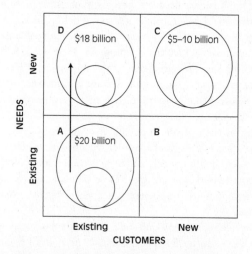

Figure 4.5   Moving into supplying services as well as equipment to its utility customers opened up another $18 billion in potential business, enlarging Power Systems' pond to as much as $48 billion.

prospective basis, not the historical basis. And indeed, Nardelli says, "We were looking at the industry through a rear-view mirror. We were building products based on where we thought the industry should be headed, rather than on shaping our business based on what the industry needed given the realities of global deregulation and customer convergence."

As the distinctions between industry segments began to blur and global energy companies that spanned the entire playing field emerged, Nardelli and his team created a service company within GE Power Systems, headed by a vice president. This structure legitimized it as an entity rather than an adjunct to the core business. Thirty percent of the engineers were put to work on developing service opportunities, and the program expenditure budget for that area was tripled. Says Nardelli: "We moved them away from designing the boxes to asking, 'How can we up-rate the box? How can we improve its reliability so that the utilities could get more efficiency and lower emissions without the heavy capital investment?' "

Frank Blake and his business development team started to look—"feverishly," says Blake—at potential technology-based acquisitions that might supplement the Power Systems service capabilities. The acquisitions helped the business do everything from perform more nondestructive testing to rewind generators faster in the field.

Simultaneously, in 1996, Power Systems plunged into the "Six Sigma" quality and productivity training that Jack Welch had mandated for all GE businesses. This was particularly important at Power Systems, where overcapacity and fierce global competition were driving down prices in the core product market. The results were phenomenal, but they were a requirement just to stay in the game.

It's driven by the outside in perspective. Power Systems works with customers in what it calls the Customer Dashboard program to identify their most critical quality needs, and targets these for Six Sigma projects. Metric Improvement Teams ensure there is a linkage all the way back to the factory and that the improvements are leveraged across the entire customer base.

"Without Six Sigma we would be in terrible turmoil, given the price pressures in this industry," says Nardelli. "And it is a key driver in our being able to improve the performance, the operating efficiency, the cost, and the quality delivery that gives the bounce we need to get volume growth."

From the Wellhead to the Consumer

Turning a business's viewpoint from inside out to outside in is rarely an instant process—but neither is it necessarily a long grind. "We didn't hit it right the first year," acknowledges Nardelli. Adjacent segments, for example, weren't even on the company's radar screens. But within two years, GE Power Systems had nailed down some $1.4 billion of revenue commitments for long-term service contracts and operation and maintenance in that $48 billion pond.

And gradually, the company began to broaden its pond to something much bigger. "We were taking an incremental approach," says Nardelli. "And last year we said, 'Let's take a bolder view. Let's define our playing field as $700 *billion*—the energy industry.'" Before, the pond had been pretty well limited to power plants. The new pond would include everything "from the wellhead to the consumer"—a phrase that became the guiding motto of the company's ambitions. (See Figure 4.6.)

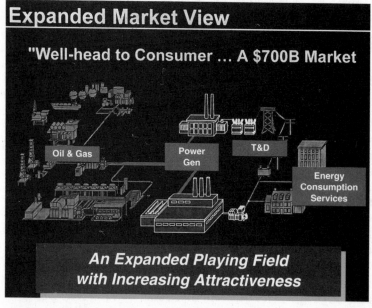

Figure 4.6 In the phrase that would become the guiding motto of their ambitions, Power Systems' leaders redefined their market as everything from the wellhead to the consumer.

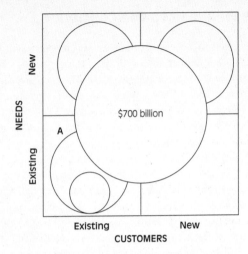

Figure 4.7 GE Power Systems' 1998 pond is the entire global power industry—and at $700 billion, it's almost 37 times as big as the market it defined as served three years previously.

Like Roberto Goizueta, Nardelli had, in one stroke, defined an immense pond of which his company's current share was a tiny fraction—a pond, in short, of almost infinite opportunity. (See Figure 4.7.)

Defining the new pond opened the door to developing all sorts of adjacent segments. Power Systems acquired its way into many of these segments, picking up small companies that occupied critical parts of the wellhead-to-consumer value chain. As Blake puts it, "If we were elephant hunters before, we became duck hunters. The duck hunting might have been small, but as a market it was just as big as the elephant hunting."

The opportunities he and his team identified included smaller products used in distributed power. For example, GE Aircraft Engines sold turbines derived from aircraft engines through packagers—companies that buy components, assemble them, and install them for utility customers. "And that led us to packaging," says Blake, "again, a market every bit as large as the elephant-hunting market we had been in before." Early in 1998, the company completed the acquisition of the gas turbine division of Stewart & Stevenson Services, Inc., an entrepreneurial, fast-moving company that had essentially created the packaging market and was strong on direct relationships with customers. "Their packaging is the most efficient in the industry," says Nardelli. "But it's their entrepreneurial spirit that will really help us change the game."

Another segment of elephantine potential is management of the power transmission system—the whole energy grid—which Nardelli likens to serving as the air traffic controllers of electrons. In 1997 Nardelli worked out a joint venture between Power Systems and Harris Corp. The opportunities for GE Harris Control Systems, as the venture is called, seem boundless. Says Nardelli: "There's a lot of software content; you start getting into the very basics of how power is distributed in the grid."

In the three years since it began to look from the outside in, GE Power Systems has totally transformed itself through a dramatic redistribution of its revenue mix and an upgrade of talent that has brought an innovative, entrepreneurial spirit to an old line industrial business. Power-generating equipment, which previously accounted for almost all of its business—and of its people's share of mind—in 1994 is now about 50 percent of the total; The rest is energy services. Assuming it stays on its new trajectory as planned, the company will be more than half again as large in 2000 as it was six years previously, with half or more of its revenues coming from services, parts, and products that it did not provide just a few years earlier.

Where Do the Ideas Come From?

Critical to your success in broadening your pond and resegmenting your business is the quality of your ideation—the generation and flow of ideas in your company. No matter what analytical tools and technical techniques you use, you won't get on a growth trajectory unless your people bring to the party their creativity, imagination, judgment, and ability to perceive and understand change.

DuPont towered over its industry during the 1940s because it was one of the world's great engines of ideation. Apple, in its early years, was the computer industry's ideation hot spot. At Compaq, Eckhard Pfeiffer revived the ideation that had stalled under his fired predecessor, Rod Canion.[42] GE Capital is a hotbed of ideation; Gary Wendt tells his troops to "dream," and he means it.

Yet ideation is permanently at risk in most corporations. For one thing, it's easier to shoot an idea down than to help someone else develop it—especially if that someone is a rival in a cutthroat environment. Then, too, the natural tendency in business is to routinize or automate things. Just as the industrial revolution replaced judgment-based craftwork with the machinery of automation, so has the evolution of management practice tended to mechanize the intellectual side of running a business.

Leaders like Wendt, Pfeiffer, and Nardelli are leaders partly because they built organizations that encourage people at all levels to look outward and stretch their thinking. Your own company's future lies in the abilities of your people to anticipate and imagine, and in the judgment they exercise in picking the right trails to blaze.

One of your biggest challenges in designing a growth framework will be to create the *decision and social architectures*™ that support and reward ideation. We'll return to this subject in Chapter 9, "The Genetic Code and How to Change It," because the quality of ideation in any company is a direct reflection of its genetic code.

Meantime, the remaining chapters in Part II will show you how the leaders of four prominent businesses grew their companies by broadening their ponds and resegmenting their markets.

The mindset of growth starts with looking at your business from the outside in. This is a simple shift of perspective, but it's what separates the growth leaders from the also-rans. It's how you spot the discontinuities that create opportunities for enlarging your pond, defining new segments, and seizing adjacent segments. These are the fundamental means for creating new growth trajectories.

CHAPTER **5**

*H*ow John Reed Turned Citibank Outside In

Starting in 1995, Citicorp CEO John Reed transformed his corporate banking operation. He turned an inside-out organization into one that was customer-driven and outside-in. The strategy he created for sustained, profitable growth with substantially lower risk not only enlarged its pond but was also aimed at increasing return on investment. This was a fundamental departure from past practice in all respects, and it required a new mindset on the part of leaders throughout the organization.

Growth often starts only when a company's leadership breaks the lockstep thinking that has driven strategy for years. In the spring of 1998 proposed merger with Travelers Corp., Citicorp CEO John Reed parted from the rest of his industry. His bold vision was to grow by creating the world's biggest broad-based financial services empire, rather than taking the usual path and merging with another bank. But to truly understand Reed's out-of-the-box thinking, one needs to look deeper.

Reed actually rejected banking's conventional wisdom about growth during his turnaround of Citibank during the early- and mid-nineties. His masterstroke, still not widely appreciated outside of the industry, was the radical expansion strategy he devised for corporate banking (the arm that serves companies). It played a key role in lifting parent Citicorp's value in the financial markets. Arguably, the deal with Travelers would have been extremely difficult to make, if not impossible, without corporate banking's transformation.

Yet the results were evident within a year of the time Reed first articulated his new ambitions. In naming Citibank its 1996 Bank of the Year, *Euromoney* magazine took special note of "the major turnaround in strategy. . . . The firm has laid out a series of business directions that will play to its strengths in its consumer and corporate banking franchise, and differentiate it from its competitors."[1]

Breaking with the Lemmings

For just about as long as anyone can remember, corporate banking in the United States has been a lemminglike business of the worst sort, reflecting the basic strategy of the industry: Get bigger by making more loans. Bankers flock to lend wherever demand is hot—real estate, energy, emerging economies—and they vie to see who can grab the biggest share of the lending. They make ever riskier bets as the portfolio swells, because banking laws allow them high leverage on such loans.

When things finally go wrong—as they always do—they *really* go wrong. Reed learned that lesson painfully in the early nineties; bad real estate loans created such losses that some people wondered if Citibank might actually fail.[2] It was the brutal culmination of a two-decades-old goal, deeply embedded in the genetic code, of becoming the biggest bank around.

Early in 1995, with the "survival phase" of his plans concluded, Reed met with Ram Charan and some two dozen of Citibank's top leaders to look at corporate banking's future. Citibank's great strength was, and remains, its global consumer franchise, which is a century old and the most powerful one in the world. But its periodic spectacular crashes made corporate banking a serious drag on performance.

Reed was putting Citibank on course to being measured by its shareholder value rather than by the size of its assets. In itself, this was a long overdue, outside-in departure from the lockstep thinking of industry convention. Apart from the trouble it invites, simply having more assets is increasingly meaningless in a world where the real added value comes from meeting new needs for financial services—needs with higher margins and lower capital intensity.

Reed's announced goal was to grow profits at least 10 percent to 12 percent a year.[3] He also aimed to lift the price/earnings ratio of Citicorp's stock to 15 (it was then around 7[4]). By contrast, the average for the S&P 500 was 17,[5] and the average for Citicorp's peer group of major money-center banks was 10.[6]

Looking ahead over the long term, Reed realized that corporate banking wasn't even earning the cost of its capital, and concluded that it was a major reason for Citicorp's miserable price/earnings ratio.

"Corporate banking was a collection of businesses that lacked coherence, both strategically and organizationally," says senior vice president and marketing director Ed Holmes. "We had no central identity, we had different marketing approaches. We lacked a standard set of shared values, which then flowed over into vocabulary, management processes, the way we staff things.

"Some of us wondered if the business was long for Citi's portfolio. We had a big, big amount of unproductive capital invested and we needed a strategy that would let us really get an active return out of the business."[7]

Reed weighed and discarded the conventional avenues of growth. Expanding into investment banking was one possibility, but the field was already crowded with players competing on price. Acquiring a middle-market bank franchise was also a no-go; that route was well populated. Reed also felt that any expansion there would unbalance Citicorp by putting too much weight in North America, since the bank's great strength was its global scope.

Instead, after months of conversations with customers and members of his senior leadership team, Reed set a goal that went to the heart of the global competency Citibank had built up in consumer banking: "To be known as the preeminent bank for companies that value us for our globality."[8] He added, in essence, that Citibank wanted to pursue that business in a way that yielded a good return on equity, reduced earnings volatility, strengthened the organization's sustainability and believability, and realized shareholder returns that would not diminish the returns earned in the consumer business.

Reed actually articulated two major complementary strategies for the corporate banking group. The first strategy was to make Citibank an "embedded" bank in emerging markets: the largest and most global foreign bank in each country—as large as any domestic bank. Success was dramatic, particularly given that other foreign banks were busy making acquisitions in many of the same regions. By the end of 1997, Citi had added thousands of customers across the emerging markets, and lifted its share as lead bank in many.

The second strategy was global relationship banking, a thrust to make Citibank the bank of choice for global companies needing not only loans but an ever increasing number of services and solutions in a wide variety of markets around the world. Developed by a task force of senior executives over the course of a year, and launched in January 1996, this strategy rested on simple logic, confirmed by empirical evidence: If Citibank could be the most important supplier of banking services to global corporations, and could develop multiproduct, multinational relationships with these customers, it could get a higher return on equity than its competitors.

Though they were linked to fundamentally different paradigms, says Holmes, the two strategies dovetailed neatly. "The concept that you're an embedded player fits exactly with what a multinational company wants—a bank that has links around the world but that's also a serious part of the local financial scene in Asia or Latin America."

A One-Sentence Objective

Global relationship banking was summed up in a carefully crafted phrase: "To serve global customers globally, and become their lead international bank." The phrase became corporate banking's mantra. Says Holmes: "It is as clear and powerful a one-sentence objective function for strategy as I know. It's who, it's how, and it's what—what we want to become. No extra words."

The strategy was outside in from the get-go. In the old model, which was a classic inside-out approach, Citibank—like other banks—focused first on geography, and then on the bank's products. Customers were in the third slot. Now, Citibank's people and processes would focus primarily on customers and their needs; secondly on the products that could meet those needs—both existing and new; and thirdly on geography. Says Holmes: "That was new for us as a single concept and dedication, that those customers would value us for globality, the thing that differentiates us the most."

Robert McCormack, the corporate executive vice president Reed put in charge of the transformation, came from outside the mainstream of corporate banking—he had been head of real estate, deeply involved in the workout that cleaned up the earlier portfolio of bad loans. His own genetic code as a leader focused him on customers, not products.

McCormack started by spending almost half of his time visiting customers, learning about their needs, understanding and redefining the composition of the customer wallet, resegmenting customer needs, and regrouping customers in a different segmentation schema. "We want to create the products and services that customers want," says McCormack, "and not be in the equity business, for example, simply because it is a good business to be in."[9]

It was a megachange. "At other banks, you can have whole conversations with people and never discuss the customer," he says. Even at Citibank, which had more of a history in relationship banking, the customer focus tended to get diffused as managers chased after ever-larger numbers of customers. "Bankers historically think of themselves as being bigger and more important if they have more assets and more customers on the books," says McCormack. Relationship managers were happy to get even a small piece of a client's business if it could yield a profit.

In the new strategy, Citibank would narrow its relationship banking quest to a carefully chosen list of no more than 1,400 customers. But it would pursue each of these customers intensively, settling for no less than lead bank status. Says Holmes: "It's no longer acceptable to say we're satisfied at being a second- or third-tier bank, even though it might be profitable. It isn't consistent with the strategy." The goal, he adds, is to capture "anywhere from 12 percent to 20 percent of the customer's banking wallet, and the dominant portion of the global wallet."

Confining relationship banking to this select group did two things. First, by deploying human and physical resources more efficiently, it improved returns on capital. Second, Citibank substantially cut the risk and volatility of its business. "We've consistently beaten our plan on our expected credit problems because we know lots about the customers; we deal with them on multiple products in multiple places," says Holmes. "If things go wrong somewhere in the world, we're going to know about it before the center does—or possibly before their own company."

New criteria brought the target market focus down to customers who would value Citi for its global strategy. Developed with "considerable agony," says Holmes, the criteria were a mix of qualities—size, creditworthiness, the client's "management mindset toward globality," and, importantly, "the total wallet available to us."

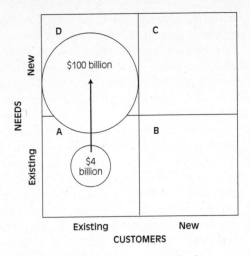

Figure 5.1 Citibank's corporate banking targeted a select group of global customers who generated some $4 billion in revenues for Citibank. They defined their new aim as this group's "total wallet" for banking services, a $100 billion pond.

And what a fat wallet it was. For the 1,300-odd customers eventually chosen, the total wallet amounted to at least $100 billion globally. (See Figure 5.1.) Citi's share of that was some $4 billion.[10] Here was a real trajectory for profitable, sustainable, and capital efficient growth.

Over the next two years, revenues grew nearly 20 percent annually. Roughly 80 percent of the business represented a growing share-of-wallet among 400 of the targeted global relationships. Early in 1998 Citi added a new strategic initiative, targeting approximately 300 customers who invest in bonds. It also combined the global relationship and emerging market banking operations under the single organizational umbrella of global corporate banking.

Mobilizing Information

A key step was abandoning the old geographical organization and replacing it with one centered on customers, clustered by industry as well as by geographical location of headquarters. "If you want to be a lead international bank, you've got to know more about the customer than any other bank," says Holmes. "But what is a lead international bank for aviation, pharmaceuticals, etc? These are different things. They have some needs in common, but it's not necessarily of value to a pharmaceutical company for you to be good at things the automotive customer group needs."

Corporate banking was reorganized into 13 industry units (with a total of 34 subsegments), ranging from autos and telecommunications to forest products. No longer were Volvo and Ericsson, for example, clustered only with other Swedish companies; Volvo was also clustered with automakers, and Ericsson with telecommunications companies.

Knowing more about the customers' needs necessarily implies knowing more about their business environment. Necessarily, the industry groups have become industry experts, drawing on a great array of resources. Each group has a senior analyst who must keep close track of trends and developments. Group members read the industry's trade and professional journals. And they share the proprietary information they gather naturally in the course of serving their global customers.

Each global industry group head is also required to create and maintain an *information knowledge advantage package* (IKAP). They're what Holmes calls living documents. They have two major components:

- ▶ Fifteen points or pages of industry lore—the key things an industry head believes his global group needs to know about their industry and the forces at work in it.

- ▶ A framework of fifteen questions—"the ones you need to ask if you want to learn more about this industry and this customer than any other bank."

The IKAPs, Holmes adds, are "sort of magnets that pull into one place all the things we know about serving these global customers, enhanced with all the stuff we've accumulated over time."

Just as important, if not more so, was the information Citibank's people gathered at ground level about their customers and industries. Mobilizing that intellectual capital became a major goal for McCormack, Holmes, and their leadership team.

"If you can have internal working sessions of product guys and customer guys, people from Asia, people from Europe, talking to each other, you not only have the information but you mobilize the information," says Holmes. "And then you're building up barriers to entry to the other guy with your superior knowledge of what the customers want, your superior access to their ideas, your command of their capabilities—your shared command internally of knowledge about those customers."

The transformation of corporate banking also required changes in the ways people defined their growth prospects. Within their regions, managers would aim to increase revenues, say, 10 percent a year. But, as Holmes says, "Revenue growth may be a spurious indicator of success. You may be happy that you've made an incremental $100,000 on a business, but if that business is General Motors, you've only dipped into the petty cash drawer. You may have even lost position in fast-growing businesses—their banking wallet may have been growing even higher than their growth rate at that stage. So we tried to get people away from being happy with incremental revenue growth."

Old ideas about resource allocation were equally counterproductive. Managers striving to maintain profits would cut down on product lines or customer bases to squeeze out the low-margin businesses. The trouble was, as Holmes puts it: "Over time, we'd be giving up share, marginalizing ourselves as other banks moved in on the spaces we'd abandoned or failed to capitalize on." Like other banks, he adds, Citibank "has been terrible about allocating the resources against the opportunities and getting where we want to. We wind up in classic rearview mirror management, saying, 'It's not a good relationship so let's not allocate many resources.'"

The Upward-Sweeping Revenue Curve

It wasn't long before Citibank learned just how powerful the mobilization of knowledge could be in generating profitable growth. With the goal of becoming a lead international bank, the corporate bankers could define their opportunities from the outside in, putting their priorities on customer needs and allocating resources accordingly. But how would they measure their progress? The answer was in a new operating mechanism that Holmes and McCormack called the "customer revenue unit" (CRU). As it turned out, this yardstick also generated an unexpected and major discovery about Citibank's new pond.

Because the quality of a lead international bank's relationship rests in part on cross-selling of products within market regions, the CRU is a sort of matrix measurement, based on Citibank's eighteen product families and the six regions it has designated on the world map. Handling a client's foreign exchange trading in North America, Asia, and the Middle East would add up to three CRUs—one product, three regions. Providing foreign exchange trading and cash management in Latin America, Japan, and Europe would equal six CRUs. Says Holmes: "What we were trying to do was get people to not think in terms of making financial increments but to think, 'Am I cross-sold; am I multiproduct, multiregion?'"

The surprise came after Citibank had gained some experience with CRUs. Holmes and his people worked up a chart, placing revenue on the vertical axis and CRUs on the horizontal. Up to ten CRUs, they found, revenues increased more or less arithmetically to a number that had long been the accepted threshold of a "really good relationship." At that point, says Holmes, you might expect revenues to start falling off with diminishing returns. Instead, revenues took off. Where there were twenty CRUs, revenues per CRU were roughly twice as high as at ten CRUs.

"'Why so?' we asked," says Holmes. "This is more like what you associate with the *law of increasing returns* [emphasis added], the stuff you hear people talking about in relation to knowledge-based businesses, rapidly consolidating businesses, software, and so forth.

"And we found out that, to a degree, relationship banking is indeed a knowledge-based business. The more you know about the customer, the more the customer knows about you; the more you're sharing information back and forth, the more you're dealing with each other. And your revenue per relationship continues to take off.

"What happens further out? We don't know; but at least in the portfolio we have today, the more CRUs, the more revenues per CRU. After a point, it starts to be what I call the upsweeping CRU curve.

"And upsweeping curves like this are real bad news for the other guy. Not only are we dominating the customers' wallets, we are creating competitive barriers to entry at the relationship level based on superior knowledge of the customer in multiple dimensions."

Changing the Genetic Code

The new focus was a major wrench for the leaders and managers. The geographic divisions, for example, were deeply embedded in the genetic code. Regional leaders not only identified themselves by their geography but also ran their businesses differently from each other. Says Holmes: "If I had the Nordic countries and you had the Iberian countries, we were almost as different as different banks."

Predictably enough, it was toughest for older, more senior managers. "People don't like to take risks they don't understand," says McCormack. "This is an old principle of community development; I learned it in the Peace Corps. Their families have to eat, so they do things that they know work, and only change when you show them that the new way actually works."

McCormack and his team carefully chose managers whom they judged adaptable to the new order, and coached them extensively. Says Holmes: "We spent a lot of time talking about global customers, and articulating that our job was to serve them globally." It helped that a predecessor group in corporate banking had done similar things with a smaller group of clients, says McCormack. "It was a strategy that had already worked, not born out of whole cloth and totally off the wall."

What really swung people around was the results that started coming in. Once the leaders gained experience in dealing with clients on an industry basis, says Holmes, "It turned out to be about a tenth as difficult as we thought it would be, and the number of border skirmishes fought by old geographic barons was virtually none. Why? Because they found that it had value—'Gee, it really helps me in marketing to Ericsson to be able to draw on the telecommunications experts.' Or, 'I'm much more impressive when I'm talking to a leading global airline by bringing in the aviation specialist who really knows how to finance planes on a global basis, rather than just talking to them in their language and taking them to good restaurants.'" And fortunately, the global economy was strong during the new strategy's formative years, so the results were plain and compelling.

The benefits to be wrung from Citibank's global knowledge of industries were particularly apparent in emerging markets. "Companies there are desperately interested to know what they ought to know as incipient players in the global world," says Holmes. In turn, the intimacy with those clients pays off when a Citibanker can say to a European client, "Do you know that out in Malaysia there's a components company in your industry that's looking for a joint venture partner?" (The response, Holmes adds with a laugh, is apt to be, "Well, we know about this, of course, but, um, maybe we could go a bit further with it at lunch next week . . .")

A major change in mindset for the corporate bankers was developing the patience to capture "share of mind"—the prominence in the potential customer's mind that would make Citibank bank of choice. Developing share of mind requires a persistence that wasn't part of the old way of doing business. To help the bankers visualize the process, Holmes created another operating mechanism, using the S-curve diagram shown in Figure 5.2.

The vertical axis is the bank's share of the customer's wallet; the horizontal axis is time. The slowly rising curve during the first two years is the tunnel—a time of much work and little evident return. "People in the tunnel would be working hard and not getting anywhere, so after a while they'd just give up—not quite waiting the next ninety days, at which point they might have been marching to the head of the line." Once they got the chart's message, and understood themselves as "tunnelers" on a journey with a clear destination, their persistence became more natural. As Holmes says: "To get out of the tunnel, you need consistency and a level of effort that eventually causes the share-of-mind breakthrough."

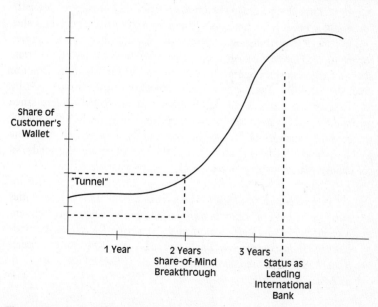

Figure 5.2   Typical Three-Year Pattern for Gaining the Desired Share of the Citibank Customer's Wallet.

Farther out on the chart, where growth flattens because Citibank has gained nearly the maximum share it can squeeze from a customer's mind and wallet, the bankers can focus on tradeoffs in resource allocation—going after the business with the highest value added, and leaving less profitable lines to others.

For all of its early successes, global relationship banking at Citibank is still a work in progress. Among other things, the bankers are intent on improving the speed and scope of communications within industry and client groups so that people in these groups can share more of that all-important knowledge of their customers. The goal, says Holmes, "is to activate the network so that everybody who's touching that client anywhere around the world is getting information in one place." The resulting creation, transfer, and proper use of knowledge create shareholder value and differentiation against competition.

The biggest job in any transformation is changing minds, and it's especially hard in conservative businesses like banking. For example, says McCormack, "Traditionally in Citibank we have a mania about financial numbers. I'm convinced one reason the relationship managers have been successful is because we have not spent a lot of time managing the financial impact of everything—going through the monthly report results of, for example, France, Germany, or Canada. What we're saying is, 'Don't show me the results for Spain; show me the results for Telefonica [a major Spanish customer].' Even so, a lot of country heads just can't get it."

To keep the changes rolling, Holmes and his fellow leaders stress again and again the need for "consistency, continuity, and collaboration," the guiding principles of the new approach. "We're partway there," says Holmes, "and a lot further along than I think most people expected. But the change management process is a big part of what we're doing."

In a classic example of looking from the outside in, John Reed redefined Citi's corporate banking according to needs that offered a profitable, capital efficient growth trajectory. Unique in the banking industry, the new business is also less risky and volatile than the previous one, and is helping Citi command a higher price/earnings ratio.

Eckhard Pfeiffer
THE METHODICAL RADICAL OF COMPAQ

Change has been swift and relentless in the computer business. The industry of mainframe makers that was in its youth just two decades ago has been effectively wiped out by leaders who were nobodies back then. None took a more ambitious approach to change than Eckhard Pfeiffer. After saving Compaq Computer Corp. from oblivion, he went on to redefine the game for everybody with his vision of a company that would bundle hardware, software, and services in a quest for the customer's total computing wallet. After his downfall, many questioned the strategy. The problem was not with the idea but in the execution: Attempting to do too much too fast, Compaq lost its competitive edge. But for anyone aiming to enlarge his or her pond, Pfeiffer's approach remains a model.

Compaq Computer Corp. was a $3-billion-a-year company stuck in a shrinking niche when its board pushed out founder Rod Canion late in 1991 and made Eckhard Pfeiffer CEO. Its high-priced PCs were rapidly losing ground to machines from the likes of Dell and Gateway. Pfeiffer, a virtual unknown from Compaq's European operations, had been in the U.S. less than a year as COO.

Thus it was no surprise that jaws dropped in 1992 when Pfeiffer said Compaq would pass IBM as the world's number one supplier of PCs by 1996.[1] Many people in the industry and on Wall Street snickered at the German's bravado. But Pfeiffer doesn't do bravado. Growing revenues at a compound annual rate of about 63 percent and profits at just over 100 percent[2], Pfeiffer met his goal two years ahead of schedule.[3]

He then redefined Compaq a second time, announcing that it would play across the entire spectrum of computerdom—serving the enterprise (corporate) market with networked servers that would do the work of mainframes. In July of 1996 he did it again, declaring that Compaq

117

would by 2000 be one of the world's three largest computer companies, with revenues of $40 billion.

Compaq was then number 5, up from number 16 in 1992; its 1995 revenues of $14.8 billion lined it up behind IBM, Fujitsu, Hewlett Packard and NEC.[4] Fewer jaws dropped this time—competitors and investors had learned that Pfeiffer delivers on his promises. By the end of 1997, revenues had climbed to almost $25 billion and profits stood at $1.9 billion[5]. Compaq's p/e ratio, around 11 in 1992, was around 19.[6]

The January 1998 deal to acquire Digital Equipment Corp. (DEC), following the 1997 acquisition of Tandem, put him once again on target well ahead of schedule—combined revenues of the companies amount to $37.5 billion. When the deal is complete, only IBM will exceed Compaq in computer sales.[7]

It was a bold move, strategically brilliant but with considerable risk on the execution side. Integrating DEC will draw on every bit of Pfeiffer's leadership abilities. And as a company that plays at the edge, Compaq is watched closely by Wall Street. Early in 1998, for example, it missed a profit target and suffered from an inventory pileup. Compaq's stock, already in decline, plunged further. As of mid-June it was down 42 percent from its peak of roughly 39⅛.[8] Inevitably, Pfeiffer will hit more speed bumps as he navigates the express lanes.

Nevertheless, Compaq's transformation under Pfeiffer provides a model of how to combine boundless ambition with clear strategic vision. Today its product line extends from handheld computers to multimillion dollar failsafe servers. Compaq defines its pond as not only sales of hardware but virtually anything that existing or new customers might do with their computers. It's after as much of the total computing wallet as it can get, whether from big corporations, small business, or individuals.

Compaq's strategy is exemplified by the "lifetime cost of ownership" paradigm it stresses to business users. The hardware purchase price, it points out, is just 20 percent of the total lifecycle cost; administrative costs, technical support, and end-user operation make up the rest.[9] As the low-cost lifetime provider, Compaq wants to sell you everything from the hardware—complete with support and integrating software—to training and maintenance. When replacement time comes, it will finance the purchases and cart away the old equipment. Not incidentally, the service business offers considerably higher profit margins and requires less investment. Unafraid to cannibalize existing products, Compaq even aims to keep customer costs low by designing simplified machines for applications that don't require the full capabilities of a PC.

How did Pfeiffer transform a near basket case into such a power-house? First with a growth strategy that can be summed up in three words: radical, methodical, and fast-moving. In less than five years he completely redefined his company—and enlarged Compaq's pond—three times. And each time, the changes were executed quickly but only after extremely thorough and dispassionate analysis of customers, competitors, the business model, and Compaq's own capabilities.

Second, he changed Compaq's genetic code. Compaq could not even *set* its ambitious goals, much less achieve them, if the entire company were not marching to the same drummer. We'll look at that part of the Compaq story in Chapter 9. For now, the point to keep in mind is that Pfeiffer has taught Compaq's people to look always from the outside in, anticipating and defining new needs as the computing environment changes and evolves.

Overtaken by Change

The story begins with Pfeiffer's outside-in understanding of his business environment. "The industry is constantly changing, your competitors are constantly changing, and you have to anticipate those changes," he says. But nothing, he adds, is harder than casting aside the old thinking that initially made a company successful. "Companies need to learn how to unlearn."[10]

In the eighties, Compaq had been hugely successful as a builder of top-quality, expensive PCs for corporate customers willing to pay a pre-mium for the best. But by 1991, the mass market was growing, powered by lower-priced computers using the so-called Wintel architecture: Win-dows operating systems combined with Intel microprocessors. As these components became the industry standard, they lowered costs and barri-ers to entry into the marketplace, raised performance, and broadened de-mand by standardizing the look and feel of PCs.

Compaq's leaders, mostly engineers schooled in the old theory of the business, were still looking at the market from the inside out. Says Pfeif-fer, "We were too much focused on one competitor, and that was IBM. And they were doing so poorly that outdoing them and ignoring all the other competitors had made us very complacent. Our costs were too high; the pricing was much too high."

Compaq's leaders made what Pfeiffer calls "one last-ditch attempt" to turn the company around by getting costs in line. They succeeded to the extent that the pursuit of productivity became a core part of the genetic code and a permanent element of the company's success in the marketplace. But by itself, cost cutting was not enough; it was clear that the problem lay deeper. The old game was disappearing fast, and Compaq's previous strategy was no longer tenable. "So we were under tremendous pressure to come up with a new statement of direction for the company," says Pfeiffer.

The new statement came out of a ruthless outside-in analysis of how the industry was changing. A relentless asker of questions, Pfeiffer piped scores of them into his organization. Because he was equally relentless in demanding straight answers, the questions forced people to confront the new reality. "Would this company be a high-performance, high-priced niche player?" he asked for openers. "And would that be a good future?" Except for diehards steeped in the old mindset, the answer was clearly no. The next question took note of Compaq's true core strength. "We were the technical leaders of the PC business. But we had left the midrange and the lower end to others. Were we in a better position than anyone else to spread that across the entire spectrum of PCs?"

He set a tight deadline for answers, and made it clear that they had to be good ones. Leaders who couldn't rise to the challenge—the ones who were fixated on cutting costs and unable to play the growth game— were replaced. Those who could immersed themselves in studying market trends, customers, competition, and the company's strengths and weaknesses.

He also led his executives toward the answer. The industry, people agreed, would "ultimately become so competitive that you either play at the most competitive, most aggressive level, or you crawl way down in the rankings."

It quickly became apparent that the future lay in enlarging the pond. Pfeiffer was convinced that the PC could be made to do almost anything a mainframe could, and that Compaq could use its technical prowess to lead the way. "The PC industry provided enormous potential to leverage the technology that we had in a much broader way," Pfeiffer says. "So the fundamental decision was that we would play across the entire PC business community." Henceforth, Compaq would think of itself as a PC company.

That goal developed into a new central idea—one that people in the company still use to define their mission: "To expand the definition of the PC so that there's more room for innovation than there appeared to be."

In its old niche market for high-end PCs, worth some $8 billion, Compaq had a 50 percent share and nowhere to go but down. In the newly defined $80 billion market, Compaq's share would be less than 10 percent and, with the right execution, its opportunities would be immense.

"This was the starting point of the new Compaq," says Pfeiffer. "We called it the New Era."

Compaq's leaders resegmented its existing markets, breaking them down into home, education, small business, and enterprise (corporate) customers, and responded to the needs of those segments (Figure 6.1). They strengthened distribution channels by expanding dealerships more than tenfold, to some 38,000 worldwide. New product introductions more than doubled, to some 200 in 1995.

In an imaginative and immensely important move, Compaq's leaders poured resources into developing servers. Other manufacturers weren't paying much attention to them, but Compaq—using them to link its own global operations—saw what the others didn't: Networks of servers could compete with minicomputers and mainframes for the enterprise market, providing most or all of the same capabilities at much lower cost and with greater flexibility. They would also be more profitable than PCs. Compaq began going after the market in earnest in 1993 using alliances with networking companies to help it develop the systems. By 1996, the enterprise business driven by servers was worth $4.7 billion to Compaq. Sales of servers, says Pfeiffer, "are growing at incredible rates, and most other people don't even want to acknowledge it. Why? Because it's eating into their base."

In fact, servers were Act II: meeting existing customers' new needs and taking Compaq into quadrant D (Figure 6.2).

One reason Compaq was able to take the lead in servers was because its leaders had refocused the PC as a building block based on the Wintel architecture. The same architecture would serve for everything from a palmtop to a linked network of servers powerful enough to compete

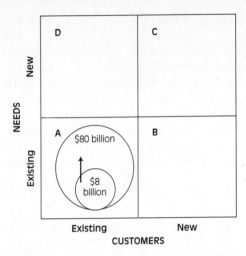

Figure 6.1   Act I: Existing customers, existing needs. Compaq had almost half the market for high-end PCs in 1992. But facing competition from increasingly capable lower-priced machines, Eckhard Pfeiffer decided to build midrange and lower end PCs as well. That broadened Compaq's pond to roughly $80 billion, of which its share in 1993–1994 was around 10 percent.

with mainframes. As FORTUNE magazine stated in 1996: "The 'Wintel' architecture is relentlessly creeping into virtually every form of computer. Pfeiffer has engineered the company so that the further PC technology goes, the further goes Compaq."[11]

Wintel also is emblematic of the partnerships and alliances that Compaq has used extensively to leverage its core competencies and to hold down its capital intensity. Over years, it has reaped the benefits of Microsoft's and Intel's combined research and development. Today, Compaq is a master of "co-evolution." Among its dozens of other partners are companies as diverse as Novell, Oracle, SAP, Cisco Systems, EDS, and Andersen Consulting. As part of its plan to build a major future presence on the Internet, for example, it's working with Microsoft, Intel, and Cisco to develop what it calls Web-Based Enterprise

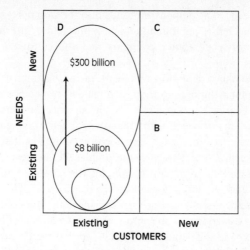

Figure 6.2 Act II: Servers, linked to provide most of the capabilities of mainframes, gave Compaq its entrée into the roughly $300 billion enterprise market. It further enlarged its presence by adding financing, maintenance and other related services and products, using alliances to leverage its resources.

Management—tools that will let any customers use any Web browser to manage a variety of systems, networks, and applications.

With alliances like these, Compaq can expand far more widely and quickly, while keeping investment low. Its research budget, for example, is just 2.2 percent of sales,[12] compared with 7.2 percent for Hewlett-Packard.[13] And partnering is central to the integration and "scalability" the company offers customers—the ability to integrate systems and expand them to meet growing needs.

The problem with "open-standard" arrangements such as Wintel is that the same popularity that makes entry easy for one manufacturer makes it easy for all. Computer hardware has become a commodity, which is one reason why its margins keep declining. From the outset, Compaq sold not only the boxes but the expertise, including help for customers in designing and maintaining their systems. Apart from being more profitable than the boxes themselves, the expertise paved the way for what was to become a major move into adjacent segments.

In 1995, the PC Company morphed into the Computer Company—becoming, as Pfeiffer put it in his annual-report letter, "the perfect blend of the enterprise computer company and the consumer electronics company."

Although the redefinition was years in the making, it emerged at Compaq's annual Innovate Forum, a three-day conference attended by thousands of executives, top customers, and strategic partners, and one of the company's major operating mechanisms for generating growth strategies. When the meeting ended, says Pfeiffer, "it was as if someone had thrown a switch. One day we were the familiar 'PC and server giant.' And the next we were the company 'reinventing the economics of mainframe computing' and 'mounting a challenge to the giants.'" This was a clear growth trajectory—one that once again changed the rules of the game.

The new direction was an expression of the central idea laid down in 1992: "to expand the definition of the PC so that there's more room for innovation than there appeared to be." But this iteration would enlarge Compaq's pond to include just about anything anybody might do with a computer. The opportunities were starting to look infinite.

The Same Old Organization

Pfeiffer wasn't quite ready at that point to announce another jaw-dropping goal to the world. As in 1992, formalizing the new direction generated incredible excitement and energy throughout the organization. "Everybody wanted to run for this new, great opportunity and be on the leading edge and participate," says Pfeiffer. But then performance began to suffer. "Nothing too serious," he says; "we took the eye off the ball of running day-to-day operations a bit. But listening to what was going on, I sensed that we were shooting off in too many directions. While before we were very focused, now that seemed to open up a lot more opportunities, and we hadn't organized around it properly.

"It was still the same old organization. And you know what that brings along. It doesn't show what all is happening; it doesn't get proper resourcing; it doesn't get proper management attention. In fact, it may kill your best newly borns. It may do all kinds of harm."

Characteristically, the moment he identified the problem, Pfeiffer dealt with it thoroughly and swiftly. The result was essentially a re-invention of the company through a new set of strategic directions, a new organizational structure, and new key genes—leaders at critical nodes who could carry the new plans forward.

The operating mechanism, which came to be known as the Crossroads, was extraordinarily intense and broad-based. Where another company might have brought in consultants and engineered a reorganization from the top down, Compaq turned to the layer below. "It was bottoms-up," says Pfeiffer, "an internal process that seemed almost voluntary. We said, 'Let's bring together groups of people who are the best inside the company to deal with the issues.' We formed 12 teams—typically, the next management level below my direct reports." There were teams for service, strategy, desktop, and distribution. All told, some 150 people were involved. The teams were cross-functional and cross-divisional, and cross-geographic; members included the most knowledgeable people on the subjects, naturally, but also "anybody who we felt could contribute, including people from Europe and Asia.

"We had to move very, very rapidly, but it needed to be a good job. And one of the conditions was: It's hands off by senior management [his direct reports]. We didn't want direction-setting or manipulation by them."

Pfeiffer nonetheless kept a firm hand on the steering wheel. He gave the teams eight weeks to rethink Compaq's entire management structure and process. After they reported back, worldwide division managers reviewed the results at Compaq's quarterly Joint Division Review. To say that top management was impressed is an understatement. Says Pfeiffer: "It was overwhelming for the entire management team to see the level of depth, the level of really solid, detailed work." The operating mechanism was also a great developmental experience for the participants.

Three major strategic directions were identified. First, Compaq would stick to its financial models and not dilute them. Second, the company would invest "significant amounts strategically in a recommended list of businesses."

Pfeiffer describes the third strategy as "the recognition that we truly had the opportunity to double the size of this company again in a similar time frame." It was based on the summary of all the five-year business plans, or related budgets, that the groups working on existing and new business strategies had been asked to produce. "As they integrated the whole thing toward the end," says Pfeiffer, "the anticipated growth came to the '$40 billion by 2000' number."

Crossroads also produced a new organizational structure. Existing and new divisions were pulled into four customer-focused global products groups: (1) Enterprise Computing, (2) PC Products, (3) Communications Products, and (4) Consumer Products. The 5 previous geographical sales groups—or "geos," as they were called—were to be consolidated into one worldwide sales, marketing, service, and support organization.

Pfeiffer thought twice before going public with the $40 billion forecast. He was haunted by the memory of IBM CEO John Akers, who, not long before he was replaced, predicted that Big Blue would be a $200 billion company by 2000. Even as Akers spoke, IBM was losing ground.[14] Besides, the $40 billion seemed incredible to veterans at Compaq. "We said: 'Is this real?' You think you'll grow the business, but you don't think in these huge leaps," says Pfeiffer.

"On the other hand, this was really solid work. We felt the only thing that could stand in our way was the competition, but we felt pretty good about that. There was a lot of very good competitive analysis with each of the proposals."

The implementation was just as quick and thoroughgoing. In a matter of months, Compaq was pushing into new categories of business: workstations, handheld PC companions, high-speed network connections, and computer equipment financing. All told, the company introduced some 250 new products in 1996; many resulted directly from Crossroads.

"The workstation business is the best example," says Pfeiffer. "It did not exist when we did the Crossroads. Nine months later, we were in it." By mid-1997, Compaq had at least a significant share of every major market; in some locations, the share was more than significant. In the United Kingdom, Compaq rose to number one in microsystems, with more than 23 percent of the market, just six months after selling its first workstation.

Compaq was still short of all the elements it needed to go after the ultimate pond that Pfeiffer had staked out, however. During the first six years of his leadership, the company made only two acquisitions—both in 1995, and both small.[15] In 1997 Pfeiffer went on a relative shopping spree. Microcom, a maker of remote access equipment, now helps to build Compaq's offerings of networking gear. Not long after, Compaq and Intel agreed to jointly develop other network products, such as, switches and hubs, which route data among computers.

More substantial was Tandem, whose high-performance, fault-tolerant computer systems are used by banks, airlines, and other users with critical high-volume transaction needs. The acquisition provided access to high level decision makers in enterprise customers, and a sales and service force skilled in dealing with complex systems. It was Pfeiffer's first "building block" acquisition for the new strategy.

The DEC acquisition in 1998 capped all Compaq's purchases and changed the rules of the game for the entire industry. Most notably, it added some 22,000 highly regarded service and consulting people, whom Compaq desperately needed to realize its goal of being the premier systems integrator and lifetime service provider to its enterprise customers.

And so we arrive at Compaq's current place on the growth 2 × 2 (Figure 6.3). The company is now a full-fledged player in the broad pond, second only to IBM. Compaq now has an inestimable pond. The best approximation would be the total world expenditures on computer sales and service, excluding mainframes—something on the order of $600 billion, and, growing by the minute.

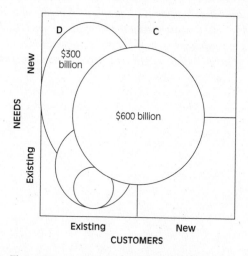

Figure 6.3   Act III: New needs, existing and new customers. With the additions of Tandem and Digital Equipment, as well as acquisitions and alliances in networking products, Pfeiffer has made Compaq into a full-line supplier to consumers and businesses.

In the months before he abruptly resigned, Pfeiffer was attempting to integrate the two big acquisitions and build new core competencies for servicing and selling large enterprise customers for their life cycle computer needs. He was also looking for ways to broaden the pond to include Internet-related products and services. If executed well and with edge, these plans will position the company for the next thrust of profitable growth.

Redefining Compaq's pond again and again, Eckhard Pfeiffer turned a failing niche player into the world's second-largest computer company in just a few years. By early 1998, its opportunities looked virtually infinite. But then the company stumbled badly. Expanding ahead of its ability to execute, it was unable to turn the vision into reality. The new model seemed to be Dell Computer Corp., the fastest growing, most profitable company in the industry and the clear leader in creating shareholder value.

Business history is full of visionaries whose legacy lives beyond their failures—like William C. Durant, who assembled General Motors, but had to watch from the sidelines while Alfred Sloan made the assemblage work. If his successors can pull off a Sloan, Pfeiffer's strategy will be vindicated as one of the computer industry's great business ideas.

CHAPTER

John Trani and the New Frontier of Service at GE Medical

Every growth trajectory flattens out sooner or later. The ultimate test of a company's leaders is how well they anticipate that moment and respond to it by finding new needs they can meet. GE Medical Systems CEO John Trani responded by broadening his company's pond twice and reengineering its genetic code. Result: Today GE Medical System is the most global of GE's businesses, and a leader in GE's move into services. It is capturing the greatest market share, and most of the profits, in its pond.

On the surface, GE Medical Systems (GEMS) looks like a company that's grown easily over the past two decades. The $4.5 billion-a-year maker of diagnostic imaging equipment such as X-ray and MRI machines and CAT scanners is the global leader in its industry.[1] But look more closely and you find a business whose leaders saw life-threatening change coming again and again, and adapted by broadening their pond. In the process, they fundamentally changed old strategies and mindsets.

Originally a maker of X-ray machines, GEMS led in developing the new diagnostic technologies from the mid-seventies through the mid-eighties. What followed was a classic period of natural, product-driven market expansion. Spending on health care in the United States was growing as if there were no tomorrow, and hospitals and clinics couldn't wait to get their hands on the latest gee-whiz equipment.

But easy success makes for hard falls. In the mid-eighties, the growth faltered; the domestic market flattened out. At the same time, tough foreign competitors moved in, Toshiba from Japan and Siemens from Germany. GEMS was a company driven by technologists—engineers who

129

were brilliant at product design but didn't know much about marketing. And costs were out of control—far higher than the competition's.

Globalization was high on CEO Jack Welch's agenda at that time. In August 1986, he appointed a new leader, John Trani—formerly head of GE's mobile radio business—and gave him a mandate to globalize GEMS. (See Figure 7.1.) The expansion would position GEMS in a much bigger pond—worth some $120 billion (versus the U.S. market of $48 billion) and growing rapidly.[2]

GEMS already had a controlling interest in a Japanese medical equipment company, Yokogawa Medical Systems. The medical equipment operations of Thomson, were acquired in late 1987 as part of a major swapping of businesses with the French electronics giant.

So Trani had an ostensibly global entity—except that it wasn't global. The GEMS leaders in Waukesha, Wisconsin, didn't have a clue about how to attack the global marketplace or integrate their management with the newcomers. That had to change—fast. GEMS, Toshiba, and Siemens

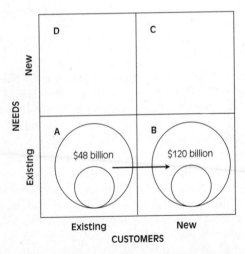

Figure 7.1 The equipment pond: With growth stalled in the U.S. market, (quadrant A), GE Medical Systems CEO John Trani staked out a global pond in which his company's share was just a small percentage (quadrant B).

dominated their respective domestic markets, and whichever company globalized first would clean up, bigtime, in the world marketplace that was starting to take shape.

First, Trani organized task forces to wring out some $80 million in costs. Working seven days a week, with full authority to do what was needed, they got the desired results within months. Concurrently, Trani asked us to help him jump-start the globalization. He had worked with both of us at Crotonville, GE's outstanding in-house training center, and wanted a Crotonville type of operation for teaching his executives how to think and act in this new environment.

We will explain in Chapter 9 how the Global Leadership Program, as it came to be called, jump-started the new genetic code at GE Medical. For now, what's important to understand is that it transformed the GEMS leaders. They began the program as inside-out thinkers, narrowly focused on their own operations and, creatively, cooped up in silos. They left it as a globally networked and customer-focused team, fired up to have GEMS grow aggressively around the world. They also learned how to teach their point of view to their troops. GEMS was back on a growth track.

An Operating Mechanism for Sharing Knowledge

Trani also developed a key operating mechanism for translating customer needs into fast action. He'd visited Wal-Mart's headquarters and had come away deeply impressed with its powerful intelligence-gathering system (see Chapter 9). "It was like a revelation," he says. "I felt like I'd found the holy grail."[3] GEMS didn't need anything so elaborate, so Trani rapidly devised a variant that suited his own purposes.

Called Quick Market Intelligence (QMI), it brings together, on a Friday morning, all of GEMS' geographic-region and business-line heads in a phone or video conference where they share information and act on it quickly. A simple example: San Francisco is losing a sale of a machine because of an order backlog. But Boston had a cancellation, so San Francisco can have the machine.

If an issue starts to consume too much time, the CEO steps in to say, "We'll take it up later offline." That's not a synonym for, "We'll sit on it." It's a rule that the issue has to be dealt with in a week or less.

Each business within GEMS has its own variation of QMI; one may meet weekly, another monthly. Depending on the issues to be dealt with, participants can range from a handful of key people to groups of 100 or more, including representatives of every unit from field sales and service to manufacturing, finance, engineering, distribution, and legal.

QMI became a central mechanism for breaking boundaries, integrating globally, and linking customers with all levels of the organization. It made information flows filter-free—undistorted—and fast. As Trani explained it some years after he devised the system: "This is how we took the top of the organization and the bottom and married them. We can get an idea from the bottom—a salesperson—to the top in one day, and that top will respond somehow to you, on the bottom, in a week. Guaranteed."

QMI is not only a powerful tool for meeting customer needs swiftly, but also an unparalleled operating mechanism for accumulating worldwide intelligence. At one meeting, for example, the American sales manager reported that a major competitor had raised prices in the United States. There was a chuckle from the sales manager in India. "No wonder they increased the prices here yesterday," he said. There was a hushed silence as all of the participants realized that they had developed a snapshot of the competitor's global pricing strategy—just days after it was executed.

"The Lower Your Share, the Better"

Expansion of the GEMS service business, its third stage of growth, came out of another nascent crisis. "In 1992, we were in a wonderful position," says Tom Dunham, the head of the service business for North America. "We were in a high-growth industry where the product side was growing by leaps and bounds, with new technology coming on almost every four to five years." Then came the health care upheaval. With costs suddenly under sharp scrutiny, the market for expensive medical technology imploded. "We had to do something differently," says Dunham.[4]

The inspiration came from another GE leader: Gary Wendt of GE Capital Services. Unlike GE Power Systems (Chapter 4), GEMS had developed service into an independent, and strong, profitable business that dominated the market for service of its own machines. "I was always sort of proud that we had a fairly large share of the GE service market," says

Dunham. Then he heard Wendt explain *his* take on market share. "Capital's view was just the opposite," says Dunham: "The lower your share, the better—it means you get more opportunity." As he mulled that one over, Dunham thought about a group of small companies already competing in his marketplace. Their competency was providing "multivendor service"—servicing equipment made by numerous manufacturers. And some customers were servicing their own equipment.

"That was about all it took to get the 'Aha,'" says Dunham. "We started looking at how we redefine our marketplace, and we recognized that the customer may be interested in a less complex situation: Why deal with three, five, six, twenty, a hundred suppliers when they could deal with maybe one, more effectively or more efficiently?"

Suddenly, GEMS had a whole new pond to explore: the needs of its equipment customers for a single, reliable, easy-to-deal-with supplier of related services. GE's own equipment amounted to a service pond of some $1.5 billion in annual revenues. The new multivendor pond would be three times as big. (See Figure 7.2.)

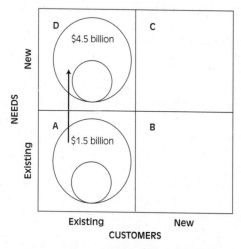

Figure 7.2   The service pond: Servicing the equipment it sold to hospitals was a $1.5 billion-a-year business for GEMS. Offering those customers one-stop shopping by taking on the servicing of other manufacturers' equipment as well, the company tripled the size of its service market.

It wasn't instantly clear that GEMS could fill the all-servicing role. "There was a lot of uncertainty," Dunham allows. GEMS faced having to persuade customers it could do as good a job servicing other manufacturers' equipment as servicing its own. And a major part of the expansion would be handling "bio-med" equipment—sterilizers, monitors, anesthesiology equipment, and the like. "Most of the equipment was less sophisticated than ours. Was it too far down the food chain? Do we bring any value to that? Do we lose our charter? We don't make any of that equipment; do we know how to service it?"

Under a different CEO, the idea could have died right on the spot. And indeed, John Trani, a tough-minded make-your-numbers man, was among the uncertain. "He wasn't thrilled about the bio-med piece," says Dunham. "It was a pretty distant neighbor from what we were doing." But Trani was also a pond-enlarger at heart, and piloting a new service business doesn't require a lot of resources. One of Dunham's core regional service managers, Steve Kellett, was eager to try. Early in 1995, he was given an office and a secretary, and invited to go after the first account. Kellett soon came up with an enthusiastic customer, a small hospital in Ohio. GEMS would be the general contractor for all equipment maintenance.

"We basically just had a model and a belief and a very supportive and proactive and forward-leaning customer," says Dunham. "There was some skepticism, but we said we'd guarantee him savings—worst case, we'd just hire the people he had doing this service anyway."

The experience taught the GEMS people a lot about how to manage a diverse group of subcontractors. They also learned to start by pitching for the diagnostic imaging (DI) business, which they knew best, and then picking up the bio-med as well, if the customer wanted them to. Most importantly, they learned they could indeed add value. Before the year was over, GEMS had signed up three more hospitals, including two teaching institutions. The adjacent segment had been defined, and the pond-broadening was underway.

The New Value Proposition— Selling Productivity

Customers were already looking for one-stop shopping. Early in 1995, one of them, a major hospital chain invited several DI suppliers and its own in-house group to bid on the business. GEMS won. It would take over management of all diagnostic equipment in the hospitals within a year, and also handle all future service needs.

A major part of the GEMS value proposition was its own productivity. "We could never service other people's equipment if we didn't have an outstanding reputation of servicing our own equipment," says Dunham. "One of our core competencies was delivering productivity year after year by utilizing technology and investing in our own service business."

To handle its own equipment globally, GEMS had built up a formidable technical and informational infrastructure, including remote diagnostics; a staff of more than 250 people online to provide technical consultation twenty-four hours a day; a global parts logistics system; and the ability to repair the digital boards that control the equipment. By focusing on process improvement, the company was able to reduce both the time it took to repair equipment and the mean time between failures. "That's what we were able to sell," says Dunham. "We said, 'If you're going to be productive at servicing your own equipment, you're going to need that same kind of infrastructure. Ours is adaptable and translatable.'

"A service contract put us and our customers on the same side of the ball. With technology driving uptime, we would have fewer service calls and the hospitals would have better equipment utilization. That was a key element of our overall strategy."

"Plant Some Seed Corn"

No less important was the fact that GEMS had taken an entrepreneurial gamble with that small Ohio hospital. "You can put a fence around an experiment easily, and it doesn't cost you a lot of money," says Dunham. "And if we had not tried that experiment, we would never have gotten in." The experience showed not only prospective customers but also its own people that GEMS could indeed add value in servicing other manufacturers' equipment. The Ohio hospital provided the all-important success that persuades people that they *can* go forward with a new venture. "The takeaway, I guess, is: Practice; plant some seed corn; you never know when they're going to build a shopping center on your little acre."

The big hospital chain also wanted someone to manage its bio-med equipment. The two companies talked about it, shortly after the DI contract was signed, and the chain's leaders raised many of the questions GEMS had earlier asked itself. The conversation, recalls Dunham, went something like this: "We said, 'We're interested.' They said, 'You don't know the first thing about it.' We said, 'We got a few hospitals.'" The reply was a skeptical, "Yeah."

So, says Dunham, "We recognized that to be successful at bio-med we'd have to acquire some competency." His marketing service head, Gary Foster, started scouting acquisitions and found a company called National Medical Diagnostics, a $20-million-a-year third-party service company. Dunham liked the fit: "They had a great franchise vehicle. They knew how to go into a hospital, do the analysis on the bio-med side, and price it. They had a good database, et cetera. We could have done all that, but it would take us probably two or three years to get there."

Dunham and his people took the proposal to GE's top management. The immediate answer, he says, was, "No way. You know: You want to spend how much to buy this little company whose assets drive home every night? And they tell you to pound salt and you've lost however much they want you to buy them for?" The brass had other worries: possible liability for being ultimately responsible for equipment made by other people; reservations about the low-tech nature of bio-med equipment—GEMS, after all, was a high-tech business; and concerns about operating margins.

It was also, as Dunham realized, a countercultural proposal. "To make money in a service business, you've got to insource—vertically integrate some of the service that is currently being done by OEM [original equipment manufacturer] suppliers of that particular institution. This is sort of the wrong direction in a company like GE—it's outsourcing everything, right? And here I am growing my workforce instead of subcontracting.

"We had a whole selling to do with ourselves and with our company. We had to learn about the business and plow some new ground in terms of employment contracts." But still the answer was no. "We tried two or three times and got turned down."

In the end, says Dunham, GEMS got its acquisition by showing how the benefits outweighed the potential risks. "We had the deal, and we just said, 'There's no way we can do it without an acquisition. We either walk away from a very big piece of business or we take a little risk on the acquisition and get some competency.'" It was an argument no pond-broadener could resist.

Acquiring New Core Competencies

GEMS got the business early in 1996 and started ramping up on the hospitals immediately. It got clearance to pick up two other companies, too, including a $50-million-a-year multivendor servicer named MMC, which also provided insurance against cost overruns for hospitals that wanted to service their own equipment.

"The whole team was very excited and charged up," says Dunham. "But we also recognized that this thing could bomb. If we stubbed our toe in the bio-med business with this large customer, they could throw us out on the DI side. So this was a 'Better do it, Tom' kind of thing.

"We were on a steep learning curve, but it was a great team, with lots of skills, lots of transferable stuff. And the National Medical Diagnostics acquisition was the key, because they had a portfolio of information, they had a system, they had a database, a way to go in and analyze."

The year ended with an increase of some $200 million in run-rate, including about $50 million from the hospital chain. "And by the way, that was fundamentally all our growth for that year," says Dunham. Equipment sales were flat.

By the end of 1997, GEMS was handling all of the customer's DI and bio-med service and had picked up several other hospital chains. Services had grown to account for some 40 percent of U.S. revenues, and the company had added about 1,000 new people to handle the new business. Work on non-GE equipment accounted for about 25 percent of total service revenues, and was growing at more than 20 percent a year.

Most recently, Dunham has begun to take multivendor service global. His operating mechanism for that is the GEMS Service Operating Council, a mechanism for sharing best practices. At Council sessions, Dunham videoconferences with his counterparts in Europe and Asia monthly, and meets with them face-to-face four times a year.

The GEMS training center, near headquarters, has turned out to be another unexpected locus of marketable skills. Like all GE businesses, GEMS devotes considerable time to training—5 percent to 10 percent of employees' working hours each year are spent in training, says Dunham. The center started simply as a place to train the company's technicians in maintenance. Then customers' operators and technicians began coming for training. "We stumbled into it," says Dunham. "Pilot error accounts for 10 percent to 15 percent of our customers' problems, so training them better pays."

Now the multimillion-dollar center boasts rooms set up with complete imaging equipment arrays, breakout rooms for study groups, and on-campus condos where visitors can stay during their training periods. (Some stay up to six weeks.) Naturally, there's plenty of opportunity for the GEMS people to schmooze and build relationships with the customers who are on-site. No competitor has anything that even approaches the GEMS center. TV studios link the center with customers' hospitals—some 1,600 are hooked in now—to facilitate on-site problem solving and remote training.

Other "near neighbors" are making a contribution too. When pond-broadening gets established in a company's genetic code—when thinking about new ways to capture every dollar the customer has to spend becomes a way of life for energized people—the opportunities are almost endless. GEMS executives now meet with customers in seminars and workout sessions, to help them improve productivity. "We know how to do management processes," as Trani put it. "If customers want to, we can do them on a consultancy basis, sharing 50–50 in the productivity gains." The Business Solutions Group, formed in 1995–96 to package the best practices of GEMS, was a $10 million business by the end of 1997, and growing rapidly.

The economics of information are compelling. Shortly before he left to be CEO of Stanley Works at the end of 1996, Trani explained it this way: "It's an inverted pyramid, with products at the bottom, then service, then information. As you move up, the base gets bigger.

"And you make more money as you move up. Because both competitive intensity and capital requirements are less."

Indeed. Early in 1998, GE Medical CEO Jeffrey R. Immelt was able to tell GE shareholders that "we posted record ongoing earnings during 1997 despite continued price erosion in a slow-growing worldwide diagnostic imaging [equipment] market." Part of the growth, he added, came from GE HealthCare Services's revenues of more than $200 million. Moving higher on that pyramid, GE Medical was acquiring businesses which, said Immelt, "have given us a strong global position in the rapidly expanding medical image information segment."[5]

So long as a company doesn't bet the ranch, the risk of an entrepreneurial gamble is lower than the risk of not growing. The seed corn GE Medical Systems planted in Ohio is yielding bumper crops. Apart from the added revenues it generates directly, the new service business model creates longer-term relationships with customers. By improving customer retention, the cost of selling equipment in the future is usually lowered. The resulting growth has created a new competitive advantage—a new core competency.

── John Trani's Second Act: "GROW or DIE!" ──

Since John Trani took over the leadership of the Stanley Works at the end of 1996, he has been drastically reshaping the company's strategy and genetic code. The job has taken longer than he or his investors expected. The century-and-a-half company's culture was deeply rooted, its operations were extremely complex, and the inevitable surprises took their toll. Nevertheless, Trani's changes are gradually taking hold.

Despite a powerful brand name in the tools business, Stanley's revenues had averaged only 6 percent a year growth over the previous six years, and earnings had been shrinking at a 1.5 percent annual rate.[6] Applying the leadership skills he honed at GE Medical Systems, Trani formed several task forces to look at every aspect of the business. Out of these came a host of cost-saving moves, including plant closings and pruning of support infrastructure, along with a reallocation of resources into product and brand development, new ventures, and further cost-saving investments to drive prices lower.

Stanley's leaders—including many new genes—also restructured the company by product groups, geography, and functions such as brand development, operations, and technology. As Trani reported in his 1997 letter to shareowners, "Essentially, we have moved from a portfolio company to an operating enterprise. This will enable us to present One Stanley to our customers while fostering people and process development, as well as freeing up resources to grow."[7]

The company's growth framework, he added, "involves three elements and a singular glue: the Stanley brand. The elements are new products, distribution expansion, and adjacent or 'near neighbor' market development." New product development got a 50 percent increase in resource spending, along with a new, outside in approach—using, for example, input from customers "to ensure new products solve real problems." Trani's long run goal, reminiscent of 3M's, is to derive 25 percent of annual revenues from products introduced within the previous three years.

Trani has broadened Stanley's pond from $16 to $27 billion of "fragmented, profitable hard goods markets that Stanley serves or should serve." Many of these are near neighbors, such as garden tools, electronic tools, commercial entry doors, and European hardware—and services, such as installation, repair, and maintenance. Stanley is also focusing on specified segments to develop. For example, says Trani, Stanley doubled sales to manufactured housing producers in 1997 "simply by focusing specifically on their needs and making it easier for them to do business with us."

Any doubts about the growth mindset Trani is striving for should be dispelled by the annual report itself, its bright yellow cover emblazoned with the word "win" in huge black type. His letter is no less fervid in tone and content. "Growth is the essence of any institution," he writes. "All organizations and organisms either GROW or DIE! Growth energizes people, provides a purpose for restructuring, delivers opportunities for career enhancement, adds to wealth, and is the 'like to do' side of becoming a Great Brand."

GE Capital Services
CAPITALIZING ON CHANGE

What's the secret of GE Capital Services, General Electric's celebrated growth machine? Simply this: A leader who finds opportunities for enlarging his pond everywhere, and has replicated his point of view in the company's genetic code.

For sustaining profitable growth, no company compares with GE Capital Services. From 1983 to 1997, revenues expanded at a better than 20 percent rate, to $39.9 billion, while profits rose at an 18 percent rate.[1] Indeed, it has been the primary engine of GE's growth. According to Prudential Securities analyst Nicholas Heymann, its revenues contributed more than half the gains in the parent company's top line from 1991 to 1996.[2] Profits, which grew 17.5 percent a year over the same period, reached $2.8 billion in 1996—39 percent of GE's total.[3] If GE Capital were a separate company today, it would be bigger than Citicorp.

Whether the economy is up or down, no matter what the competition is doing, regardless of financial crises, Capital—as it's known within GE—just grows. So reliable is this record that Wall Street views it in a class by itself compared with its peers in financial services. As Heymann told FORTUNE magazine: "The market is learning that Capital is different from cyclical financial-service firms, that its better-than-15 percent growth rate is practically guaranteed."[4]

GE Capital began in 1933 as a captive credit arm, financing refrigerators and the like. But any resemblance to the credit operations of other major industrial companies, such as Ford Motor Capital, GMAC, or Westinghouse, is purely coincidental. Today, among other things it is the world's biggest equipment lessor, owns the third-largest reinsurer in the United States, competes with banks in providing commercial loans, residential mortgages, mortgage insurance and private-label credit cards, and supplies life insurance and computer services.

Capital's strengths are many, ranging from superb risk management to some that reflect its relationships with the parent company—such as low cost of money and the contacts, intelligence and knowhow gleaned from GE's other businesses (several of Capital's leaders come from the industrial side). Business acumen is another asset; unlike executives of typical financial services companies, Capital's leaders are hands-on managers. When some of its airplanes came off lease in a down market early in the 1990s, for example, Capital turned them into cargo planes and set up its own freight airline, Polar Air. They also know how their customers' businesses work, sometimes better than the customers themselves, and can run them in a pinch. In the early 1980s a big borrower in the railcar leasing business got into trouble; Capital took it over and became a profitable railcar leasing company. So well do they run the business that their cars were in revenue service an average of 74 days during 1996—vs. 11 days on average for cars owned by railroads.[5]

Hands-on aptitudes also play a role in Capital's highly successful acquisition program. Acquisitions account for a fair share of Capital's growth—it made more than 100 from 1992 to 1997,[6] spending $11.8 billion from 1995 through 1997[7]—and the company is masterful in spotting opportunities, understanding the risks, and evaluating potential acquisitions. It has also learned how to integrate them with extraordinary thoroughness. "GE Capital has been working to make acquisition integration a core capability and a competitive advantage," according to the *Harvard Business Review*. The process starts in the due diligence phase, and continues long after the company is folded into Capital.[8]

That's one reason Capital was able to develop its latest business, IT (Information Technology) Solutions, as fast and well as it did. IT Solutions provides the full range of computer services for corporations, from financing purchases to hooking up networks and monitoring systems offsite. After getting experience in the business with a small Canadian acquisition, Capital plunged in during 1996, with a string of some 12 acquisitions in the United States and abroad over two years. By the end of 1997, the business was producing annual revenues of about $6 billion.[9]

Institutionalized Entrepreneurialism

While superb execution makes it all work, GE Capital's success is rooted in a mindset—an institutionalized entrepreneurial approach to business rare in big corporations. That mental architecture, present in leaders at all levels, largely reflects the leadership of Gary Wendt, Capital's CEO since 1986. It has three major components:

1. **Capitals people are passionate about growth.** Growth is woven into the very DNA of the organization. At GE Capital, there's no such thing as an existing pond. There's only, as Wendt puts it, "a continuous series of looking for the next generation of opportunity. And the job of a leader is to find the next activity that the company goes into."[10]

2. **They thrive on change.** It's worth repeating Gary Wendt's quote from Chapter 3: "You always look where there's change. Change is what creates opportunity." Opportunistic and entrepreneurial, Capital's leaders at all levels excel at capitalizing on demographic, economic and regulatory changes, spotting emerging trends and buying into new segments cheaply when they are in upheaval and turmoil.

3. **GE Capital is the king of adjacent segments.** More than perhaps any other company, Capital has segmented and resegmented its marketplace, identifying new needs and developing each into a fast-growing business. Each of its 28 major businesses represents a segment, and within each of these, new segments are constantly being pinpointed. Its diversity is not only the source of its growth but also one reason why economic cycles don't greatly threaten its profitability.

There's no point in showing a 2 × 2 for Capital, because expansion is so central to its genetic code that it's been going everywhere for years. Wendt doesn't think of his company as being in the financial services industry but rather as serving an endless series of markets and customer bases with needs for an endless variety of products. The industry definition, he points out, is just a way for people to report on a diverse packages of related services; as a definition of a business it's useless.

Wendt's own definition is a classic statement of adjacency: "We consider financial services to be almost anything that everyone else calls financial services, plus the things that are tangential to things we already do," he says. The segmenting approach arose naturally out of Capital's history. Commercial financing, added during the sixties, was a segment-specific business unit, as was leasing, added during the seventies. But it was Wendt, arriving in 1975, who institutionalized the process of creating new segments.

"We have a chart of the world, and our world has just hundreds of little segments in it," says Wendt. Most were identified and defined by Capital itself, and developed into their own small businesses. Its organization chart shows a constellation of 28 "bubbles"—that's what they're called there, and ambitious people speak of having their own bubble some day—grouped broadly under headings such as equipment management, mid-market financing, and consumer services. Each bubble started as a segment; each now operates like a small business, with its own P&L. Says Wendt, "It is one of the top three or four secrets of why GE Capital has grown."

For one thing, it keeps leaders close to their markets and customers. Selling an auto insurance policy in Des Moines, Iowa, doesn't have much in common with financing a power project in Indonesia, he points out, "so a set of practices on how to do one will not necessarily help you in the other. Applying the small business approach lets us narrow in on specific niches and focus on them and understand them for what they are." Focused on a specific set of customers, the leader of each group understands the customers, can be flexible in what he or she offers the customers, and can react quickly to change.

Strategy from the Outside In

As president Denis Nayden puts it, "If you really understand what your market focus is and your customer focus, then you can better define for yourselves the next growth opportunities. What are all the different products I can offer? Listen to the marketplace: What are all the products that my competitors offer right now? Understand them. What are the different distribution channels that are available to me today, and likewise our competitors? Can I get into those? Can I create new ones? Can I buy them?

"If you break the business equation down into these segments and zero in on the customer group, step by step, growth becomes a tangible issue you'll be able to get your hands around—instead of this great, generalized 'Of course we want to grow.'"[11]

Spotting opportunities isn't always the result of some disciplined segmenting process. At Capital, it's part of a mindset built into the genetic code. While managers in many companies tremble at the prospect of change, Wendt and his people tend to lick their chops in anticipation. That's always been Wendt's view of the world—"Change is what creates opportunity."

In 1981, for example, Wendt got wind of a proposed law aimed at lowering corporate taxes. On the surface, says Wendt, "it had absolutely nothing to do with leasing." But he went down to Washington to find out exactly how the proposal would work, talking to lobbyists, senators, and the University of Virginia professor who came up with the concept. "By the end of that day, honest to God, we figured it out. And the impact was just overwhelming." In fact, it would create a huge new demand for equipment leasing, something few if any of Capital's rivals grasped. Before the ink was dry on the tax bill, Capital had gone out and taken orders for some $3 billion of new business.

Two years later the rich tax benefits were eliminated, the result of a backlash to the huge and highly-publicized breaks corporations were getting (including GE itself, the most prominent beneficiary, which drew flak for winding up with a $1.6 billion windfall).[12] Anticipating just such a turn, and its negative impact on equipment financing and leasing, Wendt had already started to develop a business in equipment *management*—the operation and maintenance of everything from railcars to truck fleets.

"We thought, 'Well, we better find something else to add value to get revenue, to get return on that equipment financing we do,'" recalls Wendt. "And it turned out to be owning the companies that actually managed the equipment." Once again, growth would come from adjacent segments. "Our definition wasn't, 'We finance equipment.' Our definition was 'What can we do with equipment?'"

Today equipment management and leasing is a major sector at Capital, including nine segment-specific business units: fleet leasing, trailer leasing, container leasing, truck leasing, satellite leasing, commercial air leasing, modular structure leasing, computer services, and railcar services. It generated an estimated $716 million of Capital's profits.[13]

The top secret of why GE Capital has grown is Wendt himself, with his absolute passion for growth. The need to dissect change, generate ideas, look constantly for new sources of ideas, and convert them into growth trajectories is understood throughout the company. "Growth is everybody's business," as he says, because he makes it so.

Gary Wendt is a restless, creative, and relentless leader with a thoroughly entrepreneurial mindset. After graduating from Harvard Business School in 1967 he went to work for a real estate developer in Texas. (Within a month, at age 25, he was in charge of the business.) "I never had any interest in big business whatsoever," he says. " I always thought of myself as an entrepreneur, and I still do."

Many leaders set numerical growth targets to stretch their peoples' minds and ambitions. Wendt's view is that any pond can be as big as you choose to make it. "It's not like, 'Well, should we grow 4 percent this year, or should we grow 8 percent, or should we grow 28 percent?'" says Wendt. "The simple answer for us has always been that you grow as much as you possibly can." But if there's no ceiling, there *is* a floor that reinforces the mindset. "We have embedded it by just demanding 15 percent to 20 percent growth by everybody every year," says Wendt. "And 25 percent of our net income should come from things we've been doing for less than about 2½ years."

Specific operating mechanisms systematize the mindset—and help speed decisionmaking and the free flow of information that sustain expansion. One such is the Preliminary Investment Committee. It's the first order of the week's business, meeting every Monday morning. *Every* Monday, 52 weeks a year. People from every region and country come in or appear on video with their latest ideas for new deals, opportunities, and directions to go. "The focus is very simple," says Wendt. "It's not to look for inventory turns but to look for growth."

The operating mechanisms are Wendt's teachable point of view translated into action. "I decided a long time ago that if I was serious about this growth thing, I had better start doing some things culturally," he says. He continually involves himself in the business unit leaders' thinking about opportunities—out in the field, one small businessman to another, asking questions and popping ideas. In forums from quarterly review meetings to informal get-togethers, he'll be questioning, suggesting, challenging, keeping the focus on understanding change and understanding the customer.

As a result, strategic planning at GE Capital is bottom-up as well as top-down. "A lot of businesses have one strategic planner trying to jam growth into their organizations," he says. "When I want growth, I have 28 leaders looking for opportunities." Above all, strategy is entrepreneurial, derived from the realities of the marketplace. Wendt stresses the point by ironically turning on its head the conventional wisdom that you start with a strategic plan and then move forward. "When you've got a good program going," he likes to say, "it's never too late to get a strategy behind it."

A Teachable Point of View on Growth

Still, in 1995, Wendt was not satisfied with the end result of the strategic planning process. The plans themselves would roll up through the general managers, through senior management, and finally were presented jointly to Wendt and GE CEO Jack Welch. The plans would be virtually finalized at that point, leaving Wendt little room to make contributions.

So Wendt went out as a teacher, sat down with his business leaders, and worked out with them a new way of developing strategies.

"Last year, rather than do the strategic plan the conventional way—sit at a table and let them present stuff—I decided to have new sessions," Wendt says. "I went out to every one of these businesses, and I just put my feet up on the table and said: 'OK, kids, what do we really think is going on in the world.' And it was just a wonderful experience." Wendt once again made his point about the importance of escaping from the confines of formalized strategic planning processes. "I told them 'We're going to talk about the future. This isn't your strategic planning process guys, this is the beginning of your strategic plan.'"

There was a certain level of discomfort—who likes the boss watching while you make your sausage? And people came to the meetings with different ideas of what he was looking for, some with old-style strategies all mapped out, others with blank slates. Wendt worked with whatever people brought him, making sure that even if they thought the plan was done, that he had the opportunity to inject himself and his experience early in the process.

Rather than test people for the carefully prepared analyses, Wendt wanted to know if they had a feel for the market—and he wanted to get a feel for the market himself. "I would say to them 'We're just going to kick it around. Tell me what your market environment is; what your competitors are doing; and what you think the best new opportunities are—give me your five best opportunities.'"

After establishing this new method for developing strategic plans in all of the bubbles, Wendt moved to engaging in the process on an "as needed" basis, using his involvement to send a message. The following year, he conducted 12 of these "dreaming sessions," focusing on both the weakest and strongest businesses. "I wanted to make sure the businesses that I think can grow understand that I think they can grow," he says. "And the same thing at the other end: I have to pay attention to these people that are having a rough, tough time."

It was in one such session that a newcomer to GE Capital got a lesson in enlarging the pond. Capital had the year before acquired majority ownership of Penske Leasing, a highly successful truck-leasing outfit with $1.8 billion of revenues in 1997.[14] The business leaders came in to the 1996 strategy process feeling great that they had growth targets of better than 20 percent. Hearing the number, Wendt sat back and looked sharply at them. "I said, 'It's not even close, guys. You shouldn't be putting percentages on your growth. You're looking at the wrong number.'" The right number didn't exist at the moment—it was whatever growth they could get.

They were also looking at the wrong definition of the market segment, focusing on their direct competitors in truck leasing rather than related opportunities. "The managers kept saying 'Ryder this' and 'Rollins this,'" recalls Wendt, referring to the competitors.

Wendt quickly redefined the opportunity from truck and fleet leasing to outsourcing of fleet management—taking over the running of other companies' entire fleets. "I began to think about it because the reason that GE Capital has gotten into other [businesses in the past] is the outsourcing that other companies are increasingly doing. So I began to ask the question 'How many total trucks are there?' Well, we started with that question and we realized that in fact only 15 percent of the market for operating trucks is taken up by ourselves, Ryder, and Rollins."

Suddenly, the market became "all the treasurers and financial vice presidents of the world that own and operate their own truck fleets. And I said, 'What would you get if you could just get ten lousy stinking percent of the whole thing?' They did the math, and it more than doubled."

This reframing caused some uneasiness in people. "They weren't sure what to do with it. Because they were doing great. They came in thinking they were doing great, going to grow 20 percent, and they left knowing they were supposed to go to two times that if they only did a small piece of the market." But he and the business leaders came up with ideas to implement their outsourcing strategy immediately, and he thinks that the changed mindset has stuck. Further, he says, "We're talking about setting up an outsourcing university to give them the GE productivity tools."

Financing Entrepreneurship

For all of its virtues, being a highly segmented company also has a downside—often, no one has the inclination or resources to develop ideas that don't handily fit into the existing structure. This gap in the "small business" organization model is filled by GE Capital Ventures, which funds and develops new businesses within GE Capital. The problem, says Steve Smith, Capital Ventures' head, is that the bubbles' leaders "look in a pretty defined space to extend their value added. And quite often ventures are a second priority."[15] Finally, in a company that typically looks for quick return on investments and writes off its losses every year, Ventures offers patient capital not otherwise available.

Some of the businesses Capital Venture seeds and incubates don't have a natural home in any of the existing bubbles; others need added or new technology; still others have the potential for cross-business synergies—within GE Capital, with other GE units, and with other partners.

The object in most cases is to get a venture to bubble status, or sell it off at a profit. In its portfolio recently were ventures ranging from commercial processing to software to digital or on-line commerce to telecommunications infrastructure and "utility outsourcing"—selling and managing remote metering systems, for example. Smith estimates that ventures might contribute between $500 million and $1 billion to GE Capital's annual net income by 2000.

Some of the most important ventures are part of a larger effort to insure that Capital is in on the ground floor of emerging businesses. None is more portentous than global electronic commerce. As Smith points out, the combination of changing transaction behavior—disintermediation, for example—with technology, deregulation and globalization is driving massive convergence and consolidation in payment systems. "It's a good time for us to get involved," he says. "People like us who have lots of global presence can play in these games." The Ventures portfolio includes a growing handful of businesses involved with payment systems and online commerce—none of which could be developed within any of the existing GE Capital bubbles.

Some will likely become bubbles themselves eventually. That's the entrepreneurial thing about Capital—no one knows when the ever-changing marketplace will elevate some little niche into a huge new segment, but everyone is ready for the opportunity when the window opens.

Has growth gotten out of balance in the expansion rush of recent years? Capital is hardly a Nokia waiting to happen, to be sure. But leaders of even the hottest growth businesses can't afford to get complacent about the basics. At Jack Welch's urging, Wendt late in 1997 was looking over the company's portfolio to screen out non-strategic businesses, and Capital is following other divisions in adopting GE's Six Sigma quality and training initiatives. Begun in 1996, the effort has paid off with better customer retention, fewer errors, and net savings after training costs of an estimated $150 million for 1997.[16]

Meantime, the world is full of the change-driven opportunities that GE Capital's leaders love, and they're going after them full-bore. Among these are deregulation and privatization in Europe, where the company has already bought or taken stakes in some 80 financial businesses in 12 countries; and acquisitions in Asia's distressed financial markets. "We will go where our skills permit us to go," says Wendt. Which suggests that Capital will go just about anywhere the next generation of opportunity is starting to be visible.

A leader must not only have clear ideas, but also must reinforce them daily in his or her interactions with all of the organization's people. GE Capital's enviable record of top line and bottom line growth reflects both Gary Wendt's conviction that change in the external environment is a source of opportunity, and his ability to instill that conviction in others. When it comes to pressing his teachable point of view on growth, Gary Wendt has few peers.

PART III

Energizing and Aligning the Organization for Growth

CHAPTER 9

The Genetic Code and How to Change It

"Business development is everybody's responsibility."
GE Capital Services CEO Gary Wendt[1]

Shortly after giving a presentation at a multi-unit manufacturing company, Ram Charan got an urgent call from one of its division heads. A highly successful cost cutter, he wasn't making his first-quarter numbers, and he didn't know what to do. Despite a lot of jawboning in the unit about putting customers first and raising forecasts, sales were down. Ram agreed to meet with him. When he arrived, the leaders' controller was with him at the meeting—the only other executive present. Ram asked, "Where's the sales manager?" They hadn't thought to invite him. Embarrassed, the leader called him in.

The sales manager reported that he'd be able to make some progress once he pulled together all of the representatives in the field and gave them a pep talk and a chance to exchange market and competitive intelligence. That would be at the beginning of the next quarter. Why not now? Well, he replied, it will cost $25,000, and the boss had cut the first quarter budget.

The sales manager had accepted that. He had not fought for what he knew needed to be done. That was just the way things worked in his company.

There was an uncomfortable silence as the division manager contemplated this. The meeting that could have helped him make his numbers wasn't going to happen because everyone, driven by the cost-cutting mentality built into the genetic code, was focusing on the need to save money in the short term.

The connection was so obvious, and yet none of these highly successful, well-regarded individuals saw it! When that pep talk finally does

153

get delivered, Ram thought as he left, it will be a band-aid, no more. Everybody is stuck in the old ways. Without a new genetic code, there will be no sustainable improvement.

Six months later, the division head was replaced.

We meet more and more leaders of companies stuck in the cost-cutting mindset who sense that they have to transform their organizations if they want growth. The standard 50,000-foot level advice they hear is to start a change process, rewrite the vision, get groups to work on strategies, and do something about the culture. They learn that, if things go well, the transformation will take shape over several years.

But the advice leaves them still unclear about what precisely to do, and about how all of these undertakings add up to a better organization. With good reason: The pieces *don't* add up, because the most critical element is missing. It's the genetic code, which drives the development of vision, strategies, and execution. If a transformation is to succeed, the genetic code must be diagnosed, understood, and re-engineered.

The Origins of the Genetic Code

It's no news that some of the most powerful forces shaping corporate behavior are intangible. All the efforts to define and understand "culture" are about these intangibles—the soft issues described variously as a company's basic assumptions, values, mindset, history, myths, language, and the like. They tend to endure through generations of management, and can play a big role in determining a company's success or failure. In companies with staying power—the P&Gs, the Intels, the Microsofts, the GEs—they can be more important, and harder for competitors to duplicate, than strategies, technologies, or products. Yet cultural change efforts rarely produce a lasting difference.

The genetic code concept defines the real drivers of culture. It's a concept we developed over time. Ram first enunciated it in the mid-eighties, while teaching at a top FORTUNE 500 consumer products company whose leadership was paralyzed by indecision. As he studied the situation, he saw that it was universally OK in this company *not* to make decisions. The CEO was a hands-off type, as were a number of his direct reports. In meeting after meeting, executives would pore over issues, nod their heads in agreement, leave without achieving closure, and return to their desks to make pocket vetoes of whatever proposals they didn't like.

Analysis paralysis, Ram thought. And he saw that the only solution was to bring in new leaders who could really lead. New genes, he called them—key genes who could alter the behavior of the entire organism.[2] Subsequently, we looked into the workings of the biological genetic code and found more and more parallels, some of them uncanny. The longer we worked with the idea, the more accurately it described the organizational dynamic. People struggle vainly to change culture, we realized, because culture in fact is a variable that depends on the genetic code.

As we explained in Chapter 1, biological and behavioral scientists debate over the relative importance of nature versus nurture. In organizations, we think, there's no argument at all. Efforts at cultural change are interventions into nurture. And as our colleague Andrew R. McGill of the University of Michigan Business School observes, the genetic code is nature—and it is the more powerful determinant. The genetic code shapes corporate culture at the most fundamental level, because it determines *both how individuals make decisions and how they work together.*

What is the natural origin of the genetic code's power? It's easy to see once you know what you're looking for. Nobody is likely to have sat down at the equivalent of a CAD/CAM terminal to design it—but it did not arise accidentally. Over time, the company's leaders created it.

In a biological organism, genes produce the RNA molecules that determine structure, organization and growth. In social organizations such as corporations, leaders fulfill the role of genes. Their thinking, approaches to decision making, and behavior set the pattern for everyone else, sending pervasive signals through the organization. As they put their stamp on the organization, those signals and cues become the organizational genetic code.

The genetic code embodies the leaders' ideas (or lack of them), the values they hold, the emotional energy they create (or fail to), and the edge they bring to the tough calls (or don't). How they see the world and act on it is translated into everyone else's behavior in thousands of ways, both visible and invisible. The code the leaders create governs all transactions and interactions. It dictates how everyone thinks, acts, and behaves. It determines choices and actions: what courses are set, which ideas fly and which ones sink. It determines how people communicate with and treat each other; it determines who gets rewarded and promoted (and sometimes who gets fired), and who gets brought in from outside.

Change efforts most often fail because the architects of change don't understand the pervasiveness of the genetic code. Think for a moment about the opening quote from Gary Wendt. In no company do all of the decisions go to one central place. Every day, at every level, people are making decisions. The sum of those hundreds of thousands of transactions—what decisions get made, how they get made, who makes them, and when they are made—determines whether a company is going to grow, stand pat, or fold.

The basic building block for a genetic code of growth is the leader's teachable point of view on growth. It includes the business ideas that drive balanced growth, the ideas that support it, the leader's ability to energize people around growth, and his or her ability to make the tough, courageous, edge decisions.

Every growth story in this book began with leaders who had the will and the ability to change the old genetic codes of their organizations.
There are three key points to understand here:

1. Growth companies grow because growth is in the genetic code.

2. A company's leadership determines its genetic code.

3. To build a growth company, its leaders have to actively change the genetic code with their teachable point of view on balanced growth—growth that is profitable and capital efficient. They must develop leaders at every level.

Decision and Social Architectures

The elements of the genetic code, unlike those of culture, can be pinpointed, quantified, compared—and specifically redesigned. The organizational genetic code has two inextricably linked components. One is what we call the *decision architecture*™; the other is the *social architecture*.™

The organization's decision architecture is the framework for what decisions get made and how they are made; what information is selected, and what analytical tools are customarily used; how that information is structured and discussed; and what types of judgments are given the most weight.

Just as each gene has its unique architecture for producing specific proteins, each leader has his or her own decision architecture. No two leaders think the same way, search the same data in the same sequence, rearrange the data in the same logic, or give them the same weights. No two leaders look at the external world the same way as they search through the morass of confusions and contradictions for avenues of opportunity. Each leader has an inherent methodology of asking questions, receiving data, filtering them, and rearranging them.

That's why two leaders, each looking at the same data, can come to very different conclusions, or set completely different goals. IBM CEO John Akers, for example, planned to split his company into multiple pieces. When Lou Gerstner replaced him, it was the same IBM. Gerstner had the same information available. But Gerstner decided not to split IBM up. His decision architecture was totally different from Akers' decision architecture.

It doesn't take long for a strong new leader's decision architecture to change thinking in the organization. The smart people know what they have to do to survive. When the new leader questions them and debates with them about the information they bring to the table, they quickly learn what he or she likes more, or likes less. They learn how the leader wants information presented, and how often, and to what purpose. They begin to architect a similar general pattern of selecting information. They look at the same data they looked at before, rearrange it and weight it according to the leader's methodologies, and discover new insights. They will also learn to look at different data, from different sources. In reviews and meetings, they will prepare to answer different kinds of questions. Thus is the decision architecture of the organization changed.

Social architecture is subtler than decision architecture, but it is just as powerful—maybe more so. Any business is a social organization—social being defined as two or more people working together—and no business transaction is without social transactions. The social architecture is the product of how people react to each other: how well or poorly they listen to each other, support each other, and respect each other; how they surface conflicts and resolve them. It includes the social relations they develop through the dialogues and decisions of work life—the relationships they build, the relationships they strain, the relationships they destroy.

Organizationally, social architecture includes informal networks of power and information flows. These are the shadow organizations sometimes called "emergent organizations." In fast-moving, less than hierarchical companies, they are most often where the real work gets done. (See Figures 9.1 and 9.2.)

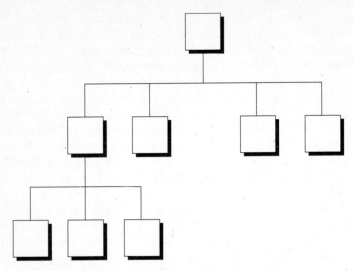

Figure 9.1   Corporation XYZ Organization Chart. They may show who reports to whom, but organization charts barely scratch the surface of how companies are really run. The social architecture chart gets to the hidden reality behind the organization chart.

Social architecture absolutely influences the outcomes of decisions. You can see it clearly by watching a meeting, that most basic unit of corporate existence, and mapping what goes on behind the scenes before and after.

The decision architecture of a meeting includes the items it deals with, resolves, or postpones, and the content and organization of its dialogue. The social architecture is how the dialogue is conducted, how the conclusions are reached; the candor (or lack of it) in the dialogue, the give-and-take, the rewards or punishment for taking risks, the dynamic by which ideas are developed—or snuffed. As everyone who has sat in a meeting knows, these can make all the difference in the quality and appropriateness of decisions.

As an example, take a typical annual strategy review. Surely you've been in one like this. You've prepared for weeks. Your staffers have gathered all the numbers and crunched them. Your targets are realistic—nobody will have trouble reaching them. Your boss has worked your plan over, making sure it doesn't throw any sand in his gears. He may have

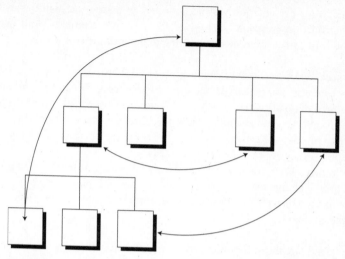

Figure 9.2 Corporation XYZ Social Architecture Chart. These lines represent the flows of information, influence, and power; the friendships and affinities, the informal relationships and unwritten understandings. They can powerfully influence whose ideas win and whose lose.

coached you on what the CEO wants—and does not want—to hear. You're smart: You will avoid any of the latter topics, no matter how important they may seem to you. You know what's good for your career.

Now it's time for that presentation you've rehearsed twenty-nine times. You stand behind the lectern and deliver it. The 20 bigwigs sitting around the boardroom table are each watching you with one eye, keeping the other on the emperor for cues about whether to ask a question. Occasionally the emperor himself asks one, and you feel good—you have a prepared answer for any he might imaginably raise. You handled them well; your boss, not embarrassed, gave you a wink and a smile each time. Finally it's over, and you leave the room feeling relieved. In the corridor, people tell you that you came away a winner.

But are you aware of an empty feeling, too? The return on your time was zero: There was no real dialogue, no creative exchange of ideas. No value was added to your business by any of the bigwigs. They were busy playing the old game, 'You scratch my back, I'll scratch your back'—don't embarrass me with any questions, and I won't put you on the spot either. Your presentation will become part of a strategic plan that will gather dust on everyone's shelves for the next twelve months. And why shouldn't it, since it has almost nothing to do with the real world?

Jack Welch's genetic re-engineering of GE began with meetings. His new rule was: No rehearsed or scripted speeches; only candor, and uninhibited dialogue where intellectual honesty rules. Wrestle problems to the ground, get into the mud, think the business issues through from a variety of angles. Participants in the meeting are not there for control purposes; they are there to generate ideas.

In fact, Welch was redrafting GE's social architecture. His new policy produced massive discomfort—and, in the end, played a significant role in transforming GE, because it became the model for all dialogues in the company.

Social architecture influences every decision-making mechanism, from ad hoc task forces through periodic business reviews. Much of its leverage comes from this cumulative total of daily transactions. For example, take a small group discussion where the social architecture does not permit candor and honest dialogue. One of the people has a far-out idea that might generate new revenues. Another individual—not necessarily the boss, but very powerful—cracks a clever joke about it. And that's the end of any creative dialogue ('Uh-oh—Ed doesn't like it'). The energy of the group collapses, and people move on to new business. No one will ever know whether it might have generated a big new revenue stream.

As you start to look for it, you'll see how the genetic code is present everywhere, every day. Its signals shape not only conscious decision making but also the basic assumptions that people don't necessarily think about but that push and tug at them constantly—affecting even the unspoken understanding they have about why they come to their desks each morning.

We all develop rules of thumb, based on what works best for us in whatever situation we're in. We filter the relevant information from the rest. We emphasize some things more than others—things we can't quantify but simply call judgment. Rarely, if at all, do we think about the filters and emphasis. We just know what's important and what we're expected to focus on, and we know not to step too far out of bounds. It's a self-reinforcing process, derived from the genetic code and perpetuating it.

Say, for example, your boss is like the division manager at the start of the chapter. In any new situation, his own ideas and values drive him to look for the lowest-cost solution. You've learned to do the same, haven't you? His filters are your filters; it's become instinctive. You don't have to think twice about your priorities. Nor do the people who work for you—or the ones who work for them.

Operating Mechanisms

The decision architecture and the social architecture are joined in the company's decision-making systems and processes. We call these *operating mechanisms*. They are where the rubber meets the road.

- ▶ Any major decision that requires tradeoffs of judgment among two or more people is produced by an operating mechanism, whether it is formal or informal, permanent or temporary.

- ▶ Operating mechanisms are the primary instruments for driving the genetic code deep into the organization. They serve as training, coaching, and feedback systems that constantly shape and reinforce the leadership's teachable point of view.

In most any company, the core operating mechanisms are those that map strategy, review and approve operating plans or budgets, and select and develop people. Other operating mechanisms range from regular meetings to the structure of daily working relationships, from standing procedures to short-term task forces. An executive committee of the board of directors is an operating mechanism, if it has the power to influence the CEO. Gary Wendt's operating mechanisms at GE Capital (Chapter 8) range from his Monday morning Preliminary Investment Committee meetings and "dreaming sessions" to the company's very structure, with its entrepreneurial profit-and-loss bubbles.

Bob Nardelli of GE Power Systems (Chapter 4) altered the annual strategy review, a key operating mechanism, by bringing into it people from all levels of the organization—including those closest to the customer—and coaching them in the art of looking from the outside in. At Citibank's corporate banking group (Chapter 5), the operating mechanisms began with the senior task force whose members developed the global relationship strategy. Others that followed included the reorganization from geographic to industry focus; the customer revenue unit (CRU) yardstick for quantifying success in reaching target customers; and the S-curve chart that the division's leaders used to help their people understand the nature of a radically new way of doing business.

The most powerful operating mechanisms are those that reinforce the change message repeatedly. They don't have to be big or elaborate—just omnipresent. For example, Citibank's S-curve chart, which tracks the share of customer wallet Citibank gains, over time, in global relationship banking, is a constant reference point. "The chart combines two things: management process and change process," says senior vice president Ed Holmes. "The change process is saying this thing over and over again. To get here is not only to believe in this stuff but to get the *whole company* using the same language, saying the same sort of things."[3]

Some of the strongest operating mechanisms center around the CEO. At GE, Jack Welch meets with each business unit every year for at least a full day, in what's called Session C. The people in the unit lay out where their organization is going, and why. They talk about changes in the external environment. They openly discuss the people issues. In these meetings, Welch's personal style—the questions he asks, the quality of the dialogues he demands—influences a lot of behavior in the company, from what people bring to the meeting to the kind of dialogue they subsequently conduct at the business-unit level.

What happens after Session C? The phones ring off the hook. People want to know what the new ideas are. They are preparing for their own Session C meetings, trying to factor in new best practices before they even arrive. The CEO himself is introducing best practices from the previous session C in subsequent ones.

This is Jack Welch's secret for managing 12 diverse businesses—implanting the same decision and social architectures in each one. It's why FORTUNE magazine called him "the ultimate social architect."[4]

AlliedSignal CEO Larry Bossidy's operating mechanisms for personally driving change include his two-day quarterly reviews for people, strategic planning, and operations and budget—plus the follow-up letters he sends out afterward (Chapter 10). As Bossidy points out, all companies have these activities, but most don't use them well. Says Bossidy: "The trick is how intense the processes are and what they yield."[5] There's no question about Bossidy's intensity. He uses his reviews not only for planning but also for coaching everybody in the room on how to think about a business. His own style is blunt, candid, and open, so that's how the dialogues develop. Such coaching travels faster and reaches deeper through a company than any jungle telegraph.

A video clip we sometimes use in presentations shows this dramatically. It was shot during one of AlliedSignal's planning review meetings. Bossidy is conducting a spirited, constructive, and energizing dialogue on a $300 million investment proposal with his CFO and the highly valued business unit manager who made the proposal.

The manager has done his homework on the numbers, the external environment, and competitive trends. Then Bossidy asks a simple common sense question that only a leader his caliber would ask: "Who will buy this product in the shop of your business customer?" A sharp, fast reply: "The purchasing guy." But, asks Bossidy, "Who really decides the specifications and ends up responsible for that decision?" Answer—not quite so sharp and fast—"The engineers."

Now there is a pin-drop silence as the dozen or so people anticipate the chairman's final question. "This is a huge investment for your business unit," says Bossidy. "Did you personally talk to the engineers who will buy it?" Pause. The unhappy answer: "No."[6]

The proposal was rejected. And the dialogue left an indelible imprint of Bossidy's decision architecture and social architecture on the minds of all who attended.

The effectiveness of the operating mechanism depends on the content, frequency, and outcomes of those dialogues—the quality and structure of the data that are presented, what is emphasized, what questions are asked; how the information is assembled; how the social architecture works in the group setting. Follow-through is just as important; it affects the quality of the subsequent dialogues, and thus the social architecture of the entire organization.

The management system Sam Walton created for Wal-Mart provides a clear example of how a single operating mechanism can link and develop a company's decision architecture and social architecture. Walton's goal was to have Wal-Mart's basket of goods priced significantly below the key local competitor. Velocity (Chapter 3) was his secret weapon—he turned inventories faster than the competition. To achieve velocity—and, not incidentally, keep his customers happy—he essentially institutionalized the small storekeeper's resourcefulness and closeness to the customer and marketplace.

Individual stores would need the freedom to reorder merchandise to suit local conditions and set prices competitively. And Wal-Mart management would need detailed and comprehensive weekly feedback on its customers and competitors, so it could know on a national basis what was changing in terms of trends, mix of products, pricing, and competitive behaviors; what was selling more, and what was selling less.

Walton's operating mechanism has by now achieved legendary status (and is the basis of the Quick Market Intelligence operating mechanism John Trani introduced to GE—see Chapter 7). As described in a Harvard Business School case, every Monday morning, all of Wal-Mart's regional managers fly out in private planes to spend three days visiting their own and competing stores in their regions. At the competitors' stores, they collect samples of goods, bring them back to the local Wal-Mart, and compare them in front of the store manager. On Wednesday evening, they return to headquarters in Bentonville, Arkansas. Early Thursday morning, they meet with senior leaders (Walton himself was always there, along with his vice chairman), advertising and logistics people, and the merchandise managers who make the buying decisions.

For four hours, changes in the marketplace are laid out and discussed by people at every level, together, in a fast-paced, high-energy dialogue among scores of people. Actions are taken—immediately. Are red sweaters in short supply because of high demand? Somebody follows through and calls a supplier. The suppliers know what they have to do if they want to keep Wal-Mart's business. Result: 100,000 dozen red sweaters are delivered next Tuesday to Wal-Marts across the nation. From the time the regional managers first became aware of the problem to the time the shortage is remedied, less than one week elapses.[7]

Driven by the outside-in view, this operating mechanism gives Wal-Mart a distinct competitive advantage. It creates speed and adaptability. It helps velocity, and it also increases margins by reducing the need for markdowns.

It reinforces and perpetuates both of the company's architectures. The decision architecture gives everyone in management, from top to bottom, the whole national picture every week. And it provides for key decisions to be made on the spot. The decision architecture works, however, only because of the social architecture of those weekly meetings. Why? The social architecture is teamwork. All the managers share the same picture of the marketplace and the competition, at the same time. They share observations and resolve conflicts. Information flows freely, from ground level to the top; nothing is witheld or fudged. We call this "zero-layer information flow."

The quality and depth of the dialogue are strengthened every week as people repeatedly and rhythmically practice their intelligence gathering and sharing. The dialogue becomes shorter, more concise, and more constructive.

Growth and the Genetic Code

In companies we've visited that can't seem to grow, the genetic code produces fairly consistent behaviors. Dialogues are mostly inward-looking, dealing with things like inventory reductions, overhead allocation and transfer pricing, increasing penetration of the existing products, and the like. The focus is on things people can control.

The social architecture resembles that of the typical annual strategy review above. No one wants to take risks. New ideas are "deviant"—and dangerous to peoples' careers. Here's the sort of thing others say about the person who champions them (this is taken verbatim from a business unit leader of a company we visited): "He can make a superb pitch for his ideas, but doesn't understand that we don't have enough time or money to develop them." And (this delivered with a curl of the lip): "He's highly optimistic." Small wonder that people with ideas leave.

In such a social architecture, people tend to wait for marching orders, often fearfully. When Glen Hiner took over as CEO at Owens-Corning in 1992, the company had spent the better part of a decade struggling to work down the mountain of debt it acquired defending itself against a hostile takeover. The genetic code Hiner found was a classic penny-pincher, bogged down in what he calls a "foxhole mentality." It was pervasive.

What struck him most, he recalls, was the sales force. "I told our salespeople, I've never seen a salesperson get fired for taking an order. And yet some of them were timid about taking orders! Why? Because they weren't sure . . . they've had so many checks and balances: I've gotta check with marketing, I've gotta check with the product guys.

"I mean, I think selling organizations have to be assertive, aggressive, have to be very self-confident. Our people weren't self-confident. Can you imagine a sales organization not self-confident? That's a tough situation."[8]

In a growth company, the decision architecture focuses people outside in. Links to the outside world are plentiful. Discussions almost always start and wrestle with external information—information about needs and change, about not only where the market is but where it's going. The decision architecture is designed to facilitate free and fast flows of information and ideas—through cross-functional teams and task forces, for example.

The social architecture is such that just about anybody can feel that he or she is capable of creating some kind of growth opportunity. People at all levels understand that growth is an essential part of a company's strategy. They are continually raising issues about new markets, new technologies, new growth opportunities. They're thinking up ways to increase their lead—everything from new packaging to new products and services for adjacent segments. They focus on *where the puck is going to be,* not where it is now. The dialogues reflect creativity and diverse viewpoints. The emotional energy is positive.

People everywhere are communicating, training and being trained, and creating operating mechanisms to develop those opportunities. They're being developed as leaders, and are themselves developing others as leaders. Ideas and brainstorming are not only tolerated; they are actively fostered. Whether people are working one-on-one or in a group, they're willing to share information with each other.

In a growth company, growth is on everybody's mind all the time; thinking about it is part of the daily routine. Sit in a GE Capital cafeteria, for example, and you'll hear people talking about it. As CEO Gary Wendt says, "Our *finance* people will say you have to find ways to get bigger."[9] Growth is in the company's genetic code.

Finance people talking about growth? You bet, and not just at GE Capital Services. At a two-hour budget meeting with several of Coca-Cola's top people in Australia several years ago, we witnessed the following dialogue about cutting costs: "We could cut $2 million from the advertising budget," volunteered the marketing head. "Over my dead body!" replied the finance director. "Building the brand is crucial to our top-line growth. Where else do we look?" To this finance officer, nothing in the pursuit of the cost side would be allowed to detract from building the brand.

Do You Have the Right Leadership Genes?

Whether leaders are born or made remains an open question, but it's our view that truly outstanding growth leaders have the critical qualities hardwired into them. Creativity—the ability to conceive of a broader pond, define a superior value proposition, and generally have fresh ideas and insights—is a unique skill. In our experience, if the top leader is not creative, it is almost impossible to sustain long term balanced growth in any institution.

A person may have inherent creative qualities that didn't develop early in his or her career, and they may flower as he or she learns how to look from the outside in. But if those capabilities aren't part of the person's mental architecture to begin with, he or she simply won't be able to do the job. It's rare to find people like Intel CEO Andy Grove, who transformed his point of view by asking himself what a new CEO would do in his place, then metaphorically walking out of his office and reentering to do it. That's one reason why the so-called "portable CEO" is becoming increasingly popular in American corporations. An outsider is brought in from a different company, or even a different industry, to lead an organization through transformational change.

Leaders of profitable growth companies have an entirely different thought architecture from those who just maintain businesses. They are realists—they see the world as it *is,* not the way it used to be or the way they'd like it to be. They constantly challenge the status quo, looking for new opportunities and ways to do things better. They're proactive—and they move fast.

They excel both as leaders of businesses and leaders of people. They understand the business basics and the methodologies of profitable growth; and they also know how to spot talent, develop leaders, and create organizations where people work well together. They design the social architecture with care.

Knowing that they have to alter mindsets and methods that were years or even decades in the making, they make it their top priority to develop operating mechanisms that reinforce new values, new goals and rewards, new ways of thinking, exchanging information, and generating ideas. They develop a teachable point of view; they coach and they listen. They create new leaders at all levels. They bring in new leaders—new genes—from outside to provide role models for decision and social architecture, and accelerate the change.

Gary Wendt's Teachable Point of View

GE Capital's Gary Wendt has the requisite ideas, values, emotional energy, and edge, and after years as CEO he still misses no occasion to reinforce his point of view among his people.

"Like anything else in your business or life, growth has to do with how much effort you put into it," he will say. "Make sure growth is part of your week. There are so many things to do—reports, meetings, presentations, things required in your job. But, know what? Growth is really required in your job. You have to sit down and say, 'I'm going to spend X percent of my time thinking about growth.'

"Give business development at least as much time, thought, attention, time-and-resource commitment, leadership, and intensity as you do anything else in your business universe. And allow time for star gazing—innovating, experimenting, and dreaming. Thomas Alva Edison supposedly said that you can't realize your dream unless you have one to begin with. In an eight-hour flight across the ocean, it's OK to say: 'Let me just think a minute about things that might be possible.'"

Wendt walks his talk. Every week, he put aside a morning to do nothing but think about growth. And he constantly asks his people questions such as these:

▶ What's the single most important change taking place that will affect the future?

▶ What are your strongest competitors going to do? Talk to your sales people to get a sense.

▶ Almost everything we do is probably going to be affected more by technology in the next five years. What's the wackiest thing you can think of in technology?

▶ What are we doing now that's a waste of time?

▶ What kind of people do you want in five years? Where will you find them, and how will you get them ready?

The questions are not rhetorical. Wendt expects answers. How well they're answered—and how well the units deliver on their promises—determines who gets rewarded and how much.

Wendt's point of view, stated clearly and repeatedly, is: "Business development can be the most exciting thing you or any of the organization can do." And everyone at GE Capital knows it.

Leaders constantly talk up the values, goals, and change-messages. They must, as Dan Burnham of AlliedSignal Aerospace put it, be "obnoxiously repetitive" because many people in the organization will resist change or just won't believe what they're hearing. There are few more effective proselytizers than Jack Welch—but even today, when a group of managers walks away from one of his presentations, only half may have gotten the point.

As they talk, growth leaders act—creating and leading operating mechanisms that incorporate and reinforce the ideas, values, and goals; and creating leaders at all levels. To transform their organization, AlliedSignal's leaders simultaneously hammered home values, coached, drove sustained Total Quality through the company, created business units whose leaders had P&L responsibility, set up cross-functional task forces and teams, and redesigned incentive systems.

They were doing what any effective change leader is doing: attacking on two fronts. They were changing both the company's decision architecture and its social architecture.

How Eckhard Pfeiffer Rewrote Compaq's Genetic Code (and Then Did It Again)

We saw in Chapter 6 how Eckhard Pfeiffer transformed Compaq from a floundering company in a niche market into the most aggressive player in the PC business. A key part of the transformation was an expansive but disciplined teamwork, part of the genetic code Pfeiffer created. This code, like his strategy, was overwhelmed when Compaq grew too quickly. Yet up to that point, it was what made the strategy work. Pfeiffer's explanation of it in 1997 shows why.

Pfeiffer himself sums up the code as "a certain mindset, a certain success model that shaped the company from the early days" after his arrival. "The industry is constantly changing, your competitors are constantly changing," he says. "So you have to observe all the things we discovered back then. You have to constantly apply them. It has to come to a way of thinking, constantly challenging what we're doing. It is a constant questioning process."[10]

The code very much reflects the leader himself. As FORTUNE magazine said, "While it sounds peculiar to say that Pfeiffer is the personification of Compaq, it's true. Pfeiffer is a highly competent, relentless, somewhat bland workaholic. Spend a few days around Compaq's monotonously identical office buildings, and you begin to realize just how archetypal the CEO is."[11]

Pfeiffer is notorious as an interrogator, and his style of dialogue realigns and redefines the corporation's decision architecture as other leaders emulate him. "The culture of the company is a huge machine that keeps asking questions," says Bob Stearns, former senior vice president for technology and development. "And Eckhard is the principal question asker. He's insatiable. He demands that you keep digging deeper and deeper into something. He wants to be absolutely thorough—and he wants to also do it very quickly." (If you don't have the answer, adds Stearns, "You say, 'I don't know but I'll find out.' The worst thing you can do with Eckhard is to try to bullshit your way through it.")[12]

The reengineering of the genetic code began the moment Pfeiffer took over. His transfer, 9 months before, from the European operations to the post of chief operating officer gave him a chance to size things up dispassionately. He was, as he puts it, "to some extent participating, but not really being involved that much, so I took a fresh look and saw a lot of things. I felt I understood why they were not working any more."

Upon being named CEO, Pfeiffer did not sit down and tell people what wasn't working. Instead, after carefully selecting a new management team, he questioned and probed: How had the competition changed? How was the industry changing? Could we stay with the strategy we had been executing, changing it substantially, or would we really have to change its focus? In near-shock at the suddenness of the company's downfall, the team responded eagerly. "They were willing to accept just about anything that wasn't foolish or incredible," says Pfeiffer. "And the managers who I would define as the old stock [or what we would call old genes] all pretty much left. So that added to the ability to have fresh thinking and nobody defending the old position."

Determining the new direction took all of two weeks. In addition to setting the company onto a new strategic course, it fundamentally changed the social architecture. The process itself sent unmistakable messages: Question everything. Set stretch goals. Act swiftly and decisively.

Pfeiffer created new decision architecture as well. A believer in flat organizations—"not because it's fashionable, but because it is being very close to the market"—he pushed considerable authority down to his management team. The leaders of each of the four new product divisions were given total authority to create products for the worldwide market. They were also given P&L responsibility—something he was amazed to find lacking when he took over. That move met some resistance at first, he recalls. "The word was that it's a hassle to collect and process and get all these things right, a major burden which right now we can least afford. I said, 'This is nondebatable.'"

How far down the line does the Compaq genetic code extend? Perhaps the clearest way to see it working is to examine the critical point where the company meets its marketplace.

Gary Stimac, who headed the server and networking operations before leaving during the 1997 reorganization, described his own style of leadership as mainly concerned with setting priorities. One priority he stressed was involvement in a new product. Everyone from engineers to salespeople had to put their heads together constantly with each other and with customers. "I basically almost insist that anyone who directly reports to me spends at least 25 percent of their time with customers, talking to real live people who use our equipment," he says. "And when we come up with what products we're going to work on, we have an interactive discussion of not only what the product is but how you're going to market it—its features and all the rest of the pieces, how you're going to sell and distribute it, how you're going to support it, how service is going to be done. What are the value propositions you're going to uniquely bring to the product itself?

"It's a dynamic set of interchanges between software and hardware engineers, marketing people, technology people. You develop the product but keep on challenging it, look at what the competition is doing, interpret what the customer may want, maybe eighteen months down the path."[13]

Compaq's Operating Mechanisms

One reason Compaq's leaders at all levels are always trying to anticipate change is that Pfeiffer's "constant questioning process" is so much a part of the genetic code that it's built into the key operating mechanisms that combine decision and social architectures.

One mechanism is the annual Innovate Forum, a three-day get-together where thousands of executives mingle with top customers and strategic partners. Another is the Joint Division Review (JDR), the action-oriented quarterly meeting with the worldwide division managers, to plan strategy. The goal is to get the views of "everyone who has to make an input or wants to make an input."

Pfeiffer describes his own leadership role as: "First, to listen. Get the issues on the table. Ultimately, guide it to some level of conclusion, that we either reach a decision on how we're going to change something, or agree at least on the next step of action that somebody will go off with and do." The division managers, he adds, get "the highest degree of authority and responsibility to act within the confines of their charters."

Changing established mindsets is tough even in a company as change-oriented as Compaq. Pfeiffer recalls his first JDR: "It was not a good meeting. It was too much the day-to-day operational stuff, and people were happy with each other and the real issues didn't get on the table." It took two or three meetings before the mechanism finally hit its stride. Characteristically, Pfeiffer advanced the process with endless questioning. "We kept coming back each time saying, 'We need to sync up here on what the next major strategic milestones are. Are we all truly focused on these? Are these the right ones? Is the company moving in that direction? Are we dealing with the issues? When everybody goes back to their jobs, are we then not executing what we said we were going to do?'"

Complementing the JDR is the Business Strategy Team (BST), which includes most of the top management team and meets on an as-needed basis. Pfeiffer calls it "the day-to-day form of corporate development." A significant part of the BST's job is to keep abreast of projects that transcend the charters of specific operations but have importance for the company as a whole. In the early days of the Internet, for example, Pfeiffer asked Bob Stearns, the head of the BST, to take ownership of it. Says Pfeiffer: "He began picking up on it and actually calling meetings where he brought in the division managers and others in the company to talk about: Where are we going? What are the ground rules? And then, after we got closer, he needed to either initiate the effort at the corporate development level or make sure that the business objectives started picking up on their piece of the action."

In 1996, Pfeiffer essentially reinvented Compaq for the second time, expanding its pond from the PC marketplace to the market for virtually all computing products and services. He did this through the massive and intense companywide process known as Crossroads, described in Chapter 6. Teams drawn from across the organization rethought and re-designed the company's entire management structure and processes, and brought their results to the company's top management in eight weeks. In several days of give-and-take, the proposals were debated, refined, and adopted.

Crossroads itself was an operating mechanism; more than a strategic planning exercise, it altered the genetic code by changing thinking. In such an exercise, says Pfeiffer: "You're dealing with a kind of constant reality check: Are we doing the things that will take us there? Where is it different, what will it take? How do we need to prepare for the next big step? And when you recognize that, your whole thought model changes."

The reorganization that came out of Crossroads ultimately reshaped the company into four businesses: enterprise systems, including servers and workstations; desktops and portables; consumer PCs; and communications products, which includes networking hardware and software. In the accompanying management changes, several longtime Compaq executives left and several outsiders were brought in as senior executives—including CFO Earl Mason, who came from Inland Steel.

The arrivals and departures led to some outside speculation that Compaq was in trouble. In fact, the changes reflected a necessary reshuffling of genes. Broadening the pond to the total computing needs of corporate customers would require a further transformation of Compaq's decision architecture—one that pushed responsibility down still more broadly in a matrix type of organization. In turn, this required leaders whose own decision architecture was attuned to the give-and-take implicit in such an organization.

Indeed, Pfeiffer draws the parallel to the client-server model in describing his organizational aims. All of the different products themselves are horizontally linked, so what would be the sense of a vertical organization? "Our organization, while having the disadvantage of being some form of the matrix thing, has served us very well in moving fast and doing all the things we do. You really have to delegate as much as you can."

Jump-Starting the Change

Changing the genetic code of an organization would seem to be inherently a lengthy process. Often it is, particularly in the absence of crisis.

But it doesn't have to be. Eckhard Pfeiffer had the benefit of crisis in his first act, but he carried out his subsequent radical changes at the same breakneck speed. Like many other leaders, he found ways to get the changes well underway—and showing results—within months.

In 1988, GE Medical Systems CEO John Trani called us in to help him build a new global organization. The process we designed turned out to be a breakthrough way of dealing simultaneously and rapidly with the hard and soft issues of radical change. It became the prototype for the genetic code-changing work we do elsewhere. Called the Global Leadership Program, it also was the model for the program of the same name that Noel Tichy founded and runs at the University of Michigan Business School.

While focused on globalization, the principles are broadly applicable to any transformational undertaking. What makes the operating mechanism so powerful is that it develops new decision architecture and social architecture simultaneously and in real time. It combines organizational development and individual development—and it delivers business results.

The operating mechanism *forces* the development of teamwork, role models, leadership skills, networks, and information sharing; the participants have no choice. There's no other way they can achieve their hard goals of coming up with strategies and business plans in a short time.

The most important point to keep in mind is that *the best individual and organizational development takes place simultaneously.* We have seen this proven time and again, and not only in our own work. Bossidy did it at AlliedSignal and Pfeiffer did it at Compaq. It's what GE's management training is all about; it's how a successful leader and social architect builds a company. We've devised one way to systematize it.

We started in February. Trani's top priority was to build an aggressive global growth company—and build it fast. This was the teachable point of view with which he would create a new genetic code, and the operating mechanisms to make it work.

The business landscape had changed dramatically with the collapse of the U.S. market for the GEMS medical diagnostic imaging equipment—X-ray machines, CAT scanners, MRI machines, and the like. Abroad, Siemens and Toshiba were poised to make their own global forays. GEMS was a babe in the woods in this environment; the inward-looking organization of engineers had known only easy, technology-led growth. True, it had acquired businesses both in Japan (Yokogawa Medical Systems) and France (Thomson-CGR). But the three organizations were poles apart.

Once we'd pulled our team together—the two of us plus Michael Brimm from INSEAD (Institute for European Business Administration) France and professor Hiro Takeuchi from Hitotsubashi University in Tokyo—we went offsite for two days with John Trani and his head of human relations, Toby D'Ambola. Our agenda was to work on John's vision and theory for where he wanted to take GEMS. We hung flip-chart pads on all four walls of the meeting room. By the end of the two days, John had laid out assumptions about the markets, products, services, channels, and strategy GEMS needed to follow globally.

That was the easy part. Also on paper was John's view of the kind of global organization he wanted—fast, flexible, action-oriented—and the values that his team members would embrace. Fundamental changes would be required in the way everybody in each of three vastly different organizations thought and acted.

We're believers in action learning—learning by doing, not just listening. The framework we laid out was for a program that would organize teams of Asians, Americans, Latin Americans, and Europeans to work together for nine months in developing the details of a strategic plan and—through practice—global teamwork, mindsets, and leadership. This would be an enormous commitment: they'd be doing this work in addition to their regular jobs. They would be working on real problems and developing action plans. A member of senior management would coach each team on the soft issues of teamwork and leadership, but would leave it to them to come up with the strategic and operating plans.

The next step was getting the top leadership team on board with John and energized to drive this operating mechanism. It started with a three-day offsite session in a suburb of Chicago. As prework, we asked John and each of his direct reports to write a FORTUNE magazine cover story on GEMS, datelined 1990, telling the story each would ideally like to have published about the company. Our intent was to force each leader to articulate a vision of growth—top-line and bottom-line, how each was achieved, how globalization occurred, and so forth. We analyzed the stories and sent them back to the group as a basis for creating dialogues leading to a common vision of what it would take to beat Siemens and Toshiba.

The dialogues were intense and sometimes contentious; each team got feedback from the others, and we pushed them to be direct, open, and candid. Contracts were negotiated among members, and specific leadership goals were set for each team. By the end of the offsite, the top group had become deeply committed to the program. They identified seven key ideas—initiatives GEMS needed to pursue, ranging from improvement in global competitive information analysis and reduction of cycle time, to technology transfer and global career development.

By June, the leadership group had picked the team members for each of the initiatives—about 55 people from Asia, Europe, Latin America, and the United States. Their first meeting, a weeklong session in Europe, started predictably enough with tension and anxiety; the attendees were uncertain about their own future in an organization about to change radically. But they believed in Trani's values.

The second day was devoted to outdoor "Outward Bound" type activities, widely recognized as effective mechanisms for breaking down barriers to communications and teamwork. By the end of the afternoon, the wall climbing, the sweating, the laughter, and the fun had done their jobs. That evening, the teams reconvened in their next workshop energized, and with a new capacity to work together.

The week ended with articulation of action plans and a feedback session in which the team members critiqued each other. The feedback, blunt and to the point, consisted of three main items: "To be a better global leader, you need to do more of [these behaviors], do less of [these behaviors], and continue doing [these behaviors]."

The next five months were intense and stressful for the team members. They were pioneering in new territory, and pushing themselves to the limit and sometimes beyond; remember, they still had their day jobs. Just gathering the information and input necessary to develop action plans was a major undertaking. Additional pain came from the novel stresses of working globally—the travel and jet lag, and the adjustment to different cultures.

Most of all, they were having to rethink the way they managed their personal time in order to work differently with the teams, groups, and organizations around them. Their November midcourse workshop was the most emotionally charged and difficult of all the sessions we and senior management had with them. At the outset, for example, the clashes of cultural as well as individual styles were prominent. Some managers were virtual cowboys who threw their weight around; others philosophized and pontificated; still others went underground, sitting silently and holding their opinions in check. Yet they were also eager for help. A new social architecture had begun to take shape, arising from the forced-draft close working relationships and intense, honest dialogues.

Each team gave a fifteen-minute presentation on the status of its efforts: the current hypotheses, the work to date, the "deliverables" (things it knew it could deliver), and the areas where it needed help. Each person got a rating from every other person in the entire group, on a scale of 1 ("not going anywhere") to 10 ("perfect"). In the feedback sessions that followed, each person got advice from individuals and groups about what he or she needed to do to improve the substance or presentation of the project.

In all, there were seven rounds of feedback, including those in small discussion groups. Everyone got experience in group process thinking and conflict resolution; everyone got a lot of tough-love coaching. The attendees went back to work having learned that they were all in this thing together, and they could tap the collective brainpower of the groups to help them solve problems. The goal was to win collectively, and they took ownership of the process.

They presented their work after six months in a final meeting with top management in Chicago. This was no show-and-tell pitch session, full of earnest pleading for approval; it was a "commitment event." They were there with specific plans, and they sought the commitment of the ten top leaders, as well as other people in the program, by hashing out their plans in real time through compromise and problem solving. Essentially, they were role modeling the new global decision architecture that GE Medical Systems would adopt.

This couldn't have differed more from the old way, which resembled the meetings described earlier in this chapter—people presenting decks of slides to a top management committee whose members had, by and large, done little homework. In the old meetings, it was almost a spectator sport to see how the boss would react and how other people would take their cues. Often, no real decisions were made. The management committee had to go back and rethink all the issues and then bring them out later on, in another agenda.

Trani's attitude was that homework was not only a responsibility but an ethical commitment, and anyone who didn't agree didn't belong on the team. Having read and annotated every report before coming, everybody was ready for honest dialogue and decision making. Through the new operating mechanism, the management committee itself would learn how to make decisions in large groups (about 60 people) efficiently and productively.

There were no long presentations. Each team had twenty minutes, maximum, to review and reinforce the material that had been read ahead of time, and to frame the decisions they wanted people to make. And again, every team in the room filled out its own feedback sheet on the other teams' efforts. This time, though, the statements ranged from "I can't support any of this" (a rating of 1) to "I can support all of it with no modification" (a rating of 10). For anything less than a 10, the raters would earmark specific points that the groups needed to change during the session's next three hours.

The senior managers and teams worked on the feedback and changes in randomly chosen roundtable discussion groups under simple rules of engagement: We are all here to make each project a win; there will be total openness and candor. At the end, each presenting team went into a separate room to meet with Trani and discuss the flipcharts that contained the key ideas from the group sessions. Trani then worked with them to firm up the plans for implementation.

In the final step, everyone came together in what we call a fish-bowl—Trani and the relevant senior officers sat with representatives from each team at a table in the center of the room. The other sixty people were an observing audience. This was a real management committee meeting: the participants systematically talked through all of the recommended changes and thrashed out disagreements. The meeting ended with Trani saying, "This is what we've agreed to do."

The program not only launched Trani's seven key initiatives; it also created a new genetic code, with global teamwork as a core element. No previous operating mechanism could have accomplished this. The participants became the nucleus of new global networks, and propagators of new shared values. The leadership and team-building skills they acquired were to cascade down through the organization in the months and years ahead.

Remember the key points we introduced at the start of this chapter: Growth companies grow because their leaders have actively worked to change the companies' genetic codes. Three levers can be used by leaders:

1. *Developing new teachable points of view.*

2. *Radically changing the organization's operating mechanisms.*

3. *Bringing in new genetic material—outsiders with different decision architectures and social architectures, fresh ideas, values, and energy.*

Developing creative leaders is critical; there's a tremendous shortage of them. CEOs need to audit their organizations for them (see "The Handbook For Growth" for more about auditing). They need to identify them, coach them, and unblock and promote the ones who have been sidetracked in the old genetic code. They must also often go outside for new genes with the requisite mental architecture for a growth company.

Creative leaders are the ultimate sustainable competitive advantage. Find them, retain them, and reward them.

In the next two chapters, we'll see how change leaders used these levers to transform two vastly different companies from lackluster underachievers to businesses with powerful and sustainable trajectories for capital-efficient, profitable growth.

CHAPTER 10

Rewriting the Genetic Code at AlliedSignal

In turning around AlliedSignal Inc., CEO Larry Bossidy faced two challenges:

▶ *Developing strategies for profitable growth in a company largely tied to "mature" industries.*

▶ *Changing the way people throughout his businesses thought and acted.*

This is the inside story of how the leaders in one of those businesses re-engineered their genetic code.

Every manager both relishes and dreads a lateral move from the Garden of Eden into a desert. Make flowers bloom and you're a hero; fail and your bones will bleach in the sun.

AlliedSignal's Aerospace sector was hurting badly when Dan Burnham joined it in 1990 to head the AiResearch group, which built aircraft engines, turbochargers, and other components. He was leaving behind the presidency of one of AlliedSignal's star performers, the fast-growing Fibers Group in the chemicals and plastics sector. "Fibers was a wonderful business—a billion dollars, profitable, lots of fun and excitement to it, growing," he says. "And I was asked to come out to Aerospace for a job at an equivalent level."[1]

The job offered Burnham, then 43 years old, a shot at the presidency of the division, the world's largest aerospace equipment maker. "But absolutely no promises were made. I knew when I came out that I was putting everything at risk with no guarantees that a year later somebody would say I've got the job." And Aerospace not only wasn't growing, it was a whole different environment. "Every element of the culture was different. Its focus on customer and on cost was totally different—it was an engineering orientation of the highest order."

The risk was worth taking: within a year, Burnham was president of Aerospace. But suddenly he was out of the frying pan and into the fire. "Roughly synchronous to my taking this job, the aerospace industry went into a complete tailspin, a depression." The great defense build-down had begun, and the division's future looked worse than ever.

Over the next several years, Burnham transformed AlliedSignal Aerospace into the star performer of the company and the envy of its industry. From 1993 to 1997, Aerospace sales grew 42 percent to $6.4 billion, and net income rose 130 percent to $515 million—44 percent of the parent company's earnings.[2] On FORTUNE's list of most admired companies, Aerospace climbed from ninth among ten in its peer group in 1990 to number two in 1998.[3] Executives from other companies flocked to it to benchmark their own operations.

Historically, the company sold manufactured products to airplane makers, commercial airlines, general aviation companies, and the military—a market amounting to some $15.6 billion.[4] The bigger pond Burnham staked out includes, potentially, almost any part, component, or service a plane maker, airline, armed forces branch, or small-plane pilot might need. The size of this pond is estimated at about $45 billion.[5]

We talked with Aerospace leaders at many levels during 1996, a year when many of the changes were clearly paying off, and others were still works in progress. Here, largely in their own words, is the inside story of how Burnham and his team transformed the strategies and genetic code of their company, creating profitable growth in spite of a deadly market environment.

"An Inner-Directed Company"

To understand their story, it's also necessary to know something about what was going on at the parent organization. AlliedSignal is one of the star turnaround stories of the Nineties. When its board brought Larry Bossidy in as CEO in 1991, the company was a muddled portfolio of disparate businesses, assembled through mergers and acquisitions during the eighties. Of its three major sectors, only the one Burnham had left—now called the Engineered Materials Division—showed much promise. The automotive sector was mature, and aerospace was in decline. Earnings had gone nowhere in six years, and the corporate stock was languishing.

From this wretched clay, Bossidy sculpted a company whose market value almost quintupled, to $24 billion, in seven years.[6] Sales grew 22 percent to $14.5 billion, and net earnings reached $1.2 billion—compared to a loss of $273 million in 1991.[7]

Bossidy arrived in July, just as Burnham was moving into his new office. Then age 56, Bossidy had distinguished himself in a 34-year career at GE, and he had most recently been Jack Welch's right-hand man. Tough-minded, blunt, and impatient, he wasted no time in sizing up AlliedSignal's problems and setting a new agenda.

Recalls Bossidy: "We were hemorrhaging cash. It was an inner-directed company, focusing mainly on itself. We had fifty-eight business units, each guarding its own turf."[8] Decisions were top-down, with little input from employees.

Viewed from the outside, what took place over the next two years had all the earmarks of the classic slash-and-burn restructuring-cum-downsizing. But it was much more. Getting costs in line was only half of the job. "Initially, we worked the cost side hard," says Bossidy. "But we knew we had to eventually get unit-volume growth. Business is really just two things: You increase sales, and you improve productivity. But the two go together."

Few business leaders anywhere have stronger views of how to make a business work—and better skills at teaching those views to others—than Larry Bossidy. His favorite and oft-repeated metaphor for galvanizing people to change was the "burning platform." "When the roustabouts are standing on the offshore rig and the foreman yells, 'Jump into the water,' not only will they not jump, but they will look at the foreman with less than benevolent regard," he would begin. "Only when they themselves see the flames shooting up from the platform will they jump. There may or may not be sharks in the water, but to stay on the burning platform means certain death, so they jump and swim for their lives."

Change starts, said Bossidy, when people decide to take the flames seriously. The leader's first job is to help everyone understand that the platform is burning, whether or not they can see the fire. So his first order of business at AlliedSignal was a reality check. "To begin the process of change, you need to decide that you're going to manage by fact. And that means a brutal understanding of reality."

Bossidy saw reality as having four specific increments:

▶ What customers believed about the company and its products.

▶ What employees thought of the company.

▶ The company's real competitive position.

▶ Whether the company was generating enough cash from operations.

The fourth reality didn't take any research. Unearthing the other three kept Bossidy on the road for two solid months, talking to employees and customers around the world.

He got an earful. The customers described a company that was, too often, subpar on quality, slow to deliver, and generally unresponsive to their problems and needs. Indeed, it often seemed oblivious to them. For example, Bossidy recalls, "While we were saying that we were delivering an order-fill rate of 98 percent, our customers thought we were at 60 percent. The irony was, we seemed to think we had to justify why we were right and the customers were wrong, instead of trying to address their complaints."

The employees painted an equally bleak picture. "In the first sixty days, I talked to probably 5,000 employees," he recalls. "We talked about what was wrong and what we should do about it. And as we talked, it became clear to me that there hadn't been a good top-down enunciation of the company's problem."

Bossidy enunciated clearly, using the same charts and message everywhere: "Here's what I think is good about us. Here's what I'm worried about. Here's what we have to do about it. And if we don't fix the cash problem, none of us is going to be around."

He met with employees not only in offices and conference rooms but also on factory floors and loading docks. "I knew intuitively I needed support at the bottom," he says. "It's important to try to involve everybody in the company."

He didn't duck the sharp questions, either. "A guy in Aerospace got up and asked me, 'Are we going to have layoffs?' 'Here's the issue,' I answered. 'We're in an environment that's weakening. We all know that. Defense expenditures are down. The commercial aviation industry is in recession. And we have too much capacity to begin with. So we're going to have layoffs.'"

Bossidy listened just as intently as he spoke. "They knew what was wrong—it's remarkable how many people know what's really going on in their company. We talked about it, and what we should do about it."

He returned with a clear and far-ranging picture of AlliedSignal's problems. Besides being inward-looking, instead of focused on customers, the company had too many managers and too many capital projects with unclear paybacks. It was clinging to underperforming non-strategic businesses; there was no emphasis on margins; managers didn't have a clue about how much defects and poor quality were costing them; and so on.

Just as important, he heard a story of alienation, disaffection, and lack of purpose. "There was a lot of drift. People had no clear idea of what they were doing. Management made all the decisions, and employees' ideas were rarely solicited. Therefore, they were rarely offered."

Over the next three years, Bossidy transformed practically every aspect of AlliedSignal. The first emphasis was on meeting commitments: making the numbers, quarter by quarter; focusing on cash and working capital turnover, margins, and competitors' margins. But every numerical goal had a subtext—to constantly improve and strengthen the three core operating mechanisms common to all companies: strategy, operations, and human resources. Thus, for example, strategic planning became not a dry yearly exercise producing dustcatcher volumes, but an ongoing, organic give-and-take—"strategy in real time," Bossidy calls it. Human resources was transformed from a bureaucratic function into the driving force for leadership development.

He began holding quarterly reviews for each of the processes, meetings with leaders down to the business unit level in which he measures and critiques progress, enunciates goals—and listens carefully. Afterward, he sends each business leader a three- to four-page letter laying out the essential points covered and actions agreed upon, and inviting the person to call if he or she disagrees. The executives make sure they are on the same wavelength as Bossidy because they know that, at the next meeting, Larry will produce that letter and say: "Uh, let's see now. . . ."

Bossidy completely reshaped the company's leadership, bringing in new genes. Within four years, he had replaced some three-fourths of senior management; more than a third of the new leaders came from outside.

Aiming for new decision and social architectures he radically redefined traditional management roles. "The day is gone when you reward the lone rangers in the corner offices because their achievements are brilliant even though their behavior is destructive," he says. "Today, managers add value by brokering with people, not by presiding over empires. That has a big impact on how you think about who the 'best' people are."

Bossidy insisted that all of his leaders become coaches. For example, when he put a new person in charge of the strategic plan, he made it clear that "an important part of his job was to make sure people are learning how to do strategy better." This was backed up with a corporation wide training program to expose people to a more external way of approaching strategy. Says Bossidy, dryly: "The result is a more exciting conversation."

No discipline was immune from the new demands. AlliedSignal had a strong central finance staff, but very little expertise at the business level. "I wanted the opposite," Bossidy says. "Good finance people are the ones who can help give real meaning to operating plans." The people he put in charge of the numbers were "not just scorekeepers but well-rounded businesspeople who contribute to business solutions—people who understand what's happening in the factories."

One such person was CFO John W. Barter. "He was terrific, but his job had been limited to corporate finance functions. When he had the chance to broaden his interest and take responsibility for the quality of the finance function throughout the company, dramatic things happened."

Total Quality became a centerpiece of the revitalization plan ("the vehicle to drive change," as Bossidy puts it). TQ is high on the list of most-abused excellent ideas and practices, but Bossidy meant business. He viewed TQ as an ongoing process—an operating mechanism for skills and mindset training that would help to alter the genetic code by changing the way people in every plant and office worked. Within 18 months, practically all of AlliedSignal's roughly 85,000 employees went through a four-day TQ training course.

Pressing a Teachable Point of View

When Bossidy convened AlliedSignal's top twelve managers for an offsite meeting to determine the company's future direction, that meant, first of all, creating a shared vision and set of values that everyone in the company could understand and own. "Each of our three major sectors had its own distinct culture, and we didn't want to change that," he says. "It makes the company stronger. But we had to unite ourselves with vision and values."

Bossidy does not lack for a teachable point of view, to put it mildly, but his coaching method is to get others to take ownership of it through debate. "We spent two days arguing—and I mean arguing—about values. At the end of the meeting, we not only had the values, we also had a specific definition of each of those values."

The values themselves don't sound remarkable, as Bossidy is the first to acknowledge: customers, integrity, people, teamwork, speed, innovation, and performance. "But they're important because they give all of our people a view of what behavior is expected of them. And if you're a leader in this company, you risk being labeled a hypocrite if you don't behave according to them. You're going to get some heat."

Translation: A lot of heat. At AlliedSignal, careers are made or broken on adherence to values. Bossidy illustrates with a reference to the Total Quality (TQ) process, which itself embodies those values.

"TQ tests us on the question of values, because we're going to encounter four types of people. We're going to have people who embrace TQ and make their numbers. We want to promote them. We're going to have people who love TQ and don't make their numbers. We try to move them someplace so they can continue to contribute. We're going to have people who don't like TQ and don't make their numbers. That's easy: we suggest they leave.

"And we're going to have people who don't like TQ and make their numbers. These are the people who will test our resolve about whether the process is going to go forward.

"Because they have to go, too. Anybody who says 'I don't need TQ' has to change or walk the plank."

After values came clear goals—targets that everybody, whatever their level in the organization, could grasp and focus on. Every year, Bossidy puts up three goals. In 1996, for example, they were:

▶ Make customer satisfaction our first priority.

▶ Drive growth and productivity through integrated world-class processes.

▶ Make all our commitments, including income and cash flow.

Finally came a vision statement: "To become a premier company, distinctive and successful in everything we do."

Again, there's nothing extraordinary about the goals or vision statement. But execution is everything: How well do leaders convey the teachable point of view behind them to the entire organization? The answers tell whether the values, goals, and vision become part of a genetic code.

Now we return to Dan Burnham and the Aerospace division, to see how the corporate design was executed at ground level.

The Aerospace Revolution

Burnham was quick to pick up on Bossidy's point of view and to make it the core of his own teaching. Still, at his first one-on-one meeting with Bossidy, he began to explain just how difficult it would be to make the targets Bossidy had set for the coming year.

"I was trying to get a few tears from him," says Burnham, "about how tough this is and how much better our goal was with respect to any likely performance by our competitors, and how we were going to beat them, all that. I started using all the charm that I was able to pull up.

"And as I'm maybe only two or three minutes into this thing, Larry holds up his hand, just like that, that big hand of his, you know. And he smiles, just smiles. He says, 'Dan, I have confidence in you,' and he reaches over and he pats me on the back. End of discussion."

So Burnham walked away to deal with a challenge unlike any he'd encountered before. "I was facing a collapsing market when the expectations of our shareowners and of my boss were to not simply do well in a relative sense, compared to other aerospace companies, but to do well in an absolute sense, relative to all companies in the market."

To drive the realities home—and, equally important, create positive energy in a scary, uncertain, negative climate—Burnham felt he had to "articulate a driving passion to our organization." He had his burning platform; most (though not all, he notes) knew the industry was in deep trouble. It also helped that he was about the only executive who didn't come from the aerospace industry. "I could see the reality of our business maybe a bit differently from others. I could see a cost structure that would have killed a business in my prior markets and industries, and a slowness of pace that was unlike anything I had ever seen before. I could see something approaching reality that others, with all of their industry-specific experience, just couldn't."

The Teachable Point of View: Productivity and Growth

In getting his point of view across, Burnham made himself visible and vocal by organizing forums and meetings throughout the company. No one was spared the message. One division, for example, had just completed a record fiscal year and fourth quarter. He brought together its top 200 people and congratulated them on their performance. And then, he said, "If you continue to do business like this, you'll be bankrupt."

But, he admits, "You can't scream 'Fire!' in a crowded theater without pointing out where the exits are." While the people were still in shock, he offered the vision that would define the new kind of company they needed to build—a clear, memorable focus. "It was all built on the premise that we had what it takes to be winners," he says. "The vision was: To be the most admired supplier in the industry."

As Burnham saw it, Aerospace had just two strategic issues: productivity and growth. "We consciously put them in that order," he says. "Productivity, then growth—driving to be the most admired supplier. Very simple; people can remember it.

"The reason it was productivity first, then growth, is that while growth creates the passion, we wouldn't grow unless we had productivity. But it was always put in that context. It was never productivity as an end unto itself, but as a fuel for growth."

The growth target would be 6 to 8 percent a year, compounded—much faster than the underlying markets would be growing.

Then he tore the organization apart and rebuilt it with new leadership. The weaknesses of the old organization were ingrained in the company's genetic code; practices and habits had been built up over decades and were being perpetuated by a leadership that knew no other way to do business. "The issue was not the willingness of the front-line employees or the front-line supervisors to be successful; these people did want to contribute," says Burnham. "It wasn't that any single constituency went out to design a system that functioned this way. It happened over a long period of time."

New Genes

Burnham replaced practically the entire top management team. The new genes came from outside and from younger leaders on lower levels. Over the course of a year, he took out two management layers and reduced the number of supervisors by nearly two-thirds. "We had staff upon staff," Burnham recalls. "People would have deputies, for God's sake; how they all didn't run into each other every day is beyond me." All told, roughly half of the top 1,000 people in the organization lost their jobs.

Aerospace was a patchwork of twenty-six business units and operations that had been accumulated over the years through acquisition and were never integrated. Each had its own procurement system, its own finance system, and its own human resources. In "a really difficult three-yards-and-cloud-of dust play," they were melded into about half a dozen organizations. At the core were five major strategic business units (SBUs): Engines, Aerospace Equipment Systems, Commercial Avionics Systems, Government Electronic Systems, and Technical Services. Each was to develop its own growth plan, focused on new product introduction, acquisitions, and globalization. The restructuring also included a major strengthening of Aerospace's global organization. European operations and staffing were overhauled, and those in Asia were significantly expanded. A large new contingent of personnel was assigned to China.

Both among the businesses and within them, the restructuring laid a foundation for a boundaryless company. "If we hadn't restructured, we could never have gotten the ability to transfer good ideas across the organization," says Burnham. "When people come here—we do a lot of interviewing, because we've hired probably, by now, 4,000 professionals in the last three years or so—often they will say to me, 'It's amazing; everybody says basically the same thing.' There is a common sense of mission, purpose, and issues."

Burnham made his changes at a blistering pace. "We recognized that we would do some things that, looking back, were too hasty, ill-advised. But if we didn't do [the change] quickly and with a certain amount of revolutionary zeal, then it would fail."

Zeroing in on Social Architecture

Like Bossidy, Burnham knew he had to change not just the structures of his business but the social architecture as well. "The social architecture is the difference between success and failure," says Burnham. "You can articulate a business strategy or scenario loaded with analysis and facts and insights, but these are a dime a dozen. The key is *execution*—and the key to execution is managing the social contract."

Aerospace had a distinct culture. "Our heritage, typical for aerospace, was engineering. If products performed safely and properly, odds were you'd win the business—it's a conservative industry. An unintended consequence, however, was that there wasn't balance. It's not that engineering was too strong—the way to create the balance was not to beat down engineering—but that other organizations were vestigial."

The very day he took office, Burnham removed the head of human resources. "If we couldn't attract the talent and create the passion, if we couldn't tap into the capability of each individual employee, then there was no way we would be able to climb the heights," he says. The new man was an outside gene: John Hofmeister, formerly the head of human resources at Northern Telecom. Originally a line executive in manufacturing and marketing at GE, Hofmeister had an activist's view of human resources as a leadership development function. He'd helped Northern Telecom build the leadership it needed to compete with AT&T's big surge in the late eighties.

As throughout AlliedSignal, Total Quality was a fundamental engine of genetic as well as operational change. In combination with the new goals and the organizational and leadership changes, says Burnham, "it gave a sort of common lexicon to the company. As a result of it, people felt that they weren't just isolated outposts. The principles of total quality made profound sense.

"The employees had seen the issues all along. They knew the place was indolent, and they were beginning to see that the aerospace world was about to change. But nobody ever asked 'em. When somebody could come in with a reason to see it constructively, it became a binding process."

Middle managers were, unsurprisingly, the hardest sell. They're the most conservative elements in any organization. No knee-jerk middle-management-basher, Burnham points out that there's a good reason for their skepticism. "We want them to be that way. They're the ones who really know how stuff happens; they have the institutional memory. They have to make it work every day."

But they could also relate to the goals of Total Quality. "Satisfying the customers—our surveys show that employees hold that as a very high value. Continuous improvement—that's not a tough sell; people can understand that if we don't get better every day, someone is going to try to take their jobs away from them. Participation by everyone—the only way we can all contribute is by identifying the problems and working together to resolve them."

The key was persuading them that the leadership was committed for the long haul. As Burnham puts it, "There has to be consistency—a belief that this will not go away, because they have the ability to wait these things out. So there has to be constant dialogue—top down, bottom up, side to side. You have to believe in what you're doing, and have the zealots communicating it and reinforcing it over and over again. You have to be just obnoxiously repetitive."

Product Development from the Outside In

A top priority for growth was to develop more new products, and develop them faster. Speeding up the cycle by weeding out waste and inefficiency would be relatively straightforward. Getting the right product ideas in the first place would be harder. The best of these are the ones that fill needs customers don't even know they have, says Burnham, and you can't just go out and ask what they want: "If they knew, they would have already told you."

This change meant getting employees to think from the outside in because, at heart, the paucity of new products reflected the genetic code of an inward-looking technical community. Innovations were conceived and designed according to the organization's own interests and priorities, rather than those of the customers.

Aerospace's General Aviation Avionics division (GAA) became a role model. In one year, it went from four new products to eighteen—without spending notably more on development. Burnham had been very clear on this point. "The quickest way to kill innovation is to throw a lot of money at it," he says. In fact, he considers the ability to innovate on a tight budget to be the ultimate proof of a company's commitment to growth. "When the organization tests you, they'll test you especially in the budgeting process. The response to that is not to blink. You say to them, 'You're in charge of your destiny; if you believe in growth, you'll find the money.' And they find the way to do it. I've seen it happen over and over again."

GAA had missed its net income targets for thirty-two of the thirty-three previous months when Greg Summe arrived to lead it. Summe, age 37, was an engineer with nine years of consulting experience at McKinsey and 1 year as a line manager at GE. He was head of GE's commercial motors business when AlliedSignal hired him.

His first job clearly was to get costs under control and product out the door—hardly the ideal circumstances for developing a new growth strategy, he says, "because you might die before you get there. You're worrying about that month; all your energies are focused on it."[9] But making GAA grow was his major goal, and he had to lay the groundwork for it at the same time.

Summe's primary growth goal was to broaden the pond by offering GAA's traditional customers more innovations. So, from the outset, he says, "We elevated the new product development process to literally the most important process in the business."

He started by giving his people a new theory of the business, a theory based on the consumer electronics industry. "All of us have more electronics in our home than we need," he explained to them. "Yet every time we walk into the electronics store, something catches our eye, and we end up buying it. Well, it's the same with our customers. They have discretionary income. If we could provide value to them in terms of new products, then they would be willing to buy those products." This strategy, he argued, would not only improve AlliedSignal's market share but would also grow the overall market.

No approach could have been more different from the old theory of the business. "That theory was that we made 'King radios,' and the King radio was unique," says Summe. "It had a sort of timeless quality in terms of the styling and the way it fit into the cockpit, and it had a lot of technical complexity—which was as much driven by what the engineers felt good about designing as by what the marketplace wanted." It had to be viewed as better than anything the competition had, so it incorporated a lot of costly, custom-designed parts.

"What was happening? The engineering community wasn't getting a strong enough lead in terms of what the marketplace needed and didn't need. It would take so long to get the product out the door that the product then had to be redesigned 'cause the marketplace had changed."

He gave his engineers three specific ideas to focus on:

▶ Demand in the marketplace is elastic and responds well to innovation.

▶ The marketplace is a series of gates or windows that open and close. "The question isn't how much time you need to do a product. The question is: Are you going to be able to take advantage of that open window over there?"

▶ Performance improvements that might be incremental from an engineer's point of view could be irresistible from a customer's point of view. An engineer might think of an easier-to-read display, for example, as an incremental improvement, and would rather focus his or her energies on a long-term project to design a new transmitter. "But the customer would be absolutely delighted by the display. Whether it had a new transmitter board or not, he doesn't much care."

GAA would keep introducing superior innovations to the customer, he told them, but henceforth innovation would be measured as a customer measures it (see Figure 10.1) and not by the degree of engineering change.

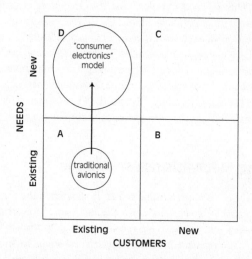

Figure 10.1 Greg Summe went after a larger share of his customers' wallets by turning new product development outside in.

Summe replaced most of GAA's leaders; about half of the new group came in from other divisions and companies. Of those elevated from within, most were from engineering and sales. "Engineering in particular was deep with people who were talented and well educated," he says. "They hadn't had the best career development or behavioral development—they hadn't had many cross-functional, cross-business opportunities. But they knew the products." The survivors of the cut had what Summe calls "the attitude that 'We could make a real difference and we're committed to making that happen; we have the energy and passion to make it happen.'"

One of the unit's strengths was that it had more than 150 former pilots among its engineers and managers, and they were good at developing pilot-friendly features. But the strength had also become a weakness: the viewpoint was classically inside out. "We had a sophisticated group of pilots, so their natural tendency was to design products for sophisticated pilots. They designed for the pilot in the office next door."

The pilot-managers were taught about market research, including the systematic use of focus groups and trade shows for gathering market intelligence. They learned to talk to distributors and to consult suppliers about the latest innovations available. And GAA was restructured into four product groups, each with revenues of some $60 to $80 million and its own P&L. The new heads—called "enterprise managers"—were responsible for product strategy, operating plans, and financial results, and were rewarded accordingly. Summe introduced six new yardsticks for success: (1) cost, (2) quality, (3) speed, (4) customer satisfaction, (5) associate satisfaction, and (6) working capital turnover.

Operating Mechanisms for Change

In a kind of shock therapy, Summe radically shortened the time frame for new product development. The new schedule was a powerful operating mechanism—it simultaneously served the strategic purposes of shortening cycle time and transforming the decision and social architectures.

"We had product development constipation, with a lot of things they were working on for years but nothing getting to the marketplace," says Summe. He announced that he wouldn't consider any product that would take more than ten months.

Sure enough, the engineers were shocked. "It was really viewed as quite unrealistic—maybe *unreasonable* is a better word." But it succeeded in forcing the mindset change and focusing on efficiency—to get products out that fast, the developers would have to use off-the-shelf components instead of expensive custom ones. And it forced closer contact with the marketplace. Using available technology, the developers could more closely correlate features and performance with current demand: "Two and a half years out, you're not half as smart about what is required, and you have to bet on technology that is not mature." Summe eventually backed off from the ten-month rule, but not before it had served its purposes.

Summe also dealt with the fear issue by teaching his people that it could be OK to fail. "When you made classics, you didn't introduce many products, and therefore you needed to bat very high. We changed the whole concept of batting average. If you introduce four new products and three of them are terrific but one falls short, it doesn't mean you've lost. Typically, we learned a lot with that one; we'd be able to turn it, spin it, sometimes turn it into a winner. Other times, it wasn't going to be a winner, but it gave us the insight and the knowledge of the marketplace to change it and come out with a replacement product that was a real winner. This kept our investment-per-product low, and kept a continual stream of products coming out. At the end of the day, that is by far the best market intelligence you can get."

Monthly new-product reviews, with engineers from Arizona to Singapore hooked in by video conferencing, underscored the importance of keeping on track and coordinating across functions. Another new type of operating mechanism, the reviews also helped meet Summe's goal of changing both decision and social architectures by empowering the project managers. "This gave them regular visibility with senior management. Those are the kinds of jobs that should attract ambitious, hard-working, tough-minded leaders who want a chance to either go up in glory or go down in flames, and that's what we provided."

Out of the product review process came a host of other ways to improve communication and coordination, such as regular small-group meetings of people from engineering, manufacturing, materials, and so forth. "We have really turned up the wick on communications that establish a two-way dialogue," says Summe. "It's got to be consistent and on a frequent enough basis for the people to get comfortable and make sure we're addressing the issues on their minds."

To develop candor, the meetings use what Summe calls a blind questioning approach: people write their questions and concerns anonymously on paper, and hand them in to the facilitator. Says Summe: "It really raises people's courage in terms of identifying the questions."

Breaking Down the Resistance

All of the changes came together in the development of a new collision-avoidance system called TCAS2, which came in on time and on budget, and was a big part of GAA's success in 1995. The project, says Summe, "not only broke down all of the barriers within the operation, it also broke down the barriers between sister divisions." But before the barriers fell, Summe had to overcome powerful resistance to change, from leaders who believed it couldn't be done.

GAA had been selling a traffic control advisory system, called TCAS1, which gives pilots a graphic display of other aircraft in nearby airspace. AlliedSignal's Commercial Avionics Systems division, in Fort Lauderdale, Florida, built the more sophisticated TCAS2 for the transport market; TCAS2 tells pilots what they need to do to avoid a potential collision. Developing a TCAS2 for general aviation seemed like a natural next step. But TCAS2 had practically nothing in common with the systems GAA made, and cost much more.

Summe put together a team of engineers from both divisions to develop a TCAS2 for general aviation, and set a time goal of nine months. The project started grudgingly. Almost immediately, the team came back to say that it couldn't be done. Summe told them that they didn't have any choice; he'd already made commitments to customers. "The team then came back and said, 'That's a very unreasonable time frame and the only way we're going to be able to pull it off is if we can reuse the software logic out of our air transport equipment and the maximum amount of hardware from the TCAS1—and even then, there's risk.' I said, 'It sounds like a pretty good idea to me; why not? What's the downside?'"

The team got down to work, but, Summe recalls, "It soon became clear that it didn't have enough passion and energy—it didn't have strong enough leadership. So within about six weeks, we replaced the project leader."

The time frame wasn't the team's only problem. "Fort Lauderdale and Kansas were not only 1,500 miles apart, they were culturally very different. They had never worked together and didn't particularly think that it made a lot of sense."

Summe solved that problem with an operating mechanism that gave the team unprecedented power and attention—literally, he empowered them. As he observes, "If people are being required to do things that are unorthodox or nontraditional, and they have the *power* to do them, then it's very liberating.

"So we made them a very highly visible team that got a lot of love and support out of the organization. The product was big enough so that instead of more formal reporting mechanisms, we put in place weekly updates on where we were. With the strong leadership, co-location, and a very tight matrix, working with them on a close basis empowered the team, forced them to take some bold actions they wouldn't normally have taken."

"Growth Was Never Part of the Deal"

Back at headquarters, Dan Burnham was very quickly broadening the division's pond, not only by lifting growth targets for spare and replacement parts, but also by setting his sights on the adjacent segment of service—a business that he could grow no matter what the demand for airplanes might be.

He didn't have much to work with at first. "We had all this stuff you need to make engineering work, but we didn't have it for growth drivers," he says. "Growth was just never part of the deal."

While the twenty-six businesses had been consolidated in the reorganization, the products and services themselves might as well have been emanating from separate companies; for each product line, there were different procedures for everything from dealing with distributors to the wording of warranties.

Problems that arose were resolved only slowly, if at all; opportunities remained unexploited. There was no way for Aerospace people to make contact with their functional peers in a customer's organization, and vice versa. For example, an engineer at Boeing who wanted to talk to an engineer at Aerospace had to go through the Customer Service organization, which had its own bureaucracy and agenda.

Aerospace was as inside-out as a company can get. "We'd never trained people in marketing or customer contact procedures and

disciplines," says Burnham. "We had no data, no supporting information systems. We did not have a strong aftermarket service orientation
because we had effectively a monopoly position on the products we provided. We made our money repairing and supplying spares, and we
thought we didn't have to prove ourselves as a service provider every day,
in order to win the business."

Getting closer to the marketplace, Burnham felt, was the key. "The
growth mindset comes first from interacting with customers on a deep
and profound basis," he says. "That means not simply asking them
what is it they want, because if they knew they would have already told
you. But we want to understand their unmet needs, and we can only do
that by getting inextricably intertwined in their organization."

Burnham brought in an outsider to turn things around: he hired Joe
Leonard away from Northwest Airlines, where he'd been Executive Vice
President of Customer Service. Leonard was put in charge of building a
new organization—Marketing, Sales and Service (MS&S)—that would
cut across all the business units and bring a cohesive, knowledgeable approach to the markets.

Leonard built MS&S from bits and pieces of the old staffs, but his
main catalyst for change came from new genes. He brought in repair
and overhaul people from airlines, and sales and marketing people from
consumer product firms such as Black & Decker, 3M, and Baxter International, as well as from computer and electronics companies.

Challenging the Organization

Voluble, enthusiastic, and down-to-earth, Leonard set up MS&S to be an
operating mechanism for change throughout Aerospace. "The whole purpose of our group is to challenge the organization," he says. "If we aren't
making people say, 'Gee, go away, that's a bad idea,' then we're not doing
our job, we're not pushing hard enough. Sometimes we're rejected out-
right and, most times, we're rejected three or four times: 'Hey, we tried
that and it won't work.' We say, 'Wrong answer. You need to listen to us a
second time around.' We're persistent, we don't go away."[10]

Leonard organized his people into Customer Account Teams (CATs,
or, to some in the division, Aerocats). A team has been created for every
major customer as well as for a growing number of smaller customers
and for regions and other parts of the world. Core members of a team

include representatives of each business unit that serves the customer, along with people from MS&S, field service engineers, and a new business development specialist. The core team for a Boeing aircraft might include twenty or more people; for a Cessna, ten to fifteen, and so on. The teams also include "virtual members"—people who come and go as special or urgent issues arise.

Customers too small to have their own CATs are being handled within another innovation developed under Leonard. In 1994, he began a test program to introduce telemarketing to an industry where it was unheard of. The program started with four people; in 1997, it generated some $30 million in sales. "We're having them call them on a regular basis," says Leonard. "Just call, 'Hello, I'm from AlliedSignal. How are things going? Is there anything that you need? Are you having any problems? Oh, and by the way, we have this new enhanced ground proximity warning system you might be interested in.' So it's both a service and sales prospecting opportunity."

CAT leaders spend 80 to 90 percent of their time with customers. And at each Aerospace business unit, an engineer acts as the customer's advocate within the organization. Though the teams typically meet formally quarterly, informal meetings occur whenever the need arises, and members routinely converse weekly or daily—or several times a day, if there's an urgent issue. All team members carry beepers, all contribute to maintaining a common data base.

Leonard's most radical departure from past practice at Aerospace—indeed, in the industry itself—was to link part of the core members' compensation to customer satisfaction. The risk part is equivalent to 20 percent of base salaries; depending on how well they do, the reward can reach as much as 50 percent. "Our objective is to pay out a lot of money," says Leonard. "We'd have a real high-class problem if we were paying out 150 percent to all the people in the pool."

The linkage generated a lot of flak at first. "When you hire people from companies like 3M and Hewlett-Packard, they can't imagine *not* having salespeople on incentive comp," he says. "But for people who spent their entire lives in Aerospace, it was just gut-wrenching."

What's more, he had to back off from his first try because MS&S didn't have good enough yardsticks for measuring customer satisfaction. It took the better part of a year to develop measurements that satisfied everybody. "First, we sat down with the customers and asked them, 'What's important to you? How are we doing against that? What are your expectations in the short run and in the long run?' Now, every quarter, we sit down with them again and measure ourselves against that. They give us their score on a scale of 1 to 10. Our goal is to improve that score 25 percent for every customer, year over year."

The customer satisfaction scorecard has only one score, for the entire organization. "So if I'm working in engines," says Leonard, "and my score is low and everybody else's score is high, I'm going to get a lot of pressure from my peers inside the company to get my score up. Because we're all in that pool together.

"We thought that was important, because we're trying to market as a single company, and we want our people within the company to not just focus on their business but have a broader perspective and help the other folks when they need some help."

Burnham, solidly behind the idea from the start, nevertheless admits that it was an extremely tough sell. "Of all the culture shifts that we tried to instill within the place, this has been the most complicated one to pull off," he says. "The majority of the people in the customer contact organization did not want to put their pay at risk. They said, 'It's not my fault that we're not growing enough or that our customer satisfaction isn't there.' And at one level, that's true. We do try to ensure there's equity in the payouts for exogenous events. But the fact is that you get 500–600 people to be passionate about customer service not by just spouting truisms but with data on our customer requirements."

Segmenting the Market

The CATs have helped Aerospace to better define its market segment and subsegments. "It's changing the whole organizational structure to focus on the actual market instead of on all the stuff we make," says Lynn Brubaker, who heads the commercial air transport marketing, sales, and service organization.[11]

One area she has defined better is leasing. It's a fast-growing business. About 20 percent of the world's aircraft are leased; for aircraft sold since 1990, the figure is 60 percent. In 1995, Brubaker organized a CAT to deal specifically with leasing companies such as GE Capital and IBD, the big Ireland-based airplane leasing company.

The interests of these companies are slightly but significantly different from those of airlines. The airlines are most interested in leading-edge technologies and cost effectiveness. "The leasing companies want to have products that are most easily placed in the widest possible range of customers," says Haluk Durudogan, a former McDonnell Douglas marketer who now heads the leasing CAT.[12]

The team scored its first big victory early in 1996: a $700 million deal with GE Capital. There's no question that the team structure made the critical difference. "My directions were to leverage AlliedSignal's capabilities as a single company," says Durudogan. "It was the first of the major package deals, the first time one book contained all the pieces of this company. And it took the creativity of the team to go outside what had been the normal practice. The customer said, 'No one has ever submitted anything like that to us before.' And even the competition said, 'We don't know what you have done, but whatever you did, we were not able to do it.'"

How did the group generate its creativity? "This team is linked up and down and sideways," Durudogan says. "You have immediate access to anybody. Beyond the account team, you can go from the chairman throughout the organization."

A small but telling illustration of the changes Leonard brought to sales and marketing is that, on the day Durudogan arrived at his new job, roughly a year after Leonard had come aboard, everything was ready for action. "When I walked into my new office February 6, they had a beeper, a handphone, and a laptop attached to E-mail, and a little card that already had my home phone numbers on it," he says. "The people walked through that door as a team, and we were able to go forward with our heads up." Among those people were some who, a scant two years earlier, had been largely clueless about how to serve their customers effectively.

The potentially biggest new growth program is Aerospace's Power-by-the-Hour arrangement. Competitors such as GE are doing this now, admits Leonard, "but we clearly led the industry." Starting with auxiliary power units (APUs) for airplanes, Aerospace is gradually expanding the concept to such other products as wheels and brakes, air-conditioning systems, hydraulics, pneumatics, and electric power components.

The concept is simple: Allied agrees to maintain the customer's unit at a fixed cost per flight-hour. "We assume the liability risk and the cost risk, but we're quite confident that we can do it cheaper than most of the people who do it today, who typically are our customers."

It's not a hard selling proposition—if you go about it the right way. That means educating the customer. "A typical negotiation for a large airline will take about six months, and about four of that is discussions over what the costs really are. It's all done open-weave. We show them what our costs are. We try to calculate what their costs are and we sit down and, at the end of the day, it's almost impossible for them to meet our costs because our economy of scale is pretty hard to match." In a typical year, Aerospace will overhaul several thousand units, while the largest airline in the world may do eighty.

Speed was another byproduct of scale and learning. When the program started, it took Aerospace the better part of a month to repair a unit. By the end of 1997, the turnaround time was down to roughly a week.

Helped by the success of Power-by-the-Hour, repair and overhaul quickly became the fastest growing part of Aerospace. From 1994 to 1996, its revenues grew by more than one-third, to $830 million. The market amounted to around $3 billion, of which Allied got a little better than half. Leonard aims to substantially enlarge that share (see Figure 10.2) by getting into the game when planes are still on the drawing board. "It can be very difficult for the airlines to move in-house work

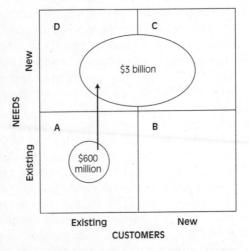

Figure 10.2   Segue into services: Power-by-the-Hour—contracting with airlines to service their equipment—broadened Aerospace's pond among both existing and new customers.

out," he says. "But it's not difficult for them on a new airplane. So we are being very aggressive about coming in early to set up Power-By-the-Hour arrangements before they ever tool up."

Learning to Embrace Change

It's one thing to create a revolution. Keeping it going, as Noel Tichy wrote about GE in *A Handbook for Revolutionaries*,[13] requires leaders to fundamentally redesign the social architecture: "It is necessary to make as many people as possible agents of change." No transition is tougher for people who have spent their careers seeking stability and predictability.

In the genetic code that Dan Burnham and his leaders created at Aerospace, people at all levels have learned to come to grips with uncertainty and ambiguity, and to embrace change. How they did it is summed up eloquently by Joe Leonard, speaking about the evolution of the new Customer Account Teams during 1996:

"We'll make a lot of mistakes, we know that. We'll back up, dust ourselves off, and go on. One thing we're not bashful about here is admitting when we didn't thread the needle and saying, 'Well, let's try something else.'

"We were trying to create something for which there wasn't a model. People would say, 'What does this look like?' And I used to say, 'We'll know when we see it.'

"We knew what we wanted to do. We had the precepts on how to work, and then we started trying to figure out precisely how it worked. This wasn't an organization that dealt real well with ambiguity, and this was certainly ambiguous when we started out. The spool-up was fairly slow—and then it just kind of took off exponentially. We made it home."

> **Epilogue:** Late in 1997, Dan Burnham was made one of AlliedSignal's two vice chairmen, with Aerospace—restructured into five business units—reporting to him. Greg Summe was appointed head of the Automotive Products group. In 1998, Burnham was recruited to be the CEO of $13.7-billion-a-year Raytheon Co. Summe was recruited to be chief operating officer of EG&G, a $1.5 billion-a-year maker of scientific equipment.

You can get people's attention when there's a crisis, but redirecting it to the long-term challenge of growth takes leaders with a teachable point of view and great persistence. Dan Burnham and his team at AlliedSignal Aerospace took charge of a business in a declining undustry understanding the necessity for balanced, profitable growth. They also understood that it could not be achieved without changing the genetic code of their organization.

Reynolds and Reynolds
CREATING LIFELONG CUSTOMERS

There is no such thing as a mature industry. In less than five years, Dave Holmes transformed a sleepy company with stagnating sales and lackluster returns into a growth powerhouse. A failed expansion into medical services hurt the company's financial performance, but the underlying strategy continues to drive its core businesses.

At the beginning of the 1990s, the Reynolds and Reynolds Co. was a $600-million-a-year bump in the middle-America corporate landscape. It made business forms, competing against giants such as Moore Corporation, and sold computer systems to automobile dealerships. In its headquarters city of Dayton, Ohio, Reynolds was a respected corporate citizen, but not the kind of company anybody thought of as a star.

Mature markets? Car dealerships sure didn't look like a growth business. As for forms, says chairman and president Dave Holmes, "We used to describe ourselves as 'in a $10-billion industry going nowhere.' "[1] Senior managers generally felt they'd taken the core businesses about as far as they could, and there wasn't much left to do but milk them. Revenues had stagnated in 1991 at about $600 million a year, with a return on equity of about 10 percent.[2]

That was the year Holmes set an ambitious goal: Grow Reynolds and Reynolds to a $1-billion-a-year company by 2000. Scarcely anybody in the organization believed it was possible—yet revenues passed the $1 billion mark in 1996, four years ahead of schedule, with profits growing at a compound annual rate of 36 percent. In just five years, the stolid forms maker had become, in Holmes's phrase, "a powerhouse information management company," with a return on equity of better than 25 percent.[3]

The picture isn't quite perfect. In the second quarter of 1997, earnings growth fell short of forecast. Auto dealers, who account for a large share of the company's profits, delayed their buying decisions amid industry uncertainty. Large acquisitions in business forms dampened profit margins, and an ambitious expansion into the larger pond of health care forms proved to be tougher than expected. As a result, Reynolds accelerated a number of cost-saving measures and took a hefty restructuring charge. Its stock, which had rocketed from about $2 at the end of fiscal 1990 to a peak of just over 29 (adjusted for two splits), fell below $16.[4] In 1998, the company sold the money losing health care division.

Unexpected negatives always confront business leaders—whether their companies are growing or not. The risks are especially high when they're trying to meet the new needs of new customers, as Reynolds is doing with its move into health care (quadrant C in the 2×2). But its stumble subtracts nothing from the essential lessons to be learned: how Reynolds grew faster and made more money than its people had thought possible in their wildest dreams. Indeed, the stumble is part of the lessons.

How did Holmes and his people do it?

1. They broadened their pond. Holmes and his leadership team moved Reynolds and Reynolds from selling business forms and computer systems to supplying "solutions"—the knowhow and the support its customers need to run their businesses better.

Besides leveraging the company's existing strengths, they made scores of strategic acquisitions, many aimed at strengthening and expanding its core competencies. They also shed old ones, including much of the company's traditional manufacturing. Business forms, the core business when the decade began, became a subset of solutions.

In the auto dealership computer business alone, this strategy expanded the Reynolds' pond from roughly a $1.5-billion market of which it had more than a 30 percent share to a $5 billion market where its share is just over 10 percent. It also gave the company a way to comparably enlarge its forms business from basically selling paper to providing document management solutions. And the fish in the new pond are fatter, because Reynolds moved up the food chain from low-margin products to high-margin knowledge.

2. They rewrote the genetic code. Sustaining growth relies heavily on winning what Reynolds calls "lifelong customers." More than a slogan, a program, or even a process, it is a combination of mindset, tools, and techniques for creating customer loyalty that borders on dependency. It works—and one reason for its success is that Holmes paid as much attention, if not more, to changing the way the Reynolds people thought, made decisions, and behaved, as he did to the basic business plan.

The old Reynolds was a company of solid, hardworking managers with limited horizons. The workforce reflected the modest ambitions of the founding-family shareholders who essentially set the agenda. Holmes taught his people to think big and look from the outside in. They learned to spot and meet customers' needs, rather than just sell the products their company made. Working with his vice president of human resources, Tom Momchilov, Holmes integrated organizational development with personal development. New operating mechanisms drove changes in decision architecture and social architecture through the whole organization. Vision, planning, goal setting, information flows, measurements, and rewards were linked into a holistic management system that's still evolving.

Holmes implanted many new genes, recruiting from companies as diverse as Motorola, Procter & Gamble, General Foods, Xerox, GE, and McKinsey. And he advanced his teachable point of view in every possible forum, repeatedly driving home the message of large possibilities for profitable growth. At Reynolds and Reynolds today, as one of his executives puts it, even the person in the mailroom knows what Dave Holmes's plan is, and what his or her role is in that plan.

Passionate, energetic, fast-speaking, and youthful-looking at 58 despite gray hair, Dave Holmes is a marketer—and an outside gene himself. Reynolds brought him aboard in 1984 to head development of a new computerized reporting system for its auto dealer customers. He'd worked twelve years for General Foods, where, among other things, he launched Shake 'n Bake; spent two years at GE as head of small appliances; and then two years at Nabisco, where he managed the salty-snack business.

When the call came from Reynolds, he remembers, "My first reaction was, 'Where's Ohio?' But I was really taken by the quality of the people here. It was very different from the bureaucracy of a General

Foods. Reynolds was a flatter organization. They appreciated the value someone from the outside could bring, and they were open—they shared the things they'd done right, and the things that didn't go so right. I'd developed what I thought were some great tools in the battle of the belly-market-share. Computers were just coming on—I'd bought an early IBM and used it regularly at home to pump out financial reports. I saw a great growth opportunity."

In 1988, Holmes was made chief operating officer, and a year later he became CEO. His values were clear. He wanted nothing more than to make Reynolds grow. Says he: "I'd rather die than maintain." For example, after he became CEO in 1989, he says, "I found myself saying to the board one day, 'We're shooting for 45 percent profit growth.' A few laughed, probably thinking, 'Isn't that crazy?'" But they didn't really think it was *too* crazy. "By then, they all knew my attitude: There's no point in hedging, but every point in stretching."

"We Look at All the Dollars"

The bigger pond Holmes saw was the need among companies not just for forms and computer systems but for comprehensive solutions to drive better business results.

The customer's biggest problem these days, notes Holmes, is not a paucity of new products. On the contrary, new products pour out all the time. "But how do you train your people on them fast enough? How do you get productivity out of them and how do you integrate them with your other systems? So companies say, 'I want a partner, I want a total systems provider, I want somebody to give me wrap around service, I want somebody who is willing to step in on a periodic basis and say, "Here's what we delivered for you. Here's the productivity we created. How do we want to raise the bar now, going forward? What are the next horizons we should take on?"'"

Or, as Momchilov puts it: "We look at all the dollars the customers spend in both the operation and the promotion of their business, and try to get our hands on them."[5]

Using the matrix we introduced in Chapter 4, this was a move into quadrant A, existing customers with new needs (Figure 11.1).

Following this approach, Holmes felt, Reynolds could learn more, and faster, about the additional needs in its chosen pond, and would be best able to leverage its relationships to fulfill those needs. As he puts it,

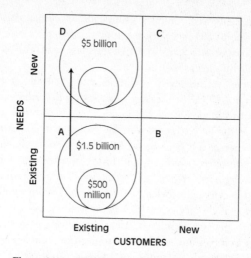

Figure 11.1 With about a one-third share of the $1.5 billion market for automotive dealership computer systems and business forms, Reynolds expanded by staking out a $5 billion pond for business "solutions"—knowhow and support its customers could use to improve their own businesses.

"It's easier to take an existing customer and surround him with added products than it is to go out cold turkey to someone new." This is what we call the concept of adjacency—a fertile area for growth used by Compaq, GE Medical Systems, and GE Power Systems, among others.

Helping Customers Grow

Reynolds and Reynolds began with auto dealerships because it already supplied them with the two basic components: computer systems and business forms. Typically, companies that offer "solutions" to customers help make those customers profitable by streamlining current processes, lowering costs, improving cycle time, lowering capital intensity, and the like. Reynolds did all of these things.

But it went beyond the norm, helping its customers to grow and to create value in their own businesses. "We started with a narrowly focused system, basically helping dealers control costs," says Holmes. "Today, we're helping them drive revenues, profits, and customer satisfaction." In so doing, Reynolds has expanded the pond through the whole value chain to create a broader prosperity and a larger share in it. This is the essence of a profitable top-line growth company.

Automotive Systems revenues climbed from $249 million in 1991 to $537 million in 1997. One measure of success is that roughly 60 percent of the company's income is earned in ongoing support and services. The centerpiece of the new strategy was the launch of the computer system Holmes had overseen. It became the ERA Information Management System, which combines computers and forms in what the company calls, accurately enough, its "engine for a broad line of retailing solutions." Surveying 1,000 dealers nationwide in 1996, the NCM automotive research group found that dealers using ERA generated an average of $200,000 more in profits per year than those using competitive systems.

With its companion SalesVision application, introduced in 1996, ERA integrates everything from sales and parts to service, vehicle registration, and customer follow-up. A document management system provides electronic storage and retrieval of paperwork. The system organizes daily staff activities and work plans, automatically schedules prospecting and follow-up calls, and plugs the dealer into online databases for parts and used vehicles. Other applications include high-powered tools for managing vehicle inventory, estimating service and body-shop work, and creating finance and insurance options for buyers. Reynolds also finances about 85 percent of the systems it sells—one factor in keeping its recurring revenue base strong.

Complementing the system is an array of related marketing services, including direct mail and database marketing. General Motors picked Reynolds to implement its Goodwrench Service Plus program, which is designed to capture a bigger share of after-warranty service. The Reynolds consulting arm, built around two companies acquired in 1995 and 1996 and now the most comprehensive in the industry, can help dealers with everything from training and systems optimization to improving customer relations. In a partnership with Microsoft's CarPoint online service, it operates a new-car buying service, connects dealer inventories through a used-car listing service, and provides dealers with "mini" home pages.

Raising customer satisfaction has become a marketable core competence. "We go in and do a baseline study for dealers and come back with customer satisfaction scores on people that have bought a new car or had their car serviced," says Holmes. "And if there are some problems we've identified, we can help them."

Providing comprehensive and integrated solutions has positioned Reynolds to stay ahead of the sea changes sweeping over its customer base, as dealerships consolidate into megadealers, manufacturers wring costs out of the distribution channel, and new competitors such as Car Max and Wayne Huizenga's AutoNation (a Reynolds customer) challenge the existing ways of doing business. As Holmes says, "If you take the outside-in view, you can drive the future of your marketplace."

Resegmenting a Mature Industry

The forms business, in that mature, low-margin, "$10 billion industry going nowhere," was a tougher nut to crack. The Reynolds people had been going after it aggressively but with a shotgun approach effectively bidding for any business they could get; as a result, a lot of what they got was scarcely worth having. Says Rod Hedeen, the division's president: "You can't grow a business if you don't know where you are going. You all need to be headed in one direction—what we call 'headed west.'"[6]

What got the Business Systems Division heading west was a breakthrough study that persuaded its leaders to resegment their market according to buying behaviors, not traditional criteria such as business size, industry affiliation, or geography. The research pinpointed four basic types of buyers; Reynolds labeled them (1) aggressive bidders, (2) systems managers, (3) convenience buyers, and (4) total value seekers. The first two were the least attractive, Reynolds concluded; aggressive bidders buy on price, and systems managers' decisions are based on other traditional purchasing criteria. Convenience buyers and total value seekers were the kinds of people Reynolds was set up to serve—people who wanted to streamline or outsource their forms management systems, appreciated the value of solutions that would improve their own business results, and were happy to pay for them.

The division's leaders abandoned the commodity paper market (after finding a partner to provide the necessary products to its customers). Nominally, this cut the pond in half, to about $5 billion. But it paved the way for reallocating resources to a much larger and richer pond. As Hedeen says, "Looking at ourselves as providers of document management and work optimization, through our own organization and those with which we partner, our industry's potential is $23 billion a year in the United States and Canada alone."

Business Systems acquired a string of weaker competitors and complementing small-fry. The acquisitions added customers and beefed up the organization, but this was not a consolidation game; as with Automotive Systems, the main goal was to build a comprehensive portfolio of products—from the traditional warehousing and distribution services through reengineering of customers' business processes.

In a typical example of how the business creates its value proposition, a major division of one of the world's largest companies brought Reynolds in to design a new reporting system, complying with the ISO 9000 international quality standards, that would link two dozen manufacturing organizations. The project started at square one: there wasn't any system whatsoever. After months of intense partnering, the customer had a system that tied all of the purchasing and manufacturing organizations together. Electronic reporting and paper forms were fully integrated, and complete supplier and product performance histories were available at the touch of a button.

New Customers and Needs

Its first-rate capability has grown revenues for the business forms segment from $350 million in 1991 to $819 million in 1997. Operating income rose from $23 million to $75 million. The new competency has also nudged Reynolds into quadrant C of the 2 × 2: new customers with new needs (see Figure 11.2). Among the scores of additions to its blue-chip customer base are GE, Nissan, General Motors, First Chicago NBD, Dell Computer, Merrill Lynch, and Turner Broadcasting.

Holmes envisioned a much bigger foray into virgin territory as the next stage. The move began in 1994, when Reynolds made its first acquisition in the health care field. Holmes bets that Reynolds can transfer its information management systems and customer-pleasing skills, which work so well for auto dealers and general business, to physician groups— a pond it estimates at $2 billion a year and growing at better than 20 percent annually. A small player in the market since the mid-eighties, Reynolds began to attack aggressively in 1994. Since then, it has been acquiring companies and merging them into Reynolds and Reynolds

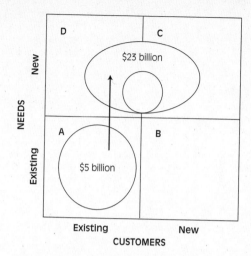

Figure 11.2 From selling business forms and forms management systems, Reynolds' Business Systems Division expanded to offering "document management and work optimization"—a pond amounting to some $23 billion.

Healthcare Systems, a business whose revenues could approach $60 million in fiscal 1998. (See Figure 11.3.)

Reynolds Healthcare Systems has won an impressive roster of new customers around the country, among them Harvard Pilgrim Health Care, the biggest such provider in New England. AMA Solutions Inc., a subsidiary of the American Medical Association, picked Reynolds as its first vendor partner in Technology Link, a program to provide the AMA's 300,000-plus members nationwide with practice-management systems.

But the essentially entrepreneurial activity of converting new customers with new needs is inherently risky, and the going has been slower than hoped. Reynolds Healthcare Systems has yet to turn a profit. For one thing, admits Holmes, Reynolds underestimated how hard it would be to sell into a highly fragmented and regional market. And as consolidation fever sweeps through the industry, many potentially attractive acquisitions of regional information management firms don't make sense "because the p/e ratios are out of sight."

"I'm not a patient person," adds Holmes, "but some things you can wrap up quickly and others you've got to take a little bit of a different

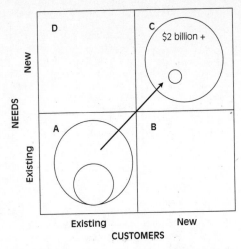

Figure 11.3   Expanding into the health care field, Reynolds hopes to bring its skills for managing information and pleasing existing customers to an entirely new set of customers and needs.

approach. This is a very large, thirsty marketplace. It is grossly dissatisfied; it has tremendous needs for information systems to help control costs, manage multiple plans, improve the practice of medicine and improve patients' satisfaction. And it builds off of capabilities that we're very good at.

"We're still building the business and developing a winning formula, but once it is finally in place, the opportunities are enormous. We are in it for the long term." He foresees doubling revenues in the next several years.

Nor has the slow takeoff discouraged Holmes from looking for more opportunities in quadrant C. In his message to Reynolds employees at the start of fiscal 1998, he reiterated the vision of the company he'd laid out earlier: "To be a highly admired company, able to attract and retain customers, associates, and shareholders." Holmes told them that acquiring a fourth major business was a critical part of that vision.

Changing the Genetic Code

The Reynolds and Reynolds leaders couldn't have realized any of this growth if they hadn't completely changed the company's old mindset.

By the time Holmes was elected CEO, Reynolds and Reynolds was in distress. The company had decentralized in the eighties and headed off on an ill-defined growth program. Its conglomerate-style acquisitions and overseas expansion were not based on a fundamental analysis of consumer need. The results: financial strain, and uncertainty about the company's direction. The first large-scale layoffs in its history had hammered morale (among those laid off were half of the R&D people who had developed the new automotive computer system). Management was divided—not only by the decentralization but also because an old guard resented the new people brought in as part of the expansion program.

"We were a sales-driven company with a lot of customer focus," Holmes says. "We had pioneered different businesses and gotten ourselves into a leadership position." The leadership was clearest in Automotive Systems, where the ERA system had helped Reynolds capture a commanding share of the market. The focus on customers, in fact, was a powerful competence. Pleasing them was deeply ingrained in the company's genetic code. Its managers—"hardworking, shirtsleeves people"— would do their best to make a customer happy.

"But we were losing ground," he admits. "There was not a lot of curiosity about competing with the world or beating it. Business plans were established without reference to shareholders or market share. We weren't focused on understanding our profitability by product line and by customer.

"And talk about radical change really scared people."

Rod Hedeen puts it more strongly. Hedeen, who had a manufacturing background at GE, came to Reynolds in 1986 and found "a company that was absolutely satisfied with the way it was and very resistant to change. People were very comfortable. If you didn't make your goal, they found a way to give you a bonus anyway. It was the exact opposite of what you see in Reynolds today."

The first priorities were to get costs under control and pull together a team of managers who could lead the company to a new growth trajectory. Top executives who couldn't get out of the old mindset left, and Holmes began to bring in more outside genes. (By the end of 1997, through a combination of direct hiring and acquisition of businesses, Reynolds had added dozens of midlevel and senior managers in marketing, sales, human resources, strategic planning, and information technology—in other words, every area of the company.) Holmes and his team also weeded out businesses that didn't have profitable growth prospects, including several that were acquired in the earlier unfocused expansion program.

Building Emotional Equity™

Holmes was convinced that Reynolds had the potential to grow, but he wasn't about to rush ahead without what he called a vision—a central idea that was both clear in direction and articulated powerfully enough to capture the emotional energy of the Reynolds people.

Dave Holmes believes in building emotional equity™. A concept that business leaders are just starting to articulate, emotional equity™ refers to the alignment of employees—as evidenced by their psychic energy, trust, and willingness to follow leaders eagerly and give 110 percent to the effort—with their company and its goals. People with emotional equity™ in their companies work in unison and synchronization. They pay attention more to results and to being effective than to the number of hours they put in. Emotional equity,™ the psychic wellspring of excellence, is both contagious with customers and self-reinforcing.

Aggressive growth would require a major change in mindset for most of the Reynolds people. Holmes started the shift by asking the new top management group to lay out their ideas of what the company's values were, and where the company should be going. Out of this came an agreement that the future of Reynolds lay in being a powerful *information management company* that delivered "business results," was passionate about customer satisfaction, was ethical, and—of course—profitable. Holmes set a minimum ROI target of 20 percent.

Observes Tom Momchilov: "Dave's attitude was that there's always more than you think. You take the customer relationship and ask, 'How can I leverage that relationship to expand the market? How can we surround the customer, and serve him so well that he doesn't want to go elsewhere?'"

An Operating Mechanism for Radical Change

To execute a growth strategy, the Reynolds management team would need new knowledge, analytical skills, and perspectives. For some time,

Holmes and Momchilov had been working on developing an executive education program. As they talked about it, the idea evolved that the program could also be an operating mechanism for radical change—a structure for pulling the autonomous organizations together, creating the common vision and language that were missing, and stretching everybody's thinking.

Working with the executive education group at the Ohio State College of Business, they came up with four formal objectives:

1. Reshape senior management by challenging manager's assumptions and stretching their business thinking.
2. Introduce new tools and processes to help them manage better.
3. Institutionalize a customer-driven, competitive-spirited management approach.
4. Increase cooperation and synergy among business units.

Holmes and Momchilov knew many of their people would be skeptical about meeting with a bunch of academics and taking time away from serious business to do homework. So Momchilov began lobbying the concept informally, bringing it up over lunches, in meetings, and through phone calls. He reported on the unfolding status of the program at the president's monthly staff meetings.

They then asked a group of senior managers to think about the proposition and give their views. It was a carefully chosen group of fourteen persons, some picked for their acumen and insight, others precisely because they were most uncomfortable with the whole idea. Questions, based on extensive research on everything from the company's market position to its succession plans, were designed to get people debating and thinking about broad management, competitive and cultural issues, as well as about areas where training would help.

The group's response was everything Holmes and Momchilov hoped for. The executives didn't like the idea that they were stuck mainly in slow-growth markets, and they wanted to learn how to design fresh strategies. They also wanted help in developing the leadership skills they felt were critical to the company's success. And not just their own leadership skills. Any program, they said, should be driven down through the organization, and should help empower employees to take initiative and risks.

"An Unbelievable Turnaround"

The program that came out of all this was to include the top fifty or so
senior managers, and run for a year and a half. Eventually, it evolved
into an in-house training center, Reynolds University, which now provides seminars and programs for people at all levels.

The first of those early meetings was timed symbolically to be on the
first day of the company's new fiscal year. It was a day-and-a-half program offsite, conducted by Ram Charan, and it set the agenda for
change more profoundly than Holmes or anyone else had dared to imagine. As Holmes describes it:

> "It was about growth strategy. Coming in, our objective was to
> grow about 10 percent a year. But Ram talked first about growing
> from the inside out, which was historically how we'd viewed it.
> Then he led us through thinking from the outside in, from the
> markets and customers you're serving and the capabilities you can
> take to the market, using examples from successful companies.

> "That changed fundamentally how we viewed our markets. We
> learned that thinking from the outside in, you have an infinitesimal
> share of the business available, and you ask questions like: How do
> I maximize? How do I gain the broadest potential competitive
> advantage? And we learned that you keep creating and recreating
> your boundaries, rethinking them in a visionary fashion. If the
> market changes, you change your boundaries.

> "After that we broke into subgroups and analyzed what we
> thought the growth opportunities were on each of our major
> businesses. It was ground-level work, from the guts, not thinking
> from 50,000 feet. When we reported back, the consensus was that
> we were enthusiastic about prospects for a faster growth rate. We
> all endorsed 15 percent, and some of us thought privately we could
> do even better.

> "It was an unbelievable turnaround. I'd been concerned going
> in about how to move a whole management team onto a higher
> growth plane, and it was not a problem after that. In one day, the
> whole attitude began to change."

The session also exposed each of the leaders to challenges faced by their counterparts in other businesses at Reynolds. In the workshops and exercises, they defined and solved real business problems together, and shared experiences. They began to understand that they *all* would sink or swim, depending on each other's results, and there were indeed synergies to be found—people running, say, the systems business in one market could learn from those managing customer satisfaction in another. Rocket science? Of course not—but it hadn't been done before.

One thing that opened minds was the role model the CEO set. "Dave showed that he was really able to listen to criticism and change his own mind," says Momchilov. "And so he set the example that made the whole program work. Everybody there learned that good ideas are the ones that challenge everybody's most sacred assumptions."

The group came away with an action program that had specific targets and milestones. Importantly, they agreed that the program was only the first step—the changes had to be driven through the entire organization.

Holmes and his team drew a picture of the new Reynolds that everyone in the organization could understand. Called "Vision 2000," it described a company that would grow to sales of $1 billion by 2000. There would be five core values: (1) focus on customers, (2) maintaining the highest standards of integrity, (3) the importance of people, (4) the need to strive for new and better ways, and (5) the exhortation that "profits are our company's life blood."

"That caused a whole new focus," says Holmes. "First came, 'Where are our costs, where are we making money?' But that's not enough; you can clean out your cost line once, but then where are you? It takes a new fundamental direction: What makes sense strategically, where are we heading long-term, what are our customers' needs?

"Right up front, there was a lot of emphasis on pricing excellence—not the ability to jack up prices but to understand where your costs are, what kind of market environment you're in, where you can create value, and therefore what are your appropriate prices that give you a fair return consistent with your customers' perception and with your competitors."

Holmes set stretch goals for both revenues and profits, and pegged bonuses to results. "At General Foods we used to protect ourselves by spending months trying to develop plans with conservative results," he says. "Here, it was even worse." The aggressive goals had a galvanizing effect. "You could see people change dramatically from narrow functional people to broad general managers—the sales manager who used to lower prices just to sell became someone who really was concerned about the profit we'd be making.

"And it helped shift the load from the CEO. Suddenly I had an army of fifty leaders out there caring about the same things I do—shareholder value. And they're driving the whole organization."

Broadcasting the Teachable Point of View

The $1 billion revenue goal seemed incredible to most people at Reynolds, many of whom didn't have a clue about where the company was heading. "We'd reengineered the business to improve customer satisfaction and cut 50 percent out of costs, and we were feeling pretty good about ourselves," says Momchilov. "And suddenly Dave is saying, 'What I want now is completely different thinking—not incremental, but a quantum leap.'"

Holmes cranked up the decibels, explaining in every way possible, to people at all levels, why the goal was realistic. In speeches, meetings, and employee publications, he talked and answered questions. He reiterated the core values and the attitudes they embodied, stressing the continuity with the corporate history.

He began communicating his message in 1991 through quarterly videos, distributed to everyone in the company, in which he laid out goals and talked about performance. Communications vice president Paul Guthrie heavily revamped the quarterly *Reynolds World* magazine, turning it into a vehicle for ideas, in-depth features about marketplace trends, and stories about how people in various Reynolds businesses were meeting new challenges.

In the magazine and videos, Holmes also explained the company's financial results in detail, leading off with return on equity and including net income, balance sheet information, operating results, and stock performance. To foster a healthy competitive spirit among the business leaders, the results for each business were broken out.

When Holmes started his communications push, says Guthrie, surveys showed that fewer than 20 percent of the Reynolds employees felt they could explain the company's strategy. Three years later, more than three-quarters of employees at all levels—including the many who'd come in via acquired businesses—felt "extremely comfortable" about articulating it. Importantly, they could explain it to customers as a value proposition.

A major goal of both the training sessions and the communications was to get people to embrace change. "We needed to create a new vocabulary," Holmes says. "Two of the core values in particular were new directions for the company: constantly seeking new and better ways, and profits are the lifeblood. We tried to bring that home: We don't come to work every day just to perform activities, we try to create value for our customers and for our company, and these have to be compatible.

"Today, I can say to a huge audience that if we're doing business tomorrow the way we do it today we're already behind. And nobody will wince; they realize that if they want to stay ahead, they have to keep changing. If I had said that when I came first here, it would have scared the hell out of everybody."

Developing New Capabilities

The Reynolds leaders got operational changes rolling through a group of task forces. Consultants had helped Holmes identify seven areas critical to achieving the growth vision: (1) information techhnology, (2) marketing, (3) sales, (4) finance, (5) organization, (6) product development, and (7) the "Creating Lifelong Customers" initiative. "Excellence teams"—cross-functional groups, mainly officers—were organized for each area, to look at the capabilities Reynolds needed to realize the vision, and to create action plans for developing them.

For example, the customer service team identified several key goals. Among them were: higher customer retention levels, more word-of-mouth recommendations, and increased profits for Reynolds and its customers. The team looked at best practices in the Reynolds divisions, benchmarked companies noted for delivering high customer satisfaction, and pinpointed what Reynolds needed to do to reach comparable levels. In human resources, says Momchilov, "We had been recruiting in an ad hoc, not very systematic small-company way. So, in human resources, we looked at recruiting and selection—the entire process of how we source talent, sell, orient, and package the company. We also looked at how to develop skill sets, especially teaming skills for managers."

The very act of working together on cross-functional teams was a powerful change mechanism for leaders who previously hadn't spent much time talking to each other.

Goals for All

By themselves, goals, decibels, and new managerial skills wouldn't be enough. The Reynolds leaders knew they had to drive radical change throughout the organization—creating new ways of thinking and developing people at all levels who could be leaders.

To do this, they overhauled planning and performance management systems, making them into operating mechanisms for changing both decision architecture and social architecture. "We have a saying here: 'Working all the pieces,'" Holmes says. "What we're doing is not only growing the business with our customers but also focusing on growing the capabilities of the company. Because, to sustain your long-term growth, the challenge is going to be growing the people capability and the infrastructure of the organization to embrace that larger business."

Starting with the Automotive Division in 1995, Reynolds created a variation on its traditional management-by-objective approach: "Working Together For Results" (WTFR), planning and performance management system in which everyone in the company takes part in dovetailing personal goals and objectives with the larger picture.

Planning itself is a top-down–bottom-up process drawing ideas from people right down to the bottom rung of the organizational ladder. At each step—situation assessment, vision, and planning—a division's leaders meet with a cross-functional senior corporate management team to talk things through. "It's an active engagement and exchange," says Jack Proud, head of the Healthcare division. "It's an open discussion, where individuals from different disciplines and businesses can share common discoveries and common challenges."[7] The top leaders update it quarterly, with Holmes, in a two-day offsite meeting.

When the coming year's plan is written, the leaders of each business unit take it back to their organizations for a walk-through. Naturally, they introduce the positioning of products and services, and the development plans for them. But they also create specific targets for each of six key areas: (1) market leadership, (2) customer satisfaction (customers being defined as both external and internal), (3) organizational excellence, (4) continuous improvement, (5) growth performance, and (6) financial results.

Then the plan is plugged into WTFR. The business unit leaders pass it down to their direct reports, who, with their teams or work groups, add the details and specifics that they expect to contribute to the year's performance. Finally, each employee creates a personal WTFR document, detailing what he or she will contribute.

Mona Yezbak, vice president for customer satisfaction and business process, calls this a "cascading" process: objectives, strategies, and key plans at each level roll down to the next lower level, becoming increasingly tactical until they're translated into individual responsibilities. "It provides a common language for the organization, and it provides for vertical and horizontal congruency," says Yezbak. "The person in the mailroom knows what Dave Holmes's plan is."[8]

For example, the Automotive Division's objective for customer satisfaction is 95 percent. WTFR breaks that down into measurable specifics that teams, work groups, and individuals can focus on. "What it means to the person in the support center answering the phone is not that he or she is responsible for 95 percent customer satisfaction," says Yezbak, "but for answering the phone in sixty seconds and having first-call resolution with the customer, because we know that the ability to do that is one of the highest drivers of customer satisfaction. So these become individual customer satisfaction targets."

Like the business plan itself, WTFR doesn't end when everyone has created his or her personal document. It stays alive for the duration of the year, serving as a benchmark and being updated against marketplace and managerial reality in formal quarterly reviews—and informally, more often. "It's not something you put on the shelf," says Yezbak. "It's a flexible document that should be dog-eared by year's end."

WTFR also provides a mechanism for communicating the CEO's ideas about both the hard and soft issues of managing. Joe Bausman, now retired after thirty-three years with Reynolds, was head of the Automotive Systems Division when it was set up in 1994. Says Bausman: "It's really an integral part of how we do our business. It's how the chairman's ideas and what's keeping him up at night become my ideas and what's keeping me up at night. It's where you talk about setting the standard, the expectation. If there's something Dave aspires to, this is where it starts becoming real. It's kind of transferring the aspiration, the dream, down into some specific decisions you can make, strategic decisions.

"It's also a process that forces you to get outside the day-to-day desk full of things, and the mind full of things that we all have. These issues aren't new to you. But you need something that takes all these things that are in everybody's minds, that you talk about and think about, and bringing them down in a form that the whole organization can deal with."[10]

The process naturally draws together people from the different disciplines and business units. "If I want to develop a new product line, then that's the process that helps me get the people that have to do that engaged," says Bausman. "You engage, obviously, your product planning people. You engage your technology people, who can talk to you about trends. You engage your salespeople in terms of what they're seeing in the marketplace; the service people, about what the trends are in their business and what their aspirations are. You bring all these silos together in a strategic way and engage them in that process."

A key part of the Reynolds genetic code is encouraging people to stretch, and the planning mechanism helps them to do it. Says Bausman, "If my aspiration is to grow at this percentage or reach this number, and I don't know how to get there, what do I have to do to fill that gap? You make the people that have to do it work through that process. If it's not acceptable, then it's a teaching, it's a learning opportunity. It's a stretching opportunity. There's an interview process where you can decide what your opportunities are, what you need to do differently."

It helps that there's no downside risk to a career if someone falls short of the stretch goal. "You don't get paid on what you promise," says Bausman. "If you set a goal of, say, 20 percent growth and, two years later, only hit 17 percent, nobody's punished. We could take the approach of criticizing you for the 3 percent you didn't get, but we'd rather encourage people to stretch their imaginations and to identify the bigger opportunities."

Bringing the process to the other divisions during 1997, the Reynolds leaders expanded it to incorporate the "Balanced Scorecard" planning and performance management system. This specifically aims to measure and set goals for drivers of future performance, including market leadership, customer satisfaction, organizational excellence, continuous improvement, and growth performance. The Reynolds leaders expect the Balanced Scorecard to help them link pay with performance in such amorphous areas as organizational excellence. Nonfinancial criteria account for about 10 percent of senior leaders' annual bonuses, and Holmes plans to increase the proportion.

Meantime, Reynolds has set up a stock option program for all full-time and benefit-eligible part-time employees. Says Momchilov: "When Dave talks about EPS [earning per share] and creating shareholder value, and employees say, 'What does that have to do with me?'—well, now it's got something to do with practically everyone in the company."

Cultivating the Customers

Do WTFR and the Balanced Scorecard really work? Looking at the customer satisfaction component, the answer is clearly Yes. None of the attitudes and behaviors WTFR helped develop among the Reynolds people has been more important to the company's success than customer satisfaction. It's one of the company's major core competencies and competitive advantages. "We don't just talk about lifelong customers—we execute against it, it's our strategy," says Holmes. Independent surveys consistently show that Automotive Systems and Business Systems lead their industries with the highest customer satisfaction and retention ratings. (Healthcare Systems, applying the same approaches, only started its benchmarking in 1997 but was looking forward in 1998 to seeing good results.)

"In the business we're in, the ability to grow is the difference between selling a box and selling a system," says Yezbak. "It's about resolving issues, and our ability to do that depends on cultivating ongoing relationships with our customers. This is our value proposition."

The idea of customers for life is hardly an original idea—and it's meaningless boilerplate without the right kind of execution. Twenty years ago, you might have concluded that IBM had customers for life; its salespeople practically lived in customers' headquarters, ever ready to help them find uses for new products. But IBM was working from the inside out—its salespeople were there to push the company's hardware and software. Cultivating truly loyal customers is the ultimate outside-in process. It's successful in direct proportion to how intimately people understand their customers' needs, and how well they are able to convey what they've learned to the people who map segments, design products, and supply services.

Yezbak, who played a key role in developing the customer satisfaction methodology at Automotive Systems, came from Xerox where she'd been manager of quality and customer satisfaction for the integrated systems operations division. At Xerox, nothing is considered more important in meeting long-term financial goals than building customer loyalty, which the company believes can be earned only through total satisfaction of customers' needs. Yezbak brought with her that attitude, along with a host of tools and techniques for aligning an entire organization around that goal.

Yezbak allows that customer satisfaction reengineering has gotten a bad rap over the past ten years. But, she says, that's largely because it's typically a program *du jour,* layered over other programs but not driven into the genetic code. "It can all be linked to bottom-line business results—if it's pervasively the way you work," she says. "You have to walk the talk, integrate it into your mainstream business activity."

The integration at Reynolds starts with rigorous mechanisms for understanding the customers' needs and issues. They're surveyed about their satisfaction—and dissatisfaction—at every stage in their dealings with the company, from selling through ongoing usage. A Customer Satisfaction Group additionally surveys thousands of customers each year by phone; those who are dissatisfied get immediate follow-up through a closed-loop resolution process. An advisory panel of customers convenes at the Reynolds headquarters twice a year. Senior executives are expected to spend a significant part of their time with customers. There is—of course—a name for this intensive interaction: "Voice of the Customer."

All levels of employees meet regularly with their counterparts in the customers' organizations. After all, says Randy Selleck, director of customer preparation and operations support, "The customer is not just the owner of the business but every single person who uses our system." Result: In the early Nineties, he says, people in the service end of the business thought of their jobs as repairing computers. "Now they understand that their mission is to keep the customer up and running."[11]

In following up on customer surveys, the Reynolds people compare the company's methods with best practices in other industries, as well as with competitors' and their own past performance. They also interview every lost customer to find out why he or she left.

Since 1995, the company has oriented all of its people in the Creating Lifelong Customers process, using a four-hour video-based training program that managers present to their people. Managers get ongoing training in the tactical aspects at Reynolds University, the company's inhouse learning center.

Measuring ever more finely, Reynolds has most recently broken satisfaction out into "value drivers" by segment and stage of ownership. "For example, we have a pretty good idea of what our customers' value drivers are in our enterprise segment and our traditional dealer segment," says Yezbak. "We also break it down into one-year ownership, one-to-four-year, and five-to-ten, and cross-cut the information." The point is that an enterprise customer who's been dealing with Reynolds for seven years clearly values different things than the traditional dealer in the first year of operation; the goal is to be clear about what these things are.

Reynolds is working to integrate the customer information ever more tightly with budgets, planning, and strategy. "We are trying to bridge between customer satisfaction and marketing—to create a kind of combination of customer satisfaction and marketing," says Yezbak. The goal is "to link it to all of the different organizations so they can develop their value propositions by segment and stages of ownership."

Achieving targets for customer satisfaction gets equal billing with generating revenues or improving productivity. Reynolds has put a lot of effort into making information usable—"hardwiring it into the organization," as Yezbak puts it. Senior and middle managers get the results quarterly, and they're expected to act on them. They become, in the Reynolds lingo, "attribute owners." Explains Yezbak: "Attributes are the sales questions, the service questions, the training questions. In billing, for example, How satisfied are you with the accuracy and timeliness of your billing? And the vice president of finance owns these attributes."

Attribute ownership means responsibility for solving problems. "It cascades down into the organization all the way through management and individual contributors," says Yezbak. If an executive isn't on target, he or she works with the people below to improve the results. And those people are typically the ones who come up with the solutions. Says Gary Coffield, manager of customer support: "Probably 90 percent of the moves that we've made organizationally have come from the people who are out there answering the phones."[12]

Learning from Adversity

The 1997 setback slowed Reynolds' momentum, but hasn't stopped it. Toward year's end, the company broadened its pond to encompass the

United Kingdom and Europe: it paid $36 million for a 26.5 percent stake in Kalamazoo Computer Group PLC (UK-based, despite its Michigan monicker), a leading automotive dealer systems supplier. Reynolds also broke ground on the first phase of a $37 million R&D campus, located in the Dayton suburb of Kettering, among other R&D centers, advanced-technology companies, and university-related enterprises. Holmes refers to it ambitiously as "the infant stage of a Silicon Valley kind of potential."

High on Holmes's agenda for 1998 is finding yet a new pond—a fourth business where Reynolds can leverage its evolving core competencies. Why would he do that when there are still problems to be solved in the current pond? Because it takes time to identify a new pond and develop it, he says, and no company can afford to waste such time or give it away to some competitor. Holmes knows that you can't put off the search for new opportunities if you want to keep growing.

Coming after a long string of record quarters for revenues and profits, the stumble was a shock to the organization—including the thousands of employee–shareholders who saw their options suddenly underwater. But any new growth trajectory is an entrepreneurial venture, and setbacks are almost inevitable. What's important is the edge embodied in the leadership's teachable point of view—the intellectual honesty required to reevaluate actions, learn from mistakes, and move on tenaciously.

After the bad news hit, Holmes went around to each of the divisions, explaining the reasons and taking questions. Speaking from the heart, he praised the hard work that had propelled the company's growth—unimaginable just a few years earlier. He explained the plans to accelerate cost-saving measures, reiterated the importance of building shareholder value, and then talked about the lessons learned from the experience—including the need to be more flexible in planning and managing amid uncertainty. A videotape put together from these sessions was sent out as part of the Quarterly Outlook video.

"You just have to step out there and take it head-on," he says. "When you do, you can get people energized and bring out the best in the organization."

In this as in all other ways at Reynolds and Reynolds, success is directly tied to the insights people have about customer needs. Says Holmes: "When we go on a customer call, I always say, 'Guys, we're going to win one of two ways: We're going to win because we win the account or we're going to win because we gain such terrific insights into why we lost it.'

"Because another part of the genetic code here is a culture that says we're going to learn as we go and we're going to learn from our shortfalls as well as our successes—and we're probably going to get more value out of our shortfalls."

The growth journey is not a straight line that slopes smoothly upward, and it's not for the fainthearted. Growth organization leaders and their people must expect bumps, and cannot lose their nerve when they hit those bumps. It's especially bump-prone when the chosen path is the entrepreneurial push into totally new territory, which is the path Reynolds took by going into health care.

Reynolds' leaders believe the fundamentals of the strategy are right, but the jury is still out. What gives its people the confidence to persist is their collective eye on the customer, informed by total outside-in thinking, and their willingness to experiment (without betting the ranch). Learn from their experience, because the alternative to growing is certain. It is death.

CHAPTER

Can You Pass the Father Cunningham Test?

We close this book with a different kind of growth story. Three decades ago, Father William Cunningham and Eleanor Josaitis started a program to distribute food to pregnant women and infants. Today the enterprise, Focus: HOPE, is a 30-acre complex that includes everything from childcare facilities to machinist training, for-profit businesses that produce parts for the auto industry, and an advanced degree-granting institute for manufacturing engineers.

Like any good corporate growth story, this one is about leaders with ideas, values, emotional energy, and edge. Cunningham and Josaitis created their growth strategy by looking from the outside in. They constantly identified new needs, and enlarged their pond by developing new segments.

The story is also about sustainability—a genetic code so powerful that the enterprise continues stronger than ever despite the death of its charismatic founder. "Don't put my name on a building or boulevard," Father Cunningham once said. "Make my work live on." What we call the Father Cunningham test is the ultimate test of your leadership: Will the organization you built keep growing after you're gone?

On May 26, 1997, Father Cunningham died at age 67 after a protracted bout with cancer of the liver. Less than a month later, a tornado devastated Focus: HOPE. The storm caused $23 million in damage and shut down all of Focus: HOPE's activities, including production of its parts and components businesses.

Three days after the tornado, Noel Tichy and his colleague Michael Brimm arrived at 6:30 A.M. to meet with Eleanor and prepare for a day

230

of volunteer work from a Ford Motor Co. team headed by Automotive Operations president Jacques Nasser. The scene that greeted them was shocking: Roofs ripped off, windows blown out, telephone poles lying on the ground, and surrounding houses utterly destroyed. Walking up the stairs to the second floor of the old Ameritech Yellow Pages building, which Focus: HOPE had bought a couple of years earlier for a planned executive residence-style learning center, Noel ran into Eleanor. She was dressed for hard work in bluejeans and a T-shirt, a big change from her normal businesslike blue suit.

Noel was about to express his condolences when Eleanor, smiling broadly, gave him a big hug. "We did it!," she said. "We got the production line going and have not missed a customer delivery!" Then she added: "This tornado is going to be a blessing. I have always wanted to rebuild this neighborhood. Now we have the governor, the mayor, and the Feds working with us to look into how we can build new housing."

Noel thought: "Here is a 66-year-old woman who just lost her partner of 30 years, and saw a terrible natural catastrophe wreck their enterprise. But she's energized and hard at work on a new growth idea for it. We all talk about change, often devastating change, being an opportunity: Eleanor embodies this at the core. Out of destruction, she has started Focus: HOPE on a new growth trajectory."

Will your work carry on when you are gone? Will the organization regenerate? We often pose these questions in workshops with executives to get them very clearly focused on the need to teach others to be leaders. They need to understand that their legacy is in the stewardship of the people assets of their institution. The test of that stewardship is whether they have created a genetic code of continuous transformation through leaders at all levels—whether they have prepared their people to successfully create new growth trajectories.

Father William Cunningham created such an organization. Cunningham was a young priest teaching English at the Sacred Heart Seminary in 1967 when the Detroit riots erupted. Contemplating the poverty, despair, and rage that underlay them, he said: "In the terrible days of watching people be shot in front of our eyes on the street, [we felt] we had to do something."[1] He was joined by Josaitis, a suburban housewife who was one of his parishioners. Armed with studies showing that malnourished babies suffered permanent loss of brain capacity, they persuaded the Department of Health, Education, and Welfare to fund a food program for young children and mothers.[2]

Cunningham and Josaitis had plenty to feel good about. Then a marketplace reality intruded. Josaitis got a phone call one day from a woman who'd heard about the program. As Josaitis tells the story, "I went rattling on about this fabulous program for nursing mothers, and pregnant women, and babies. And then came a long, long pause. She said, 'I am 72 years old. Do I have to get pregnant before I can get some help?' "[3]

Here was an unmet need they hadn't given much thought to. But the federal money was only for young children and their mothers, so Cunningham and Josaitis hired two researchers to document the case for feeding the elderly, took the findings to Washington, and, after 32 hearings, got legislation that expanded the program.

Broadening the Pond

As successful as Cunningham and Josaitis were in serving their market, they understood that feeding people was only a palliative. In fact, they saw that hunger was a subset of a larger need, unmet by society's other institutions, for economic self-sufficiency. So long as their customers lacked training, self-esteem, and hope, they could never hold good jobs and be more than recipients of handouts. Cunningham and Josaitis redefined their pond by, in effect, creating a new value proposition for Focus: HOPE. In a phrase Cunningham was to use later, they decided to be "not in the business of saving souls but in the business of developing competitive people." (See Figure 12.1.)

In 1981, with funding help from the U.S. Department of Labor, Department of Defense, the Mott Foundation, and the Hudson-Weber Foundation, they started Focus: HOPE's Machinist Training Institute (MTI) to train students for jobs in precision machining and metalworking. They set a stretch goal: Their aim was to produce "not just adequate machinists, not even above-average machinists, but the best machinists in the world."[4] MTI graduates would not be hired as charity cases by socially conscious employers, but because they would be skilled and reliable. With a current average enrollment of about 250, MTI has graduated more than 1,500 people—armed not only with technical skills but also the self-esteem and confidence that come from meeting the program's stretch goals.

Obstacles to expansion soon arose. Young mothers who wanted to apply couldn't get child care. And finding students who were educated well enough to handle the program proved difficult. To meet those needs,

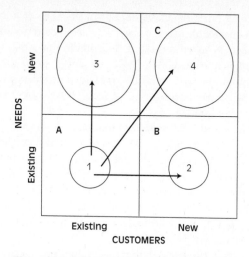

Figure 12.1 Starting with a food program for mothers and children, Focus: HOPE's leaders expanded into feeding the elderly (2). Then they broadened their pond to include the most important need society wasn't meeting for their existing and potential customers: the tools for economic self-sufficiency (3). The next step, an even larger pond in quadrant C, is training others in community development (4).

Cunningham and Josaitis organized Focus: HOPE's Center for Children. Started in 1987 as a child-care center, it is now a 26,000-square-foot facility that includes infant care, toddler care, a Montessori school program, and a before/after school program for the families of its students. Two years later they started FAST TRACK, a program that offers tutoring and remedial courses in math and language. The program has since expanded to include communication skills, computer applications, and industrial standards of discipline and personal conduct, and has graduated some 5,000 students since 1989.

A passionate speaker with a powerful message, Cunningham was able to win support from major corporations as well as government agencies. But he also invested Focus: HOPE's own human capital in the organization's growth. In 1983, MTI set up a for-profit machine shop where its graduates, along with retired machinists, could train others while producing parts for industrial customers. The venture has since grown into a quartet of enterprises whose track record would please any business leader. With sales totaling $4.6 million in 1997, they supply parts to Ford, Chrysler, GM and Detroit Diesel—and the customers aren't buying out of charity. Says Detroit Diesel president Ludwig Koci: "They are doing a terrific job for us." Focus: HOPE looks to double revenues over the next three years.

Cunningham and Josaitis realized that many MTI graduates had the potential to be much more than machinists. They also saw an unmet educational need—the need for a broader range of skills than those traditionally provided by engineering schools. They mobilized backing for their ideas from an extraordinary cross-section of the business, academic, and political communities, and in 1990 started the Center for Advanced Technologies (CAT), a unique undergraduate and graduate level engineering manufacturing program.

CAT aims at nothing less than reinventing how America teaches its manufacturing engineers. Funded to the tune of $100 million, it is partnered with the Society of Automotive Engineers and six universities: University of Detroit Mercy, Wayne State University, Lawrence Technological University, Central State University of Ohio, Lehigh University, and the University of Michigan. The departments of Defense, Labor, Education, and Commerce provide support—including, with the help of Michigan Senator Carl Levin, a $60 million special industrial grant from Defense. Cunningham and Josaitis also enlisted help from Ford, General Motors, Chrysler, Detroit Diesel, EDS, and Cincinnati Milacron. And they persuaded former GM president Lloyd Reuss to be CAT's executive dean; he has recruited numerous other retired auto executives to join.

CAT's goal is a total learning experience, one where students split their time between "real-world" manufacturing and academic pursuits. Besides design and engineering courses, the curriculum includes business administration and language training—graduates of the six-year master's degree program will be fluent in German and Japanese. Computer-based instruction takes place in a world-class electronic information center, with fully up-to-date equipment and links to the Internet. Social skills get attention, too. In the executive style dining room, students are served meals from a variety of ethnic origins. They also have to set the tables, learn manners for different cultures, and master the art of conducting appropriate business conversations.

Always looking for the next adjacent segment, Cunningham and Josaitis soon realized that their kitchen staff were developing marketable skills as chefs. Focus: HOPE has recently begun to provide culinary training as well.

Today Focus: HOPE's various operations occupy more than one million square feet of floor space in 12 buildings. More growth initiatives are pending. In addition to her goal of revitalizing housing and commerce in the neighborhood, Josaitis has global expansion in mind. She plans a 145-bed executive-quality residential learning center where individuals and teams from around the world can learn to replicate Focus: HOPE. Among the supporters are Bill Gates and Microsoft, with donations totaling $3 million, and EDS, which is donating virtual learning facilities. Ford is looking for ways of replicating aspects of the enterprise in South Africa and Brazil, and U S WEST is starting to develop a Focus: HOPE type of operation in Denver.

Decisions with Edge

Focus: HOPE's success reflects the kind of passionate, determined, committed leadership that any organization must have if it is to grow. Time and again, Cunningham and co-founder Eleanor Josaitis, looking at their enterprise from the outside in, spotted new needs to fill—and filled them. Every new problem they identified was an opportunity, every stroke of adversity a challenge to be overcome.

Like many great growth stories, Focus: HOPE's expansion may look like part of a natural progression. But things are never that easy. Cunningham and Josaitis faced tough decisions at every step. Worried supporters of the food program urged them not to start remedial education lest they spread Focus: HOPE's resources too thin. When they proposed MTI, social activists told them, "You'll never break into the auto industry." Almost everyone warned them they were reaching too far when they began to talk about the Center for Advanced Technologies. But Cunningham and Josaitis had their eye on the larger pond, and refused to settle for anything less. The calls they made exhibit the edge that distinguish growth leaders from maintainers.

And—of course—Focus: HOPE has passed the Father Cunningham test.

Could your organization pass it?

P A R T **IV**

The Handbook for Growth

Handbook

And what makes the opportunity before us so very exciting is this: never before has this company been more perfectly poised for pioneering, with a global system far more capable and far stronger than just a few short years ago. This is a business in its infancy, a true growth company with true, incomparable opportunity all over this world.

M. Douglas Ivester, Chairman, Board of Directors, and Chief Executive
Coca-Cola
February 19, 1998

GROWTH is the essence of any institution. All organizations and organisms either GROW or DIE! Growth energizes people, provides a purpose for restructuring, delivers opportunities for career enhancement, adds wealth, and is the "like to do" side of becoming a Great Brand.

In 1997, a new vision emerged for Stanley: to become one of the world's greatest brands . . . to become the Coca-Cola of the hard goods industry. Simply stated, we're going to have fun. We're going to make money. And above all, we're going to win . . . NOW.

John Trani, Chairman and Chief Executive Officer
The Stanley Works
March, 1998

Contents

Introduction

"Grow or die" has often been posed as the ultimate existential dichotomy. Not everyone will want to be quite that dramatic, but growth is clearly a key to human well-being. Psychologists have dealt with growth in their theories of personality. Abraham Maslow, for example, posited that the highest-order need culminates in a human search for self-actualization. Other theorists have effectively argued that people are energized by growing intellectually and emotionally, as well as through physical feats accomplished in sports. Growth occurs when individuals leave their comfort zones and move into a learning zone that has uncertainty, moderate stress, and opportunity for new experiences and breakthroughs. Organizations—collections of human beings striving to accomplish some common objective—become great when, collectively, the leaders have created and are perpetuating a genetic code of balanced growth.

This book has taken you on a growth journey as a leader, and has challenged your teachable point of view regarding growth by asking:

▶ What are your business ideas for bringing profitable growth to your organization?

▶ What values do you want the people in your organization to embrace, in support of your growth ideas?

▶ How will you generate, among the people in your organization, positive emotional energy around your growth ideas and values?

▶ How will you exercise the tough edge needed to make the yes-or-no decisions regarding people, investments, and strategies relative to growth?

Your teachable point of view is like a basic DNA building block. It is the key in developing the genetic code of growth in your organization.

We challenge you to incorporate these conceptual building blocks into your own teachable point of view:

1. **There is no such thing as a mature business**. Get the idea of a mature business out of your mind forever. Any company of any size in any industry—no matter how "mature" the industry—can grow, once its leaders learn how to look beyond their traditional definitions of industry and markets.

2. **Not all growth is good.** Growth at all costs, or growth for its own sake, can be a recipe for disaster. Good growth is sustainable and profitable. Don't confuse it with feverish spurts of volume that ravage earnings or steal from the future.

3. **Growth is a mentality created by a company's leaders.** It starts with the spark of a new point of view that is teachable to everyone in the company. It catches fire when everyone buys into what the leaders are teaching.

4. **Balanced growth is the key to prosperity in the twenty-first century.** Sustainable growth—growth for the long haul—requires meticulous attention to the basics: cost, quality, cycle time, productivity, continuous improvement, and all other factors that contribute to operational excellence.

5. **Growing is less risky than not growing.** You'll hear people say that growth is about taking risks. Personal risk, yes—it takes courage to stand up for new ideas. But a sustainable growth strategy, based on tightly defined customer needs, is far less risky than rearranging the furniture while your competitors grow at your expense.

This handbook is designed to help you (1) craft your own teachable point of view on growth and (2) develop the genetic code of growth for your organization.

Transformational Leadership

The goal of developing a new genetic code of growth and/or maintaining one for growth companies requires mastering revolutionary change. Bureaucracies inevitably grow complacent and inward-looking. The transformational leadership role is externally focused, with lenses pointed toward tomorrow. Andrew Grove, Chairman and former CEO at Intel, is a role model of transformational leadership. In his book, *Only The Paranoid Survive,* he describes the process of creatively destroying and remaking the Intel organization. Grove's goal was to form a new organization around new growth ideas. Our book has provided you with benchmarks created by leaders such as David Holmes at Reynolds and Reynolds; John Trani, CEO of The Stanley Works, formerly CEO of GE Medical Systems; Larry Bossidy, CEO of AlliedSignal; Eckhard Pfeiffer,

CEO of Compaq; Gary Wendt of GE Capital; Jack Welch, CEO of GE; and many others. All of these leaders embody the core requirements of transformational leadership. To join them as a leader, you must continuously lead your people through a three-act drama:

Act I. Awakening your organization to the need for change (why balanced growth is required).

Act II. Envisioning and crafting a vision of the future, and gaining your people's commitment to that vision.

Act III. Re-architecting—creatively destroying and remaking—the organization, the operating mechanisms, and the human resource systems, to fit the new vision.

The transformation drama has protagonists, antagonists, dramatic themes, and a gripping and deep plot played out over the three acts. The protagonists are the people who seek growth and set the revolutionary plot into motion. In GE's case, several dozen leaders sought to radically transform the company. Jack Welch gathered them and came to symbolize their ideas and values.

Antagonists—people who hold tightly to the company's old ideas and values—are inevitable. They must all deal with grief and deep feelings of loss as the old ways they have known disappear, and the way is cleared for new growth. Some of the antagonists must leave the company to clear the way. Eckhard Pfeiffer had to excise selectively at Compaq in 1996 and 1997, before he could form a new leadership team for new growth. The end of a corporate transformation is exhilarating; it leads to a feeling of rebirth. Then the process begins anew, and, in high-tech businesses, the repetition is increasingly frequent.

This *Handbook* is designed to help you work through your own three-act transformation as you embed a new genetic code of growth into your organization.

SECTION I
The Growth Hand You Have Been Dealt

In this section, you are asked to take a hard look at what you personally are contributing as a leader on growth: your teachable point of view, your actual experiences, and how you have developed others to grow businesses.

An important part of the hand you have been dealt is the organization you lead. What is its genetic code? Does it have a track record regarding growth?

Your role as a leader is to face reality and shape tomorrow. You cannot alter the hand you have been dealt. Your leadership will show in how you play the cards you are holding.

THIS SECTION IS A TOUGH-LOVE MIRROR TEST.

The Hand You Have Been Dealt as a Leader on Growth

As your first step in a transformation, you must come to grips with *the hand you have been dealt*. Jack Welch, General Electric's CEO, persuasively argues that leadership is demonstrated by how well you play both the personal and the organizational cards you have been dealt. You can't change history. The test of your leadership is how you take what you have and make it grow in the future.

Your first step in this *Handbook* is to candidly assess your personal growth as a leader and your organization's capability for growth. For your personal assessment, start by looking at your teachable point of view on growth and examining the personal factors that have shaped it.

Step 1. Your Teachable Point of View on Growth

As a leader, your first responsibility is to codify your knowledge. This is not an easy task. Much of what you know is tacit and inarticulate; it is implicit in your actions. Spend some time in serious thought about how to lay out your ideas and values; how you emotionally energize people about growth; and how you exercise edge regarding growth decisions.

Here are some thoughts to get you started:

▶ **Ideas.** A business starts with ideas about services or products in the marketplace. Those ideas lead the business to produce and deliver value to customers. Ultimately, those same ideas can be linked to success in the capital markets (for publicly traded companies). Leaders must be able to explain to all stakeholders how the business succeeds in creating value.

▶ **Values.** Winning organizations have leaders who can articulate values explicitly and shape values that support business ideas. Such leaders avoid using abstract terms; instead, they focus on operational values that affect the business.

▶ **Energy.** Winning leaders are motivated, and they motivate others regarding change and transition. Leaders must teach people how to energize others, face-to-face and through large-scale organizational efforts.

▶ **Edge.** Leadership is about making tough yes–no decisions. Winning leaders face reality when they make decisions about people, products, businesses, customers, and suppliers. They don't waffle, and they're willing to make decisions based on imperfect data.

This is meant to be a personal benchmark exercise. Lay out your teachable point of view as a work in progress, and modify it over time as you go through the activities in this *Handbook* and gain knowledge from interaction with others.

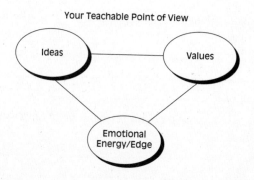

Your Teachable Point of View

Ideas

Values

Emotional Energy/Edge

A. Ideas. What are the key elements of your ideas for growth? Take some time to state them in writing.

_____

_____

_____

B. Values. What key values do you hold that support balanced growth?

_____

_____

_____

C. Emotional energy. What is your teachable point of view on how you energize others regarding balanced growth?

_____

_____

_____

D. Edge. What is your teachable point of view on how you handle the yes–no decision making around balanced growth?

_____

_____

_____

Assessing Your Teachable Point of View

▶ The major strengths of my teachable point of view on balanced growth are:

_____

_____

_____

▶ The major weaknesses of my teachable point of view on balanced growth are:

_____

_____

_____

▶ In order to improve my teachable point of view on balanced growth, my development agenda is:

_____

_____

_____

How You Developed Your Teachable Point of View on Growth

Leadership is autobiographical. Your ideas and values, the ways you energize others and deal with edge—all these were shaped by experiences throughout your life. To understand yourself as a leader and to be able to improve your capabilities in the future, it is critical that you deepen your self-understanding.

This next activity is designed to help you understand your own leadership journey line regarding your views on growth. When each team member shares his or her journey line, it is a very powerful team-building activity. We suggest that you do the activity yourself, have each of your team members do it independently, and then share the results in a workshop setting, as a way to deepen the team's mutual understanding with regard to points of view on growth.

Personal Leadership Journey Line

Life is a series of growth experiences. Not all people learn or benefit from the ups and downs of life. Winning leaders who bring successful growth to their enterprises have a capacity for taking life events and capitalizing on them. Andy Grove created a tag line, *Only the Paranoid Survive,* and was able to translate it into action and growth in all spheres of his life. In a 1994 cover story, FORTUNE reported on his handling of his own prostate cancer. Taking total charge of it as a learning experience, he worked with a dozen experts in the field and ultimately made his own decisions on treatment. He then developed a teachable point of view of the problem and shared it in FORTUNE to help others struggling with prostate cancer. Through much of his life, ranging from his days as a Hungarian immigrant through his tenure as CEO, Andy Grove's life and role as a leader are indistinguishable.

Step 2. *Your Key Growth Experiences*

Times of emotional lows often provide an effective springboard for growth. For Andy Grove, prostate cancer created a major growth opportunity. For Roger Enrico, CEO of PepsiCo, a heart attack in the early 1990s led to his launching a "Grow the Business" leadership program that has had a major impact on him as a leader and on hundreds of other key leaders at PepsiCo. Other leaders have had growth-shaping experiences as well.

Leadership Learnings from Tough Times

Coca-Cola

The late Roberto Goizueta, Coca-Cola CEO: He emigrated from Castro's Cuba with no possessions, after having grown up within a wealthy family. Reduced to a low economic status, he rejoined Coca-Cola in the United States as an R&D engineer. His growth mindset always viewed tough times as opportunities.

Compaq

Eckhard Pfeiffer, Compaq CEO: He was four years old when he and his mother left Poland right after World War II, before the Russian occupation sealed the borders. They took no possessions, and they left behind his father, who was in a prisoner-of-war camp. This experience imprinted on his mindset for life that change is an opportunity, and survivors must make changes happen first.

GE Capital

Gary Wendt, CEO of GE Capital: His pre-GE experience was gained in a number of small companies. The first job he took after getting his Harvard MBA was with a land development company in Houston, Texas, and he ended up running the company while it went bankrupt (through no fault of his own). His obsessive focus on cash and his new way of getting top-line growth go back to this early shaping experience.

Recall and list chronologically the key life events that gave you personal growth and learning. Using the framework below draw a line that captures the emotional ups and downs of your life, peaks representing emotionally positive times, valleys when you were facing negative emotional energy.

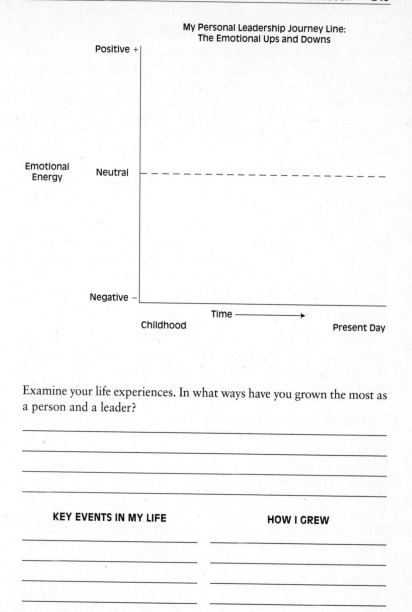

My Personal Leadership Journey Line:
The Emotional Ups and Downs

Examine your life experiences. In what ways have you grown the most as a person and a leader?

_____

_____

_____

_____

KEY EVENTS IN MY LIFE   **HOW I GREW**

_____   _____

_____   _____

_____   _____

_____   _____

Organizational Growth Time Lines

Organizations go through a variety of growth experiences reflecting new products, new markets, acquisitions, and other events. As a way to understand your organization's genetic code, identify events in the life of your organization that have resulted in growth. Plot their time line and their effect on corporate energy, following the model for your Personal Leadership Journey Line. Here are some examples to stimulate your thinking:

GM.   Alfred Sloan's concept of a car for every pocketbook, which led to the radical redefining of the auto industry, starting in the 1920s.

GE.   In the 1950s, GE launched a set of growth activities designed to accelerate top-line growth. That momentum resulted in many new areas of business (e.g., building communities and nuclear power plants) and set the stage for Jack Welch to inherit, in 1981, a huge portfolio of diverse businesses, many of them weak and poorly positioned for growth.

Intel.   Andrew Grove tells the story of betting the ranch on moving the company into microprocessing. He also talks about the development of the Intel brand as a way to get growth (i.e., the consumer branding of "Intel Inside").

PepsiCo.   Acquisitions such as Frito-Lay and restaurant chains drove growth at phenomenal rates for many decades. But the strategy, which did not emphasize *balanced* growth, also created many of the current problems facing CEO Roger Enrico, who was forced to spin-off the restaurants and revitalize the core Pepsi-Cola brand.

Do a time line of growth for your organization, reflecting the changes in total revenues over the company's lifetime (in constant dollars—guesstimate). What have been key milestones over the lifetime of your organization (new products, markets, distribution channels, acquisitions, and so on)?

My Organization's Growth Time Line

Top-Line
Revenue
(in constant
dollars)

Time ——————→

Birth of
Organization

Present Day

Analysis of the Hand My Company Has Been Dealt

1. Overall pattern:

_____

_____

_____

2. Key discontinuities (up or down):

_____

_____

_____

3. Prognosis for future growth (what you see as the future pattern of growth):

_____

_____

_____

Your Organization's Performance on Balanced Growth

Take a look at your company's pattern of sales and net income over the past few years. Do a projection of where the company is going. You should be asking yourself what these numbers say about your genetic code around balanced growth.

The price/earnings (P/E) ratio is also sending a clear message about balanced growth. The goal is to develop a genetic code that drives both top- and bottom-line improvements annually.

Step 3. Your Assessment of Your Organization— Past and Future

Actual and Projected Results for My Company
[Fill in the historical numbers and project the future estimates]

	1996	1997	1998	1999	2000	2001	2002	2003
Top Line (Sales)								
Bottom Line (Net Income)								
P/E Ratio								

What are the implications of your assessment?

_____

_____

_____

_____

_____

_____

Assess your company's leadership on *top-line capabilities,* and explain your rating:

Below Average for　　　　　　　　　　　　　**Best in Class for**
This Industry　　　　　　　　　　　　　　　**This Industry**

　　1　　　　　　2　　　　3　　　4　　　5
　　　　　　　　　　(circle one number)

Explain your ratings:

_____

_____

_____

Assess your company's leadership on *bottom-line capabilities,* and explain your rating:

Below Average for　　　　　　　　　　　　　**Best in Class for**
This Industry　　　　　　　　　　　　　　　**This Industry**

　　1　　　　　　2　　　　3　　　4　　　5
　　　　　　　　　　(circle one number)

Explain your ratings:

_____

_____

_____

SECTION II
The Growth Audit

For the leaders of an organization to achieve balanced growth, they must possess a set of critical competences. In this section, you are asked to look at the current capabilities of your leadership and project what will be required for sustained growth in the future.

A growth audit requires digging in and taking a tough look at the balanced growth capacity of your organization. What major growth levers are available? Can you assess where you are today and where you need to be in tomorrow's world? Lawrence A. Bossidy, CEO of Allied-Signal, notes that none of these activities is easy:

> We have to do a much better job at market segmentation so that we understand those markets where we can introduce niche products or broad-based products. We have to know a lot more about our customers. It takes a lot of time, attention, and digging; this is not something that is easy to do, but nonetheless it is required.

Step 1. Your Organizational Assessment/ Growth Audit

For each of the growth areas listed in the matrix on page 255, rate your organization as you see it today (Current State) and as you feel it must be if it is to be successful in the future (Desired State).

Gap Analysis. Identify the areas where your organization will have to work hardest to improve.

AREAS FOR IMPROVEMENT

_____

_____

_____

Step 2. Your Balanced Growth People Audit

Assess the capabilities of your key people to achieve balanced growth. Consider the following standards set by Jack Welch of GE. For the past several years, he has been raising the high bar at GE to have

Organizational Assessment/Growth Audit

Growth Area	Current State					Desired State				
	Weak	Moderate		World Class		Weak	Moderate		World Class	
1. Gain share										
▶ Expand reach to existing customers	1	2	3	4	5	1	2	3	4	5
2. Geography										
▶ Find new geographies (e.g., international)	1	2	3	4	5	1	2	3	4	5
3. New technology/market										
▶ Develop new technologies to open new markets	1	2	3	4	5	1	2	3	4	5
4. New distribution channels										
▶ Use alternate methods to distribute products/ services	1	2	3	4	5	1	2	3	4	5
5. Resegmentation										
▶ Identify and exploit unmet needs of customers by redefining segments	1	2	3	4	5	1	2	3	4	5
6. Services										
▶ Complement product revenues by offering services to customer base	1	2	3	4	5	1	2	3	4	5
7. Enlarging the pond										
▶ Redefine your industry	1	2	3	4	5	1	2	3	4	5

only "A" players, and to remove "C" players from the company. His teachable point of view, as reflected in the 1997 annual report is:

> [We] must raise, again, the bar of quality as it applies to ourselves. The reality is, we simply cannot afford to field anything but teams of "A" players.

> What is an "A"? At the leadership level an "A" is a man or woman with a vision and the ability to articulate that vision to the team so vividly and powerfully that it also becomes their vision.

> An "A" leader has enormous personal energy, and, beyond that, the ability to energize others and draw out their best, usually on a global basis.

An "A" leader has "edge" as well: the instinct and the courage to make the tough calls—decisively, but with fairness and absolute integrity.

As we go forward, there will be nothing but "A's" in every leadership position in this company. They will be the best in the world, and they will act to field teams consisting of nothing but "A" players. The best leaders—the "A's"—are really coaches. What coach, with any instinct or passion for winning, would field an Olympic swimming or gymnastics team, or a Super Bowl team, that wasn't made up of the absolute best available? In the same vein, what business leader worthy of the name would consider fielding a team with anything but the very best, the "A" players?

As you do the balanced growth people audit, begin developing your list of "A," "B," and "C" players. To sustain balanced growth, you need to be on the same journey that Welch is on, seeking only "A" players who are benchmarked externally, not just against the internal best.

List all of the key people you work with, and assess their actual track records for contributing to balanced growth. Even though many of them may not have had profit-and-loss responsibility, do a guesstimate of their performance in both dimensions (top line and bottom line) over a two- to three-year period. As the leader who must develop balanced growth leaders, you have to be the coach who changes your team's mindset and behavior. As Larry Bossidy, CEO of AlliedSignal, points out:

Growth is a mindset, it is an ability. When people say "I can't grow my market," I say, "You know, it is you, not the market." So I have to set the stage; I have to set a belief that growth is something you can achieve and it is only up to us to make it happen.

Plot the performance of each of your key people on the matrix on page 257.

To close any performance gaps, review the records of each of your key people. Create an action plan for getting them either out of the company or moving toward the high/high cell.

**Balanced Growth People Audit:
Plot the Names of Your Team**

The Leader's
Top-Line
Growth
Performance
(Revenue)
Over the
Last Two
Years

	High		
Medium			
Low			
	Low	Medium	High

The Leader's Bottom-Line Performance Over
the Past Two Years (Assets Utilization)

PERSON	ACTION PLAN
_____	_____
_____	_____
_____	_____
_____	_____
_____	_____
_____	_____
_____	_____
_____	_____
_____	_____
_____	_____

SECTION III
Changing the Genetic Code to Balanced Growth

In this section, we will help you plan a process for massive change in your genetic code, to ensure that you have a code that drives balanced growth. The process consists of:

▶ **Step 1**: State clearly and simply why balanced growth is needed.

▶ **Step 2**: Facing reality—there is, in any organization, resistance to balanced growth.

▶ **Step 3**: Articulating the leader's teachable point of view on balanced growth.

▶ **Step 4**: Having the top team collectively wrestle with their teachable point of view on balanced growth, and start leading the transformation effort down through the organization.

▶ **Step 5**: Completing the action-learning transformation process via projects, development, and selection or reassignment of key people.

In this section of the *Handbook*, we lay out a large-scale effort for altering the genetic code of an organization. We assume that, in order to succeed, you will have to take on the dramatic role of a transformational leader and will be willing to creatively destroy the old organization and build a new one that fits the new order of things.

Leaders have to articulate the case for change and explain why balanced growth is required—or, in the case of companies such as Intel and Compaq, explain why balanced growth in the future requires quantum changes now. Along with all its great upsides, growth also brings massive change and uncertainty, which unleash the human dynamics of resistance to change. Awakening an organization to the need for balanced growth and working through the inevitable resistance are among the toughest aspects of a transformation. Being a transformational leader means facing resistance, struggling with antagonists and protagonists, and, ultimately, building a new genetic code.

Variations of this action-learning methodology, first developed at General Electric Medical Systems (GEMS), have been used by Northern Telecom, Royal Bank of Canada, Shell Oil and Royal Dutch/Shell, Ford

Motor Company, Ameritech, and U S WEST. The process enables the leadership to drive rapid change while simultaneously developing a new teachable point of view on balanced growth.

The GEMS Global Leadership Program is a very useful model for transforming a genetic code to balanced growth. GE Medical Systems started its journey in the late 1980s. By 1987, it had become the dominant domestic player, comparable to Siemens in Europe and Toshiba in Japan. John Trani, the CEO, was given the challenge to become "the world's unquestioned leader in diagnostic imaging." To accomplish this, he had to transform a U.S.-oriented business that was providing state-of-the-art technology in a protected domestic industry into a global business that was both cost-competitive and growth-oriented.

In 1987, GE Medical Systems acquired a French medical imaging business, Thomson CGR, and 75 percent of Japan's Yokogawa Medical Systems. Building one global growth-oriented company required integrating about 6,000 French employees with 2,000 Japanese and 10,000 Americans.

This massive integration of three highly diverse cultures, along with the radical transformation of the business itself, makes GEMS a very robust model for other transformations. The chart on page 260 summarizes the plan that CEO John Trani and his top team worked out for the Global Leadership Program.[1]

The essence of the Global Leadership Program is a belief that the best individual and organizational development occurs simultaneously. The core concept is "compressed action learning." The teams are given real problems to solve. They have coaches and structured assignments so that as they work on the real problems, they are also self-consciously working on their leadership skills, team skills, and global networking skills.

Throughout this section of the *Handbook,* we will draw on the GEMS experience to illustrate the basic process for reengineering the genetic code of an organization.

Step 1. The Case for Balanced Growth

The work in the previous sections of the *Handbook* can be summarized very simply for colleagues at any level, as well as for Wall Street and the press: What is the case for radical change regarding balanced growth in your organization?

GEMS Transformation

```
┌─ ┌─────────────────────────────────────┐
│  │  The Global Environment             │
│  └─────────────────────────────────────┘
│       ▶ Olympic-Class Players Only
│       ▶ Standards Tougher/Faster
│
│       ┌─────────────────────────────────┐
│       │  The Global Playing Field       │
│       └─────────────────────────────────┘
│            ▶ Globalization of Industry
│            ▶ Cost Competition (Siemens)
│            ▶ GE Historically U.S.-Based
│
│            ┌──────────────────────────────┐
│            │  GEMS Mission/Strategy        │
│            └──────────────────────────────┘
│                 ▶ Mission: Become the Unquestioned Leader in
│                   Diagnostic Imaging
│                 ▶ Strategies: Globalization • Cost
│                   Competitiveness • Installed Base
│                   Expansion • Technical Preeminence Growth
│
│                 ┌──────────────────────────┐
│                 │  GEMS Organization        │
│                 └──────────────────────────┘
│                      ▶ Loose/Flexible Organization
│                      ▶ Blend of Hard/Soft Operating Mechanisms
│                      ▶ Global Networks
│
│  ┌──────────────────────────────────────────────────────┐
└─ │                   GEMS Response                        │
   │ ▶ February 1988—Overall Strategy Designed to Launch:   │
   │   —Global Leadership Program, March 1988               │
   │   —Middle Management Program, Summer 1988              │
   └──────────────────────────────────────────────────────┘
```

GEMS Case Illustration. John Trani, former CEO of GEMS, confronted his group with a competitive cost disadvantage, along with terrible delivery times, sloppy global coordination, and other operating problems. The mission of being number one in the world meant having to globalize faster and better than both Toshiba and Siemens, while radically accelerating the growth trajectory.

What is your case for balanced growth?

_____

_____

_____

Step 2. Dealing with Resistance to Balanced Growth

Simply making the case for change does not result in action. In fact, we know with absolute clarity that sounding the alarms for change results in the natural human response—resistance to change. This is not true of *all* people, but the vast majority will have some form of resistance. We advise you to start with a clear understanding of where you will face resistance.

GEMS Case Illustration.   John Trani faced massive resistance. Technically, it included the skills and habits of domestically focused engineers who had made their careers by selling state-of-the-art technology in protected markets in the United States, Europe, and Japan. They resisted becoming globally focused. The multifaceted political resistance to change included: the balance of power among the American, European, and Japanese managers, and resistance from the managers in the two acquired companies (Thomson CGR and Yokogawa Medical Systems), the marketing managers, and the technology-dominated old organization. Culturally, there were mindsets that had a domestic focus, were non-customer-oriented, and resistant to change.

1. Technical Resistance to Balanced Growth

Habit and Inertia. In large successful enterprises like GE, Royal Dutch/Shell, and IBM, the managers had mastered a set of bureaucratic slow-growth traditions. At GE, for example, Jack Welch had to teach and coach managers out of a complacency that had been deeply ingrained in the company for almost a hundred years. GE had reflected the GDP growth of the United States; it sold turbines, light bulbs, appliances, and other consumer products to the U.S. populace. Even though Welch started teaching growth in 1981, he was still at it, in new ways, in the late 1990s, trying to get his total company to understand that it was a global service company with products, not a global product company with some services.

Resistance to balanced growth due to habit and inertia in your organization:

_____

_____

_____

Fear of the Unknown. At Compaq, there was much fear in 1997 when Eckhard Pfeiffer started a new growth trajectory aimed at transforming the PC maker into a full-line computer company.

Resistance to balanced growth due to fear of the unknown in your organization:

_____

_____

_____

Prior Investment. A tremendous amount was invested in training people to do things the old "GE way" or the old "Compaq way." Whenever a new growth trajectory is introduced, people justifiably resist because of the sunk costs in human capital.

Resistance to balanced growth due to prior investment in your organization:

_____

_____

_____

2. Political Resistance to Balanced Growth

Growth disrupts the political system of the organization. As seemingly positive and exciting as it should be to everyone, it leads to massive realignment of resources, career opportunities, and rewards. Human nature tells us, over and over again, to expect resistance. It comes in a number of forms.

> Microsoft's earlier shift from a set of business ideas built around the PC to growth through dominant operating systems has recently given way to a totally new set of ideas built on dominating the Internet and acquiring new companies, new services, new alliances, and so on.

> Compaq's new growth strategy to become a full-line computer company has already led to acquisition of Tandem and Digital, as well as many new alliances. The transformation to this new set of growth ideas has resulted in tremendous political resistance and change, starting at the top. CEO Eckhard Pfeiffer sent several of his key executives home, to make way for a new team aligned with the new growth trajectory.

> GE's shift from its power systems, jet engine, and medical imaging businesses to an aftermarket service growth trajectory has resulted in many acquisitions, new alliances, and career and resource allocations to support the transformation.

THREATS TO POWERFUL COALITIONS. In the three examples described above, the dominant coalitions in Microsoft, Compaq, and GE were identified with the old growth trajectory; thus, most employees perceived the new trajectory as a threat to their career, their turf, and their power.

Resistance to balanced growth due to threats to powerful coalitions in your organization:

_____

_____

_____

RESOURCE LIMITATIONS AND TRADEOFFS. In 1998, GE set on a path to squeeze even more costs out of its business. There was massive restructuring and a strong drive, led by Jack Welch, to prepare for a disinflationary environment. Simultaneously, Welch was pushing for much greater investment in the new growth trajectory, in which GE's manufacturing businesses would shift to a service company. Resource allocation tradeoffs led to political resistance.

Resistance to balanced growth due to resource allocation tradeoffs in your company (List the specific tradeoffs, who will resist them, and why):

_____

_____

_____

INDICTMENT OF LEADERSHIP. In organizations that must be radically changed to launch a new growth trajectory, there is a very high probability that the leaders of the business will feel either personally indicted or defensive because they failed in the past to find the growth. This often leads to denial and ultimately having to remove the leaders, as Eckhard Pfeiffer did at Compaq or as Jack Welch did at GE in the mid-1980s, when many of his business heads could not last through the first round of his revolution. Some leaders are able to change themselves and take responsibility for having failed to achieve growth earlier. These are courageous, changeable leaders with high integrity.

Resistance to balanced growth due to indictment of leadership problem in your company (Who and why):

_____

_____

_____

3. Cultural Resistance to Balanced Growth

Developing a new culture that embraces growth and gets people excited and mobilized around growth is tough. It requires a new teachable point of view as the key building block of the new genetic code. The old teachable point of view—"We are in a mature business," "The business is cyclical, so we can't sustain growth," "There are no new ideas for growth in our industry," and so on—must be supplanted.

RESISTANCE TO BALANCED GROWTH DUE TO OLD MINDSETS.   In many industries and companies, especially those that grew up in an oligopolistic
tradition (autos, telecommunications, oil, or banking), leaders get locked
into a teachable point of view that has a mindset of "This is how we
have done it forever." The lack of a cross-selling customer orientation among U S WEST frontline people came about because, as a telephone company with its genetic code rooted in the old parent AT&T,
U S WEST did not worry about growth. Its concern was "universal service"—providing everyone with a plain dial tone. Even after more than a
decade of explosive telecommunications growth, these old mindsets are
still deeply embedded.

In the auto industry, the mindset is still "the next big product,"
and all the excitement centers on the next breakthrough car. In reality,
U.S. auto companies are selling cars at a loss, and the action is with the
customer and the adjacent segments: parts, repair, insurance, and other
services. The most difficult and subtly embedded resistance to growth is
cultural, and the shared norms are vices.

Resistance to balanced growth due to old cultural mindsets in your
organization:

_____

_____

_____

RESISTANCE TO BALANCED GROWTH DUE TO A SENSE OF SECURITY.
Companies may fail to alter the genetic code on growth because of a
false sense of security based on past or current performance. An auto
company or an oil company may have record net income and, ignoring
the fact that its price/earnings ratio is below the market average, may act
as if future performance is secure.

Resistance to balanced growth due to a false sense of security in your
organization:

_____

_____

_____

Fighting Resistance

Premise 1.   Much of the resistance to balanced growth resides in the chain of command because people's vested interests are at stake.

To counteract the resistance, you must:

▶ Stir up the total populace and begin developing new leaders for the new regime.

▶ Create a new set of values and templates.

▶ Invent mechanisms for socializing the total workforce around balanced growth.

Premise 2.   Transformational leaders overturn the current system and replace it with one of their own devising. They do not rely on the chain of command to bring about the quantum change in the genetic code. They literally grab the police, control the media, and implement the education system, much as Jack Welch did at GE.

Grabbing the Police

The staff functions of finance and human resources are historically the guardians of the "old way." At GE, Welch has successfully worked with Dennis Dammerman, the head of finance, to continuously use finance as a shaper of the new genetic code, new measures, and new partnering with the line organization. The audit staff consists of business-focused young professionals who work on growth issues. The same change has occurred with human resources, which drives both the Crotonville Leadership Development Institute agenda and the total company Six-Sigma training program. All professional employees will receive training by the end of 1999, at a cost of over $200 million a year. These training sessions support the change in the genetic code.

How can your organization grab the police to support the balanced growth agenda?

_____

_____

_____

_____

Controlling the Media

Transformational leaders take control of all their own media, both internally and externally: pronouncements by the Board, communications with security analysts, releases to the news media, or internal speeches. Jacques Nasser at Ford has a weekly "Let's chat on e-mail" message, which shapes the communication for the company and strongly reinforces growth. Larry Bossidy at AlliedSignal uses "town hall" meetings with workers all over the company, as well as skip-level breakfasts, to enhance other channels of communication. The point he makes is: This is not a delegated activity.

How can you and your organization use the media to enhance the balanced growth agenda?

_____

_____

_____

_____

_____

Implementing Education

Transformational leaders shape the training and development curriculum and require all leaders at all levels to teach. At GE, the Six Sigma training program is taught by over 1,500 line leaders, who take several-year assignments to be "black belt" trainers of others. At Ford, Jacques Nasser had had his top 1,000 managers teach all salaried employees on business leadership. The focus is on shareholder value and growth, and real projects are tied to the learning.

How can you and your organization use education programs to enhance the balanced growth agenda?

_____

_____

_____

_____

_____

Step 3. The Leader's Teachable Point of View on Balanced Growth

GEMS Case Illustration—John Trani's Teachable Point of View on Balanced Growth

BUSINESS IDEAS:
- ▶ Globalization
  - ▶ Cost competitiveness
  - ▶ Installed base expansion
  - ▶ Technical preeminence/growth
  - ▶ Emerging markets
  - ▶ Shift to service
- ▶ Organizational Form
  - ▶ Loose/flexible organization
  - ▶ Blend hard/soft operating mechanisms
  - ▶ Global teams and networks

VALUES:
- ▶ Global Mindsets
- ▶ Global Leadership Skills
- ▶ Global Teamwork
- ▶ Customer-Driven Competitiveness

John Trani spent considerable time on this outline in early 1988. His efforts culminated in a three-day offsite meeting with a faculty team made up of the authors and two of our colleagues: Michael Brimm, a professor at INSEAD, and Hiro Takeuchi, a professor at Hitotsubashi University. We worked with John Trani to clarify his business ideas, his values, and how he would energize his workforce to fulfill the teachable point of view he had articulated. He also spent time on edge—what the tough yes–no decision would be around people, products, services, distribution channels, and so on.

Step 4. Top Team Teachable Point of View

GEMS Case Illustration. At the core of the global leadership system is the top management team. Its executives need to lead and guide the process while also striving to be good role models for global managers. When we started, the GEMS top team was not prepared for this task. The team had new members; there was a great deal of provincialism—walls, barriers, and interpersonal conflicts abounded; and they did not have a common vision of where to take the business or how to get sustained balanced growth.

John Trani had each of them do some prework: Write (in March 1987) a FORTUNE article dated 1990, for an issue that would feature GEMS on the cover as the world's unquestioned number-one medical imaging company. John asked them to craft the article that they would like to be reading about the company in the future, regarding sales, profitability, products, distribution channels, services, organizations. The article also included the story of how GEMS transformed itself from 1997 to 2000. The articles were written and turned in to us to analyze prior to the session; they were also made available to each of the team members to read ahead of time.

A three-day workshop was held with the team at the Wyndham Hotel outside of Chicago. The first part of the session was spent on wrestling with the vision for GEMS. There were different opinions on how globalization would take place, what the balance of products vs. services would be, what markets would get penetrated through what tactics, and so on. The prework identified where each person's thinking was and, after a day of work on the vision, the group began to gel on a collective teachable point of view. They were then able to begin to figure out what key strategic actions were needed to implement the change. This work led to a set of strategic decisions regarding the distribution of products among the design and manufacturing facilities. For example, the United States would have manufacturing responsibility for premium CAT Scan and Magnetic Resonance products, as well as certain X-ray products. The Asian pole would design and manufacture other CT and MRI products and a variety of ultrasound products. Other operating issues that had to be sorted out included integration of the functions of marketing, financial reporting, and human resources.

Seven key areas that would accelerate the transformation of the genetic code of GEMS were identified:

1. **New technology development**—how to beat Siemens and Toshiba in coming up with breakthrough technology.

2. **Competitive cycle time**—how to beat Siemens and Toshiba in the speed of product development on a global basis.

3. **Competitive analysis**—how to build an outside-in capacity, throughout the organization, for making competitor intelligence an obsession with everyone and getting information shared throughout.

4. **Worldwide cardiology market**—how to transform the concept of one of the company's most important markets as being global, not multidomestic.

5. **Worldwide product planning process**—how to design a global process for product planning, recognizing that Thomson CGR and Yokogawa Medical Systems had just been acquired.

6. **Global careers in GEMS**—how to merge three domestic companies (one European, one Japanese, one American) and the domestic careers involved. A global company with global careers was needed fast.

7. **Product quality/Customer satisfaction**—how to fix some pretty awful quality problems in the United States and Europe, and how to be the best in the world—fast!

The top team owned these seven areas, framed projects, and then formed global teams from among the top fifty-five managers worldwide. The Global Leadership Program (GLP) was built around the projects; six or seven managers were assigned to each. Person-by-person, cross-functional teams of French, Japanese, and American employees were formed. They decided whom they wanted to work with and why. The top team was forced to decide what networks they wanted to create for the future, which team members they wanted to stretch outside of their function, and how much expertise they needed on each team.

The top team members became coaches to teams that were outside of their own area of responsibility, which meant that they, too, had to stretch, grow, and coach, not take over.

HOW WILL YOU ENGAGE YOUR TOP TEAM?

A. PREPARATION WORK:

_____

_____

_____

B. WORKSHOP DESIGN:

_____

_____

_____

C. PROJECT FRAMING AND PARTICIPANT ASSIGNMENT:

_____

_____

_____

Step 5. The Global Leadership System—Compressed Action Learning

GEMS Case Illustration.   Over a four-year period, four programs, involving about fifty-five participants each, worked through twenty-eight projects. The top team taught and was actively involved throughout.

An overview of the process is laid out on page 272.[2]

Stage 1 was a five-day workshop to build the teams, deal with the GEMS global vision and strategy, and launch the projects.

Stage 2 was work on the projects, while team members also carried out their full-time responsibilities in their respective roles. They coordinated via phone, fax, electronic mail, videoconferences, and face-to-face meetings. At the halfway point of Stage 2, all the teams met with the faculty for three days in Japan to work on their projects, their global processes, their team skills, and networking.

Stage 3 was the final stage of developing implementation strategies for each of the projects in the program. Real decisions were made as to what would get implemented, and people were asked to make major resource commitments. CEO John Trani and the top team made the final commitments. In addition, the total group assessed learnings from the process and extracted best global practices to disseminate to others at GEMS.

The new teachable point of view on balanced growth was ingrained in the top several hundred leaders, altering forever the genetic code of GEMS.

Program Overview

Timeline

0

> *Prework*
> Readings, Data and Leadership Feedback Collection: Extensive work framing and packaging projects by the Global Leadership Program (GLP) staff and faculty.

> *Stage 1: 5-day Workshop*
> Fundamental concepts: Globalization, Cross-Cultural Awareness, Teamwork, Networking. Project teams established, initial work plane set.

> Interim Period 1: 2 team meetings, 1 video conference. Project work by teams in conjunction with day-to-day job responsibilities.

> *Stage 2: 3-day Workshop*
> Check progress on the projects, as well as process within the teams. Make midcourse adjustments.

> Interim Period 2: 1 team meeting. Teams prepare final recommendations on projects.

> *Stage 3: 3½-day Workshop*
> Review achievements/recommendations. Commitment process with all participants and the GEMS Group Staff; Implementation and action plans committed to. Global learning and personal action plans.

> *Stage 4: Followup*
> Ongoing monitoring of project implementation.

9 months

Stage 1

Day 1	Day 2	Day 3	Day 4	Day 5
Opening GEMS Vision Operating Mechanisms Team Project Introduction	Global Issues Leadership Feedback and Challenges Global Mindset Team Building	Cross-Culture Senaltivity Leadership and Changes Launch Project Work	Project Work Testing High-Performing Teams Project Work	Feedback to Team Members Closing Session Adjourn

Stage 2

Day 1	Day 2	Day 3
Opening	Team-on-Team Counsulting Project Feedback	Project Feedback Action Planning by Team

Stage 3

Day 1	Day 2	Day 3	Day 4
Opening How We Will Work	Projects Commitment Process	Projects Commitment Process	Projects Commitment Process Best Practices Feedback to Team Members Closing Celebration

Altering Your Genetic Code, Using Compressed Action Learning

The fundamental building blocks incorporated into the GEMS approach are outlined on pages 273–274.[3] Incorporate them into your design for altering your genetic code.

STAGE 1 DESIGN:

_____

_____

_____

STAGE 2 DESIGN:

_____

_____

_____

STAGE 3 DESIGN:

_____

_____

_____

Fundamental Building Blocks of the Global Leadership Program

The Global Leadership Program (GLP) is both a lever for transforming GEMS and a powerful leadership experience. A unique set of building blocks, "social technologies," are used in GLP to achieve the results. There are five primary goals for GLP:

1. Deliver on the global projects—to make changes in GEMS.
2. Develop "global mindsets."
3. Develop "global leadership" skills.
4. Develop "global team skills."
5. Develop "global networks."

Each of the major building blocks is described on page 274, along with the impact it has on each of the five goals.

The GLP is delivered by creating a temporary system—that is, building a social organization with its own structure, leadership, and values. Compressed action learning puts individuals and teams under intense time and performance pressures. They must deliver strategic change to GEMS, while acquiring new skills and immediately using them to deliver on the projects.

Impact Scale

○ = Little or no impact

◐ = Moderate impact

● = Strong impact

Building Blocks	Global Projects	Global Mindset	Global Leadership	Global Team	Global Network
GEMS Top Team Leadership: Ownership of the projects, selection and sponsorship of participants, and full involvement in the commitment process.	●	●	●	●	●
Cross-Cultural Faculty: Multicultural, multilingual, and multidisciplinary faculty leading the process.	◐	●	●	●	●
Coaching Role: Each team has a process consultant—someone selected and trained from the previous GLP—who coaches the team.	●	◐	◐	●	◐
Process Learning: Team-building activities, including "Outward Bound," learning about high-performing teams, systematic attention to feedback for each other.	●	●	●	●	●
Learning Feedback Loops: Collection of data and feedback to GLP participants: (1) survey pre-GLP (self and others' ratings of global leader behavior); (2) team members provide feedback (3) coaches give feedback; (4) another team analyzes and feeds back data; (5) research team collects data and feeds back as part of program.	◐	◐	●	●	◐
Commitment Processes: Throughout GLP, individuals, teams, and the total group actively and publicly use processes for contracting and making "who, what and when" commitments.	●	○	●	◐	◐
Concepts/Ideas: The GLP faculty present participants with new conceptual tools dealing with GEMS global strategy, global operating mechanisms, time-based competitiveness, process loss, change processes, and leadership.	◐	●	●	◐	◐

SECTION IV
Outside-In Behavior

In this section, you will wrestle with the key behavioral change required, if a critical mass of people in your organization is to develop sustainable trajectories of growth. You will work on how you, the leader, can resolve the following:

▶ No more inside-out thinking.

▶ How to frame needs and customers.

▶ Unleashing creativity—ideas for growth trajectories.

The fundamental leadership challenge is to turn thinking upside down. The traditional business view is represented as:

YOUR COMPANY ⟶ YOUR CUSTOMER ⟶ THE FINAL USERS

The organizational behavior that ensues is: we produce something; we sell it to our customers; our customers sell it to the final users. This schematic leads people to think in terms of a set of assets they have (their core competences, a brand name, wide distribution), and then try to build on those assets. People look for ways of selling more, which leads them to see the future in terms of present-day operational technical thinking. They think along the following lines: "I'm in this industry. Where is this industry going, and how can I make more money out of it?" This was the IBM view with the mainframe mindset of the 1980s, the Sears view of mature retailing, and the DEC view of minicomputers. Ken Olsen, the founder and former CEO of DEC, once dismissed PC's as "toys." He was obviously looking from the inside out.

Your leadership challenge is to turn the old schematic around. The following flow is the new way of thinking:

THE FINAL USERS ⟶ YOUR CUSTOMERS ⟶ YOUR COMPANY

This starts a different set of behaviors and thought patterns. As a leader, you are looking at the drivers of change—often radical change. You are looking at *needs*. What do people out there in the real world need? How are their needs changing? From this standpoint, what you make and sell is subject to a new set of questions. Do the changes mean that what we're producing today is on its way to being obsolete, or a subset of some new need? What's a different way of doing it? How can we meet the needs better than anyone else? Can we create new needs?

Growth starts with looking at your company from the perspective of your once and future customers. What's happening out there?

Step 1. Symptoms of Inside-Out Thinking

Take some time to assess how much inside-out behavior there is in your organization.

1. **Personal examples of inside-out behavior.** What actions have you personally taken that exhibited inside-out behavior and were or could have been detrimental to the growth of your company?

_____

_____

_____

2. **Other leaders' actions.** List examples of actions others have taken that exhibited inside-out behavior that was detrimental to the growth of your company.

_____

_____

_____

Shifting to Outside-In Behavior

Here are some examples of companies and leaders who have effected growth through outside-in thinking and behavior.

Taco Bell. During the 1980s, Taco Bell CEO John Martin was able to continuously redefine his chain's market or pond. Initially, Taco Bell viewed itself as being in the Mexican fast-food business. Martin's first expansion moved Taco Bell into the quick-service restaurant business, competing with all other fast-food chains (from pizza to burgers). The next expansion of scope came when Taco Bell redefined itself as being in "the business of feeding people." This definition forced Taco Bell to reexamine its distribution channels; they were expanded to include many more points of access, such as stalls and kiosks in airports, malls, convenience stores, and high school and college cafeterias. As a result, Taco Bell broadened its market from $80 billion to $800 billion, and the company is doing all it can to capture a greater share of that larger market. Profits rose almost 300 percent from 1984 to 1993.

Nike.   In 1984, Nike had about one-third of the U.S. athletic foot-wear market. In this same year, Nike learned an invaluable business lesson: in a blindsiding move, Reebok cut Nike's market share by half. The cause: segmentation of the market. Reebok had quickly risen to new heights of success by segmenting the athletic shoe market—specifically, designing shoes for women's aerobics. Learning from the success of its competitor, Nike went on to define segments and create products for the segments in basketball, tennis, cross-training, and aquatic footwear. Today, it has half of the U.S. athletic footwear market, and is expanding around the world.

Nike has broadened its pond even more by moving into apparel, accessories, and retail stores. Anything that can be associated with fitness is Nike's new market. Of the total industry sales, estimated at over $100 billion, Nike's share today amounts to a mere 12 percent. In 1998, Nike has been redefining itself again, to ward off attacks by Adidas and other competitors.

Chrysler (Minivan).   Lee Iacocca created the minivan by examining the market from the outside in. He noticed that a small but significant number of people were using commercial vans for domestic hauling. He also noticed that station wagon sales were flat or declining. What did this indicate about Chrysler's future customers? Families were growing, and more and more people were having trouble fitting all the kids, the dog, and the 4 × 8 sheets of plywood into a car. The solution was to design a vehicle that handled like a car but had the capacity of a light truck. The result was the minivan, and family transportation has never been the same since. In 1998, Lexus is redefining the market with a hybrid between a luxury car and a sport utility vehicle.

Target.   Target CEO Bob Ulrich was able to identify the needs of retail customers and position Target to capitalize on those needs. What did he notice? Many Wal-Mart and other discount retail customers wanted merchandise that was just a cut above the quality and service available at Wal-Mart. This is exactly where Target positioned itself: a cut above Wal-Mart, but still with low prices. Target also provided a higher quality of service and a nicer in-store image than other discount retailers. Target strongly positioned itself to go after Wal-Mart's slightly more affluent customers, even making Target stores easy to find for Wal-Mart customers by placing them near Wal-Mart locations.

Coca-Cola. Faced with the soft-drink market, which everyone *knew* was "mature," Roberto Goizueta, shortly after taking over as CEO, asked his managers a simple question: What was the per-capita daily consumption of *fluids* by the 4.4 billion people in the world? The answer was: Sixty-four ounces. His next question was: What was the daily per-capita consumption of Coca-Cola? The answer was: Less than two ounces. Suddenly, managers realized that their competition was not the other soft drinks; it was all the other fluids in the world. This simple realization played a large role in making the threatened market leader in soft drinks one of the greatest market value creators ever.

GE Capital. In one of what Gary Wendt refers to as "dreaming sessions," his managers came to him with projected growth rates of about 20 percent in the truck-leasing business. As the managers were detailing the specifics of their position, Wendt noticed that they kept mentioning Ryder and other truck-leasing companies as competitors. He then had the realization that much of the trucking market was done by individuals, not by the Ryders or the GE Capitals of the business. He then posed a question to his managers: How could they capture the business of the individuals who did the trucking themselves? The result was a smaller share of the larger market, but the growth rate of GE Capital's truck-leasing business more than doubled the 20 percent that the managers had initially projected.

Step 2. Changing the Mindset—Defining Needs from the Outside In

The key from the examples above is finding opportunity in change. As a leader, you must be able to:

▶ **Look outside for discontinuities in the environment.** What are some of the discontinuities you should be focusing on?

_____

_____

_____

▶ **Define the needs that the discontinuities create for existing or new customers.** What needs do the discontinuities create?

_____

_____

_____

▶ **Match the needs to your strengths.** Which needs match which strengths?

_____

_____

_____

Step 3. Defining a Sustainable Growth Trajectory

The outside-in matrix shown below is your conceptual tool for outside-in thinking. As described in the text chapters, it gives you not only a framework for looking at the world of opportunity in a totally new light, but also a teachable point of view for mobilizing others to think outside-in.

Needs are always changing, and new ones are arising. But what is a need? What do people in your marketplace want? Once you've pinned

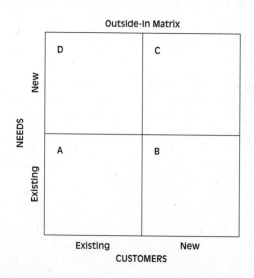

Outside-In Matrix

that information down, your task becomes strikingly simple. But until then, it is usually not obvious, even to a customer.

Do not limit your thinking by viewing yourself as being in one industry or another. In an industry with a traditional definition—aerospace, banking, retailing, semiconductors, software, utilities, and so on—the industry is the denominator of goals and core competencies.

That's the wrong denominator today. In this age of deregulation and the Internet, of manufacturers segueing into services and selling their expertise, players in different industries are realigning. Industries are crossing over into each other and reshaping the game for everyone.

▶ What is your traditional industry definition?

_____

_____

_____

▶ What are some possible crossovers in the future?

_____

_____

_____

Examples of Growth in Each Cell of the Matrix

Even though the most desirable outcome of outside-in thinking is growing the pond, there is much growth to be had in every cell of the matrix.

Quadrant A.   Companies like Rubbermaid, Procter & Gamble, and Gillette get continuing growth from their universe of existing customers with existing needs because they're constantly resegmenting markets, and learning to fulfill needs in innovative ways while keeping costs down.

▶ What are the growth opportunities for you in quadrant A (existing customers with existing needs)?

_____

_____

_____

Quadrant B. Michael Dell started by selling computers directly to companies, then expanded into the consumer market. Coca-Cola expanded to new customers by going global.

▶ What are ways that you can grow with existing needs and new customers?

_____

_____

_____

Quadrant C. Technology is often the driver in meeting new needs for new customers. Motorola launched its cellular phone business with a huge bet on an unproven need in a market it had never served. Hewlett-Packard generates growth by moving into adjacent segments—from printers to computers to fax machines and so on.

▶ What are ways that you can grow with new customers by meeting new needs?

_____

_____

_____

Quadrant D. Meeting new needs for existing customers usually allows the quickest breakout from a mature market. In 1994, GE Power Systems had half of the approximately $20 billion world market for power-plant gas turbines, a sterling reputation, strong relationships with the CEOs of major utilities—and a business that was suddenly going nowhere. An acquisition of a European company, Nuovo Pignone, opened up some $5–10 billion of new market segments in the oil and gas industry (Quadrant C). But the big challenge of outside-in thinking was to look at the GE franchise, the 11,000 units worldwide in their installed base. GE found that the pond could be enlarged to $38 billion—the total of power-plant equipment and service expenditures worldwide. To exploit these opportunities, the CEO of Power Systems, Bob Nardelli, and his team created a service company and allocated 30 percent of the best engineers to developing service opportunities. They nailed down some $1.4 billion of revenue commitments for long-term service contracts in the $18 billion pond.

▶ What are ways that you can grow with existing customers by meeting new needs?

_____

_____

_____

By early 1998, Nardelli had taken the biggest step in redefining the pond. He said: "Let's define our playing field as the $700 billion energy industry." Before, the pond had been pretty well limited to power plants. The new pond would include everything from wellhead to customer. This became the GE Power Systems guiding motto. (See page 283.)

The new pond opened the door to developing all sorts of adjacent segments, such as Whole Energy Grid Management, a joint venture with Harris.

▶ What are ways that you can radically alter your pond? What is your equivalent of the Coca-Cola's 3 percent of the world's 5.7 billion consumers' daily liquid consumption, or of Gary Wendt's Penske Trucking Group's going after total logistics handling for companies?

_____

_____

_____

Step 4. Teaching Others Outside-In Behavior

Take some time to plan ways that you can develop outside-in behavior among your colleagues and staff.

▶ What I can teach them:

_____

_____

_____

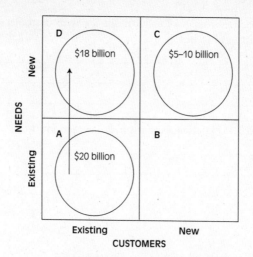

Pond Defined as the Total Power-Plant
Equipment and Service Expenditures Worldwide

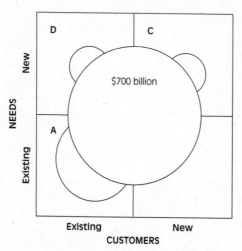

Pond Defined as the Energy Industry

▶ Experiences they should have outside with customers, other industries, and so on:

_____

_____

_____

▶ Leadership experiences that can be created for them:

_____

_____

_____

Section V
Building the New Genetic Code—The Teachable Point of View

In this section, take the time to rethink the elements of the new genetic code for balanced growth in your organization. Start with what has to be excised from the old genetic code. Next, articulate your teachable point of view on balanced growth, and, finally, start teaching it!

Step 1. The Old Genetic Code

What specific elements of the old genetic code, as represented in the leaders' teachable point of view, need to be destroyed?

▶ BUSINESS IDEAS (this is a mature industry; maintain rigid industry boundaries, and so on):

_____

_____

_____

▶ VALUES ("If it ain't broke, don't fix it"; be cautious and risk-averse; invest in known solutions):

_____

_____

_____

▶ EMOTIONAL ENERGY (how we energize people, through threats, speeches, bureaucratic procedures, and so on):

_____

_____

_____

▶ EDGE (how to make the tough investment/business/people yes–no decisions; consultants are no better than the people who recommend them; how hard it is to decide to get rid of anything; people stay forever . . .)

_____

_____

_____

GE Capital Services

Growth: How To Get It!

**MEETING
THE CHALLENGE
OF**

**WENDT'S TOP 10
IDEAS FOR STIMULATING**

GROWTH

General Electric   12 Businesses

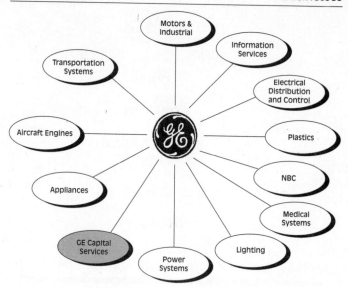

GE Capital Services   Earnings Growth

($MM)

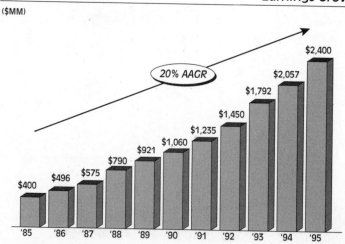

20% AAGR

'85	'86	'87	'88	'89	'90	'91	'92	'93	'94	'95
$400	$496	$575	$790	$921	$1,060	$1,235	$1,450	$1,792	$2,057	$2,400

But, No Matter What Else You Try. . .   *Tip #1*

GROWTH

SUCCESS   FORMULA

Give
Business
Development
<u>At Least</u>
<u>As Much. . .</u>
➡

THOUGHT
+
ATTENTION
+
**TIME & RESOURCE
COMMITMENT**
+
LEADERSHIP
+
INTENSITY

As You Do
Anything
Else in
Your
Business
Universe

Make It A Part Of Your Culture And Your Being!!

Necessary Element For Successful Growth Culture   *Tip #2*

. . . Allow. . .

STAR GAZING

– Innovating
– Experimenting
– DREAMING

Outside Tools To Help   *Tip #3*
Many Aids Exist To Provide A Path, If You Wish

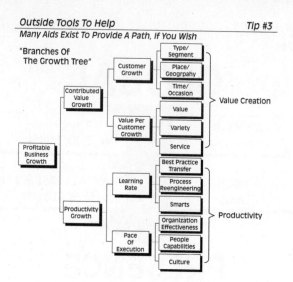

"Branches Of The Growth Tree"

Seizing Opportunity   *Tip #4*

Whenever Possible

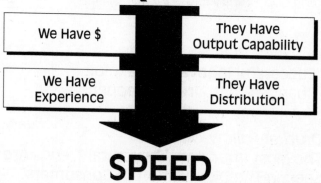

ACQUIRE

| We Have $ | They Have Output Capability |
| We Have Experience | They Have Distribution |

SPEED

In A Fast Changing World

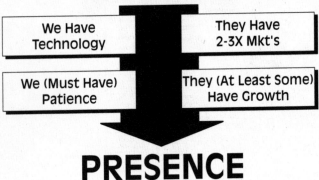

Get

GLOBAL

We Have Technology	They Have 2-3X Mkt's
We (Must Have) Patience	They (At Least Some) Have Growth

PRESENCE

In An Ever Smaller World

Drucker's Rule
"Successful Innovations Exploit
Changes That Already Happened."

Drucker Follow-On
The Most Important Structural Trends Are
Seen In The Distribution Of Consumers'
Disposable Income.

Where To Look For (Conceptual)   *Tip #7*
Make Change The Opportunity (Not The Problem)

- Demographic <u>Changes</u>

- Technological <u>Changes</u>

- Political <u>Changes</u>

- Competitive <u>Changes</u>

- Value/Taste <u>Changes</u>

Practical, Proven Management Techniques
For Getting Broader Involvement In Growth   *Tip #8*

- Strategic Time Management
  - Plan Your Week

- "Innovation Councils"

- Establish A Separate Futures Budget

. . . And, Of Course. . .

- Reward <u>Forward</u> Movement

- "Stretch"
  - Keep The Challenge Meaningful!

Who Should Focus Your Business Development Efforts   *Tip #9*

**Wrong
(Old Way):**   Business Development Is
The Responsibility Of The
<u>Strategic Planning</u> Department

Right Way: <u>Business Development
Is Everyone's Responsibility!!!</u>

Get The Proper Focus   *Tip #10*

"Don't Be Ashamed
Of Profits!" a)

---

a) i.e., It Should Be The Focal Point For Why You Need Business Expansion Activities

Step 2. The Balanced Growth Architecture

Drawing on the material in the text chapters and the exercises in this *Handbook,* redo your teachable point of view on balanced growth. A presentation prepared by Gary Wendt, describing GE Capital Services, is reproduced as a model. It includes ten tips for your own adaptation.

John Trani, now CEO of Stanley Works, has this teachable point of view as noted in his 1997 Annual Report:

> *Our growth framework involves three elements and a singular glue, the Stanley brand. The elements are new products, distribution, and adjacent or "near neighbor" market developments.*
>
> ▶ *New products are the heart of a manufacturing company. Our intention is to double the spending in product development over the next several years. A new process is being implemented across Stanley to deliver products so unique that customers will demand that retailers carry them.*
>
> ▶ *Distribution expansions will occur as we move to One Stanley. For example, prior to our new organization, the manufactured housing industry was being served by only one Stanley business. Today, our manufactured housing sales team takes all Stanley products to market. As a result, our opportunity in this growing market tripled from $100 million to $300 million.*
>
> ▶ *Near neighbor market opportunities abound. A number of adjacencies have been identified which are complementary to our current offering and build upon our core competences. Examples include storm doors, wood entry doors, tool kits, and garden tools. These adjacencies expand our overall market opportunity from $16 billion to $27 billion. Our challenge is to capitalize upon those which prove viable and successful and to promptly terminate those which prove unworthy of further resource commitment.*

Trani points out that, to get energized people, he must build in stretch and must stress winning. He views benchmarking as a key lever:

> *Benchmarking is not just an intellectual exercise. It provides the measure of the competitiveness of an enterprise. That knowledge will*

cause us to STRETCH . . . to adopt without change if possible . . . to adapt if necessary . . . and to advance ultimately. An example: if inventory turnover is four in a factory, the plant manager might consider achieving five an excellent performance, since it's a 25% improvement. That is, until benchmarking reveals the best plants have 18 turns . . . almost 5x! The goal then isn't 5, it is 18. The only question is how long it will take to get there. Without benchmarking, incrementalism reigns.

. . . The Stanley Works has long stood for integrity, respect, value, and quality. To that we want to add a strong desire to win . . . to compete and to commit to excellence. We want everyone in our company to love to compete and commit themselves to reaching for the excellence achieved by best-in-activity companies. That means incremental thinking and behavior are out—for example, budgets that are mostly exercises in minimalism. Quantum improvement and stretch are in. We must all realize that it is the beauty of the execution, not the brilliance of the idea, that matters; performance, not plans—commitment, not agreement. Over the next few years, our goal is to show this is not rhetoric but reality.

What will be the elements of your new genetic code?

▶ BUSINESS IDEAS on balanced growth:

_____

_____

_____

▶ VALUES supporting ideas on balanced growth:

_____

_____

_____

▶ EMOTIONAL ENERGY (how you energize others about balanced growth):

_____

_____

_____

▶ EDGE (how you exercise edge around balanced growth):

_____

_____

_____

Step 3. _Teaching the Balanced Growth Teachable Point of View_

Now that you have articulated your teachable point of view, you need to design ways of teaching it to others. This can happen in one-on-one situations, in the context of business or strategy review, or in formal development classroom settings.

▶ **One-On-One Teaching Opportunities**

With Whom	What I Will Do
_____	_____
_____	_____
_____	_____

▶ **Teaching in Conjunction with Business/Strategy Reviews**

Event	What I Will Do
_____	_____
_____	_____
_____	_____

▶ **Formal Development Experiences (part of leadership training, and so on)**

Event	What I Will Do
_____	_____
_____	_____
_____	_____

SECTION VI
Growth Social Architecture

Organizations operate through complex weblike social networks. *Prescribed networks* are the formal structures most often pictured in organizational charts. *Emergent networks* reflect the information, influence, and affinity flow; they are of primary importance to any leader because they represent the way the world works. In fast moving, less than hierarchical organizations, work is accomplished through these shifting emergent networks. Increasingly, the role of a leader is to architect these networks in a way that will lead to success in tomorrow's environment. Emergent networks accomplish organizational objectives while fulfilling individual needs for information, influence, and friendship.

Balanced growth requires leaders to build networks, both internally and externally, to support innovation and new business opportunities for their organizations.

This section of the *Handbook* provides you, the leader, with some guidelines for building the social architecture necessary to drive balanced growth in your organization. A key component of the social architecture is the human resource system—the staffing, appraisal, reward, and development processes. To ensure that the balanced growth genetic code gets reinforced, all these processes must be aligned.

Step 1. The Current State of Your Social Architecture

Map out the key elements of your social architecture. Start with an analysis of your own networks. Put yourself in the center and identify the key people in your role set—the people with whom you interact, and who have expectations regarding your role as a leader driving growth. Indicate the nature of the exchange, and then, for each of those people, take the interaction at least one step further. To whom are they connected, and what is the nature of their linkages? The example on page 297 can be used as a guide.

As you map your social network, ask yourself:

▶ What changes would increase the outside-in behavior?

▶ What new linkages are needed?

▶ Who should be dropped?

▶ How should the linkages among people change?

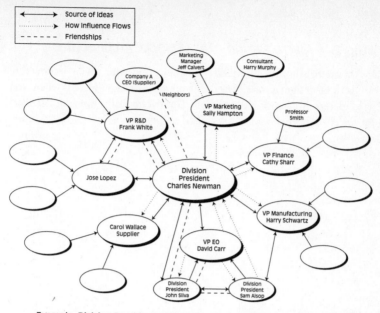

Example: Division President of Company X—Balanced Growth Network

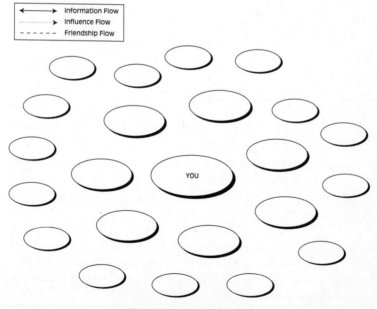

Map of Your Social Network

Step 2. A Macro Design of Your Social Architecture

Many of you lead thousands of people, and your social architecture needs to be designed for all levels of your organization. Here is where you can create a number of interventions. *Draw a formal organizational chart for the current state of your prescribed organization.*

Now go back and *overlay* on the chart:

- ▶ Key influence linkages: use arrows to indicate who influences whom.

- ▶ Key information flow: use arrows to indicate who shares information in which direction.

- ▶ Key friendship linkages: use arrows to indicate the degree of reciprocity.

Are changes in the prescribed network required, to support balanced growth? Should you move to a business unit structure, create a matrix, be more functional, be geographic? Every situation is different, and you, as leader, must wrestle with the tradeoffs.

AlliedSignal CEO Larry Bossidy says:

Organizationally, I pair marketing with technology so that I can make sure that they are working together. In the past, the marketing people were working on what they wanted to, and the technology people were working on what they wanted to, and products never got to market on time.

Emergent Network Creation

Leaders can greatly influence the building of infomal, emergent networks through events, through the creation of temporary systems such as special task forces, through physical architecture (where people have their offices), and through the use of various electronic networks. Developmental experiences, such as GE's use of the Crotonville leadership development center, provide ways to build lifelong networks by putting people through intensive action-learning experiences.

▶ What changes would help with outside-in behavior?

_____

_____

_____

_____

_____

▶ In what ways can I bring about change?

_____

_____

_____

_____

Step 3. The Human Resource System

A key determinant of balanced growth behavior in any organization is the human resource system. The genetic code of the organization is implemented and reinforced through the system, which includes *staffing* (who is hired, who is promoted), *appraisal* (what is measured and by what standards), *rewards* (how performance is rated and how exceptional performance is acknowledged), and *development* (what capabilities we teach our people to bring them to a higher level).

The diagram below is a simple framework for both diagnosing and changing a human resource system. As shown, the system must be mutually reinforcing. Staffing—finding the right people to put into particular roles—is the first step; the goal is to find people who can contribute to balanced growth. Staffing involves external recruiting and hiring as well as internal movement of people. After hirees are in positions and performing, the human resource system provides mechanisms and tools for appraising them, in terms of their current performance and, increasingly, their future capabilities and developmental needs. The appraisal data can then be used as a guide for allocating rewards such as money, stock options, recognition, promotions, and so on. In the diagram, an arrow from appraisal connects to development. This reflects both ongoing developmental efforts for driving performance on the current job, such as teaching people marketing segmentation skills if they are in a product management job, or future-focused developmental experiences that would prepare someone for a promotion (the dotted arrow into the staffing component).

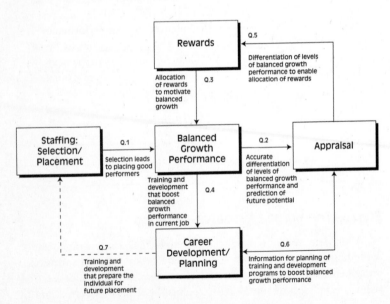

Some key points must be noted when using this simple framework. As a system, it is only as strong as its weakest link, which, in most organizations, is appraisal. Without good appraisals, you cannot allocate rewards fairly, nor can you make informed decisions on development. A major appraisal problem is lack of courage and integrity. Many managers give inflated appraisals to avoid the difficult tasks of honest tough-love coaching of their people. The easy way out is the overinflated appraisals that occur in most companies. The culture of the system encourages a 360-degree feedback process: Rate everyone high because the implied contract reads, "If I rate others high, then others will do the same for me." In companies with 360-degree feedback on leadership capabilities, we have seen the top leadership team receive very high ratings while the companies lumbered along with terrible performance. No one from the outside would ever think of hiring away any of these leaders with high internal ratings. They were using inside-out thinking to rate themselves.

Step 4. Diagnosis of Growth Performance

Examine your organization for balanced growth performance, keeping in mind its actual track record. Review the present human resource practices. Do they help or hinder the balanced growth performance? Answer the questions below by rating your company's actions as "very little," "moderate," or "very great." (See the rating scale on the next page.)

Using the rating scale below as a guide, indicate your evaluation of your company's actions or awareness in response to Questions 1 through 8. Write your rating (1 to 5) in the brackets alongside each question.

Very Little		Moderate		Very Great
[1]	[2]	[3]	[4]	[5]

To what extent:

[ ] Q.1. Are key people selected for their positions based on their capability to achieve balanced growth?

[ ] Q.2. Are key people promoted due to balanced growth performance? Explain. _____

_____

Very Little		Moderate		Very Great
[1]	[2]	[3]	[4]	[5]

[ ] Q.3. Are key people rewarded for balanced growth performance? Explain. _____

_____

[ ] Q.4. Are key people trained and developed for their positions to deliver balanced growth? Explain. _____

_____

[ ] Q.5. Does the appraisal of balanced growth performance affect the rewards key people receive? Explain. _____

_____

[ ] Q.6. Does the appraisal of key people's balanced growth performance affect the training and development they receive? Explain. _____

_____

[ ] Q.7. Does the training/development/career planning key people receive prepare them for placement into a new, higher, and larger position requiring balanced growth performance? Explain. _____

_____

[ ] Q.8. Overall, to what degree is the human resource cycle—as in integrated unit—supportive of balanced growth performance?

Step 5. Architecting Human Resources for Balanced Growth

Based on your diagnosis above, develop plans for changing your organization's human resource system to drive more balanced growth performance.

Selection and Placement—Examples

▶ **Ameritech.** When Dick Notebaert became CEO of Ameritech, he had a very specific plan to unleash balanced growth performance:

he would hire 25 percent of the top 200 people from outside the company, and mostly from outside the industry. He hired many people away from consumer companies such as Kraft, American Express, and GE. This was his way of quickly bringing in new genetic material to his company.

▶ **GE Power Systems.** When Bob Nardelli set up his Power Systems Service Company, he took 30 percent of his best and brightest engineers and moved them to that new business.

▶ **Reynolds and Reynolds.** CEO selection by the Board was the key human resource lever. Dave Holmes, whom it had made CEO, had come from outside the company. With a totally new teachable point of view, he altered the genetic code.

What specific changes will you make in your selection and development systems to support balanced growth?

_____

_____

_____

Appraisal Systems—Examples

▶ **AlliedSignal.** Larry Bossidy has goals and objectives for each of his key businesses and leaders. The objectives state how much growth is expected, over what period of time.

▶ **Coca-Cola.** To ensure the discipline of balanced growth, Coca-Cola makes extensive use of economic value added (EVA®) measures in assessing the performance of its units and leaders.

What specific changes will you make in your appraisal system to track balanced growth performance and the developmental needs of your people?

_____

_____

_____

Reward System—Examples

▶ **Coca-Cola.** The reward system is tied to profitable growth of the business; EVA® is a key factor in allocating rewards, thus supporting the discipline of balanced growth.

▶ **Royal Dutch/Shell.** In many of the operating companies, the oil products businesses have worked with Professor Larry Selden of the Columbia University Business School to set *growth* and *return on average capital employed* targets. Teams and individuals at all levels are then rewarded based on how they meet those targets.

What specific changes will you make in your reward system to drive balanced growth performance?

_____

_____

_____

Development System—Examples

▶ **AlliedSignal.** Larry Bossidy sees to it that growth is a key part of the development curriculum at the AlliedSignal leadership development center.

▶ **Ford.** As a part of a leadership development and transformation process, called Capstone, Alex Trotman and the executive committee have allocated one of four teams to look at growth for Ford Motor Company. This six-month team mobilized resources and ideas both from within the company and through external benchmarking. The findings are to be a catalyst for the leadership of the company to accelerate its development of a new growth trajectory for Ford. The team also developed a teachable point of view on growth that they and other senior executives are helping teach to others.

▶ **GE's Crotonville Leadership Development Institute.** GE incorporates action-learning projects into all of its four-week leadership development programs. The majority of these projects in the past five years have been focused on growth. Topics have included possible joint ventures or acquisitions in Southeast Asia, service opportunities for GE Medical Systems and other businesses, and how to play for growth in the Information Age. Growth is woven into all programs.

What specific changes will you make to your development system, to drive balanced growth performance?

_____

_____

_____

SECTION **VII**
Growth Decision Architecture

The genetic code is built into everyday leadership action through the regularly recurring operating mechanisms of the organization. Your teachable point of view plays out over and over again in the strategy process, the budgeting process, and the people (personnel review) process. This section gives you a framework for analyzing and redesigning your growth decision architecture.

How can you build operating mechanisms for balanced growth? There are three core leadership processes for driving organizational performance: (1) the strategy process, (2) the budgeting process, and (3) the people process. Through these three processes, the genetic code is played out in the fabric of the organization. As an example, Larry Bossidy uses his operating mechanisms to inculcate his teachable point of view on growth into the leadership of AlliedSignal. He states:

> *We have three processes which cut across everything: an intense people process, which obtains people, trains them, appraises them, and promotes them; a good strategic planning process; and a good operating plan or budget process. Those are the same across the whole company.*

He goes on to point out that all companies have these processes, but most don't use them well. The trick question is: How intense are the processes and what do they yield?

Each operating mechanism emerges from activities that can be analyzed as having three phases:

1. **Preparation.** What goes into getting ready? What is generated and how is it analyzed? Where are ideas generated? Who is involved in what, and how do people work together?

2. **Face-to-face decision making.** No important strategies, budget decisions, or people decisions are made without a face-to-face meeting of the key parties involved. What materials and people are present at the face-to-face meeting? What is the agenda? Is the meeting run in a climate of openness and candor? How are conflicts and decision making handled?

3. Follow up. The implementation part of each of the operating mechanisms indicates what will happen with the decisions or issues that emerged from the face-to-face meeting. If follow up is weak, the whole cycle will deteriorate and the next round of preparation will feed off how people feel when there is poor follow up.

Step 1. Analyzing Current Operating Mechanisms

Use the form below to assess what occurs in each phase for each operating mechanism. For example, begin with the Strategy/Preparation

Assess the operating mechanisms by asking: How well do they drive the balanced growth teachable point of view?

Rate each element in each cell of the matrix on a scale of 1 to 5:

1 = Little or no reinforcement (negative)

2

3 = Moderate reinforcement (slightly positive)

4

5 = Strong reinforcement (very positive)

	Preparation	Face-to-Face Decision Making	Follow Up
Strategy	Ideas Values Energy Edge __ __ __ __	Ideas Values Energy Edge __ __ __ __	Ideas Values Energy Edge __ __ __ __
Budget	Ideas Values Energy Edge __ __ __ __	Ideas Values Energy Edge __ __ __ __	Ideas Values Energy Edge __ __ __ __
People	Ideas Values Energy Edge __ __ __ __	Ideas Values Energy Edge __ __ __ __	Ideas Values Energy Edge __ __ __ __

phase. To what extent are innovative ideas generated? To what extent are the core values of your organization embodied in the strategy preparation? To what extent are tough yes–no decisions made? To what extent are people energized by the preparation? Next, move on to what happens with each of these elements in the Strategy/Face-to-Face phase, and then in the Strategy/Follow-up phase.

Step 2. Doing a Qualitative Assessment

Use your diagnosis based on numbers, and think about each of your operating mechanisms.

1. What are the biggest weaknesses?

Strategy Process:

_____

_____

_____

Budget Process:

_____

_____

_____

People Process:

_____

_____

_____

2. What are the results?

Strategy Process:

_____

_____

_____

Budget Process:

_____

_____

_____

People Process:

_____

_____

_____

As benchmarks for new ideas, read the examples below. Would any of these tactics suit your organization?

Gary Wendt at GE Capital: Early Strategic Input

Gary Wendt, CEO of GE Capital, decided several years ago that waiting to review his business heads' strategic plans in the Face-to-Face phase, with no real involvement or input, is not a way to influence his company's ideas and values. He has about twenty-seven businesses, and by the time managers complete their strategic planning and go to him for a presentation, they are in a selling mode, not a creative-ideas mode.

In the operating mechanism Gary started, he injects himself into the strategy process on the front end, before the managers start work on their formal presentation. He goes out to the business and has brainstorming, blue-sky sessions; he does not allow the leadership team of that business to come with a presentation. They all spend about a day talking about the business and pushing for out-of-the-box thinking. In one of these sessions, he got the Penske team to realize that their market was not in going after Ryder; it was in every company that needed help on logistics, from order to remittance process to physical handling of stuff to helping with just-in-time delivery, etc.

Jack Welch at GE: Discipline and Follow Up

The face-to-face meetings are run by Welch with extreme discipline. For example, the agenda for his people review, what GE calls "Session C," is shared across all the major businesses. The agenda for the session influences the preparation, the nature of the face-to-face meeting, and the followup.

One of the most effective ways to teach and embed the teachable point of view on balanced growth is through the followup and execution phase of the operating mechanism. Welch uses a variety of tools here. First, there is a very disciplined staff followup. Depending on the session, strategy, people, and budget, the appropriate staff person will have been an active participant in the meeting and will have a written followup set of action items with dates and other details.

Welch always uses the face-to-face session as a teaching and coaching event. There will be verbal real-time feedback; many times, there will also be a handwritten note to the parties involved. One of Welch's techniques is to follow up the people reviews with a videoconference within a month, to discuss the action items and priorities.

Carlos Cantu at ServiceMaster: Keeping Leaders Energized

One of CEO Cantu's rules as a leader is: If he fails to energize his team members, he fails them, because they then put pressure on the organization. If someone leaves one of his meetings deenergized, he will seek out that individual in his or her own office and will reenergize that person. He feels that a deenergized division president can wreak a lot of havoc on an organization, so he is obsessive about tracking energy.[4]

Larry Bossidy at AlliedSignal: Put It in Writing

Larry is compulsive about following up *every* face-to-face meeting, in all four areas, with a written letter to his direct report—often, a two-page statement of what he views as the outcomes of the meeting. These letters are tracked and retrieved the next time a review takes place. Most importantly, the letters are a psychological contract between the head of the business and the CEO. They are written in informal, direct, no-nonsense language, and they constitute a working understanding between Larry and his leaders.

Step 3. Building Balanced Growth into the Operating Mechanisms

What specific new architecture for each operating mechanism would help you embed the new genetic code of balanced growth?

Take the time to make concrete changes to your operating mechanisms (below), so as to embed your teachable point of view on balanced growth. Think about idea generation, value reinforcement, where the tough edge decisions are required, and how to emotionally energize people.

	Preparation	Face-to-Face Decision Making	Followup
Strategy			
Budget			
People			

Step 4. Designing Other Operating Mechanisms for Balanced Growth

Creative leaders can build an infinite variety of operating mechanisms to reinforce their genetic code of growth. Take some time to design other mechanisms for reinforcing your teachable point of view on growth. The examples that follow may suggest some innovations.

▶ **GE's Quick Market Intelligence (QMI).** GE leaders benchmarked Wal-Mart and were very impressed by the ritual of the key leaders' going out into the field to visit stores, competitors, and suppliers all week. Wal-Mart pulls all the information together on Friday and then downlinks it, via the Wal-Mart communication system, to all stores on Saturday. This schedule allows quick responses to competitors' moves and to changes in customer behavior.

   GE copied this concept; every GE business has what the company calls a Quick Market Intelligence (QMI) process. Basically, once a week, a team and the CEO at the center involved meets with an extended electronic network of sales people in the field. At Major Appliances, about twenty-five key managers sit around a large horseshoe-shaped table, listening to sales managers from around the world report on what is happening in the marketplace. The purpose of the meeting is to make quick decisions about dealing with customers and growing the business. At one meeting, GE got wind of a Whirlpool discount planned for the coming Friday, and was able to come up with its own discount before Whirlpool implemented theirs. In another meeting, the group discovered a problem with refrigerators. The head of manufacturing stopped production on the spot, until the flaw was fixed. Both of these problems would have taken weeks, if not months, to fix in the past. At GE Medical Systems, all the heads of modalities—CAT Scan, MRI, and X-ray—are on a conference call with sales managers around the world to do a quick round-robin in sharing and decision making.

▶ **GE's CEC Meetings.** Jack Welch holds quarterly off site meetings with his heads of businesses and key corporate staff. Held at Crontonville, these are informal, high-energy sessions for sharing and generating ideas. The sessions reinforce the GE teachable point of view on growth and Six Sigma performance.

► **Compaq Annual Innovate Forum.** This three-day conference is attended by thousands of executives, top customers, and strategic partners. It is a hotbed of ideas for growth at Compaq.

What additional operating mechanisms do you need for balanced growth?

_____

_____

_____

SECTION VIII
Continuous Transformation: Can You Pass the Father Cunningham Test?

The ultimate challenge for leadership is creating an organization that can sustain growth. Our closing example is the story that concludes the book, and it's worth repeating here in short form.

Three decades ago, Father William Cunningham and Eleanor Josaitis started a program to distribute food to pregnant women and infants. Today the enterprise, Focus: HOPE, is a 30-acre complex that includes everything from childcare facilities to machinist training, for-profit businesses that produce parts for the auto industry, and an advanced degree-granting institute for manufacturing engineers.

Leaders with ideas, values, emotional energy, and edge, Cunningham and Josaitis created their growth strategy by looking for the outside in. They constantly identified new needs, and enlarged their pond by developing new segments.

They also created a genetic code so powerful that the enterprise continues stronger than ever despite the death of its charismatic founder. "Don't put my name on a building or boulevard," Father Cunningham once said. "Make my work live on." What we call the Father Cunningham test is the ultimate test of your leadership: Will the organization you built keep growing after you're gone?

On May 26, 1997, Father Cunningham died at age 67 after a protracted bout with cancer of the liver. Less than a month later, a tornado devastated Focus: HOPE. The storm caused $23 million in damage and shut down all of Focus: HOPE's activities, including production of the parts and components businesses.

Three days after the tornado, Noel Tichy and his colleague Michael Brimm arrived at 6:30 A.M. to meet with Eleanor and prepare for a day of volunteer work from a Ford Motor Co. team headed by Automotive Operations president Jacques Nasser. The scene that greeted them was shocking: Roofs ripped off, windows blown out, telephone poles lying on the ground, and surrounding houses utterly destroyed. Walking up the stairs to the second floor of the old Ameritech Yellow Pages building, which Focus: HOPE had bought a couple of years earlier for a planned executive residence-style learning center, Noel ran into Eleanor. She was dressed for hard work in bluejeans and a T-shirt, a big change from her normal businesslike blue suit.

Noel was about to express his condolences when Eleanor, smiling broadly, gave him a big hug. "We did it!" she said. "We got the production line going and have not missed a customer delivery!" Then she added: "This tornado is going to be a blessing. I have always wanted to rebuild this neighborhood. Now we have the governor, the mayor, and the feds working with us to look into how we can build new housing."

Noel thought: "Here is a 66-year-old woman who just lost her partner of 30 years, and saw terrible natural catastrophe wreck their enterprise. But she's energized and hard at work on a new growth ideas for it. We all talk about change, often devastating change, being an opportunity: Eleanor embodies this at the core. Out of destruction, she has started Focus: HOPE on a new growth trajectory."

Will your work carry on when you are gone? Will the organization regenerate? We often pose these questions in workshops with executives to get them very clearly focused on the need to teach others to be leaders. They need to understand that their legacy is in the stewardship of the people assets of their institution. The test of that stewardship is whether they have created a genetic code of continuous transformation through leaders at all levels—whether they have prepared their people to successfully create new growth trajectories. Father William Cunningham created such an organization.

Preparing Your Organization for Continuous Transformation

Step 1: Name five successors who are ready now to drive balanced growth.

1) _____

2) _____

3) _____

4) _____

5) _____

If you don't have five, don't be discouraged. Very few do—the challenge is to build them.

Step 2: What actions are you going to take in the next several years to develop more leaders, capable of continually creating balanced growth?

_____

_____

_____

_____

_____

_____

The Final Exam: Passing the Father Cunningham Test

Draft a brief article dated sometime in the future when you see yourself leaving the organization. Tell the story you want told, your vision. Imaging FORTUNE, *The Economist*, or *Business Week* were to write your ideal "Father Cunningham" story about you in the future. Be sure to describe how other leaders are "carrying on your work":

_____

_____

_____

_____

_____

_____

_____

_____

_____

Endnotes

Chapter 1 Thinking Clearly About Growth

1. Deogun, Nikhil. "Advice to Coke People from Their New Boss: Don't Get Too Cocky." *Wall Street Journal,* March 9, 1998, 1.

2. Fahri, Paul. "Coca-Cola Chief Goizueta Dies." *Washington Post,* October 19, 1997, B08.

3. The p/e ratios of the Big Three are based upon year end values. As you can see, in 1993, GM had an unusually high year-end ratio. The number steadily declined and returned to normal rates by first quarter 1994.

Year	Ford	Chrysler	GM	S&P
1997	5.6	8.5	7.0	24.5
1996	5.7	6.5	9.2	20.8
1995	5.2	9.9	7.4	17.4
1994	3.7	4.8	6.8	16.9
1993	9.4	8.0	25.8	22.9

Source: Bloomberg Financial Markets: Price/Earnings Chart.

4. Ford Motor Company Annual Report 1997, 65.

5. New York: Harper Business, 1997, 3.

6. Speech at the University of Michigan Business School, Multi-Disciplinary Action Project (MAP) Kickoff, March 10, 1998.

7. Loomis, Carol. "Forty Years of the Fortune 500." FORTUNE, March 1995, 182.

8. Interview with Ram Charan, Noel Tichy and Charles Burck, June 1997.

9. Rosenbush, Steve. "MCI Lures AT&T Callers with Frequent-Flier Plan." *USA Today,* April 21, 1998, 1B.

10. Business Ranking Annual (Brooklyn, New York: Gale Research Publications 1998), 45.

11. As of April 14, 1998. (Source: Swanson, Stephen. "Merger Wave Engulfs BancAmerica, Nations." *Chicago Tribune,* April 14, 1998, N1.)

Chapter 2   There's No Such Thing as a Mature Business

1. Interview with Charles Burck and Eli Cohen, January 1996.

2. Interview with Noel Tichy and Charles Burck, January 1997.

3. Interview with Charles Burck, October 1995.

4. Henkoff, Ronald. "A Year of Extraordinary Gains." FORTUNE, April 28, 1997, 194.

5. Eyal, Jonathan. "Conspiracy of Silence." *The Guardian* [London], December 11, 1995, 15.

6. Davis, Bob; Wessel, David. *Prosperity: The Coming Twenty-Year Boom and What It Means to You.* (New York: Random House, 1998), 28.

7. For more information on this topic, please see Ram Charan's article "The Rules Have Changed." FORTUNE, March 16, 1998, 159.

8. Initially undertaken in 1990, and updated annually, his work shows that companies in the top quartile of market value creation achieved annual top line growth of 12 percent and return on assets (after taxes) of 16 percent. The parameters will be different in today's environment of lower inflation and consolidation among and across industries, but the point is the same: Market value creators excel at both.

9. Lubove, Seth. "It Ain't Broke, but Fix It Anyway." *Forbes,* August 1, 1994, 56.

10. Tully, Shawn. "So Mr. Bossidy, We Know That You Can Cut, Now Show Us That You Can Grow." FORTUNE, August 21, 1997, 70.

11. Speech at the University of Michigan Business School, Multi-Disciplinary Action Project (MAP) Kickoff, March 10, 1998.

12. AlliedSignal Communications Department, May 1998.

13. AlliedSignal Annual Reports, 1997, 20; 1994, 4.

14. Speech, March 10, 1998.

15. Calculated on an annualized basis from 1978–1991. (Source: American Express Annual Report 1991, 5; 1978, 6).

16. This rate refers to sales growth from 1984–1997. Nike Corporation Annual Reports, 1997, 42; 1995, 20; 1990, 15; 1987, 16.

17. Revenue growth is calculated from 1985–1997. The profits grew at increasing rates in every year except for 1988 and 1994. (Source: GE Annual Reports, 1997, 45; 1992, 34; 1989, 28; 1986, 41.)

18. Interview with Ram Charan, Noel Tichy, and Charles Burck, July 1996.

19. "Travelers Group and Citicorp Agree to Join Forces in $83 Billion Merger." *Wall Street Journal,* April 7, 1998, A1.

20. Levitt, Theodore. "Marketing Myopia." *Harvard Business Review,* September/October 1975, 28. (Originally printed in 1960.)

21. Gates, Bill. *The Road Ahead* (New York: Viking, 1996), 35.

22. Scheier, Robert. "What's in it for you?" VARBUSINESS, February 2, 1998, 56.

23. Schlender, Brett. "Bill Gates and Paul Allen Talk." FORTUNE, October 2, 1995, 68.

24. Myerson, Allen. "Rating the Bigshots vs. Rockefeller." *New York Times,* May 24, 1998, 4.

25. Microsoft's opponents argue that Microsoft is violating the Clayton Anti-Trust Act of 1914, which prohibits the sale of one product based on the condition that the consumer must buy a tied product (in this case, the browser). In defense of the computer software giant, economists argue that displaying monopoly power involves charging a monopoly price for the tied good. Moreover, even if Microsoft were to hold a monopoly position within the industry, it is not sustainable because of the rapid rate of technological advances. (Sources: Becker, Gary. "Let the Market Judge Microsoft." *Business Week,* April 6, 1998, 26. Klein, Joel. "Computer Bugaboos." *Chicago Tribune,* May 15, 1998, 10.)

26. Hills-Moore, Alicia. "Mr. Gates Builds His Brain Trust." FORTUNE, December 8, 1997, 85.

27. Grove, Andy. *Only the Paranoid Survive.* (New York: Doubleday, 1996), 89.

28. Grove, 90.

29. Grove, 89.

30. Grove, 93.

31. Grove, 84.

32. Grove, 96.

33. Grove, 95.

34.

1958	1998
1. General Motors	1. General Motors
2. Standard Oil	2. Ford Motor
3. Ford Motor	3. Exxon
4. **U.S. Steel**	4. **Wal-Mart**
5. General Electric	5. General Electric
6. Chrysler	6. **International Business Machines**
7. Socony Mobil Oil	7. Chrysler
8. **Gulf Oil**	8. Mobil
9. **Bethlehem Steel**	9. **Phillip Morris**
10. **Swift**	10. **AT&T**

The companies that have been added or removed since 1958 are in bold. Standard Oil has since been renamed Exxon and Socony Mobil Oil is currently known as Mobil. The 1958 listing is based upon the largest U.S. industrial companies, while the 1998 list includes all areas of business. Both lists are based upon revenues. (Sources: "The Largest Industrials." FORTUNE, July 1958, 50. "The FORTUNE 500." FORTUNE, April 27, 1998, F-2.)

35. Sellers, Patricia. "How Coke Is Kicking Pepsi's Can." October 28, 1996, 70.

36. Rahul, Jacob. "The Resurrection of Michael Dell." FORTUNE, September 18, 1995, 118.

37. Jacob, 120.

38. Jacob, 120.

39. In a June 1994 brochure, the company noted that it had doubled its business roughly every five years for three decades. Annual revenues had reached $25 billion, and the company employed 400,000 people. Said PepsiCo: "By the year 2000, we may become the first company on earth with one million employees."

40. Sellers, 70.

41. Sellers, 70.

42. "Coca-Cola Profits Rise 8.6%." *Los Angeles Times,* April 16, 1998, D13.

43. Perman, Stacy. "The Man Who Knew the Formula." *Time,* October 27, 1997, 102.

44. "Stars of the '97 Business World . . ." *The Toronto Star,* January 22, 1998, B6.

45. PepsiCo spun off the restaurant division into Tricon Global Restaurants Inc., 1997. The company raised $5.5 billion in the process, which will be used to pay off short-term debt and increase its stock buy back program. (Source: "PepsiCo to Tricon . . ." *Chicago Tribune,* October 7, 1997, N22.)

46. Edmondson, Gail; Elstrom, Peter; Burrows, Paul. "At Nokia–A Comeback and Then Some." *Business Week,* December 2, 1996, 106.

47. Sources: Nokia Annual Report 1997, 25 and Ericsson Annual Report 1997, available at *www.ericsson.com*

48. Edmondson, 106.

49. Nokia Annual Report 1995, 25.

50. Edmondson, 106.

51. Edmondson, 106.

52. Edmondson, 106.

53. Nokia Annual Report, 1997, 3.

54. Sales in 1997 totaled $90.8 billion. (Source: GE Annual Reports, 1997, 45; 1981, 39.)

55. Market value is calculated by multiplying the shares outstanding by stock price for the same time period. At year end 1981, shares outstanding equaled 230 million and the stock price was 57⅜, resulting in a market value of $13 billion. The shares outstanding on May 8, 1998 were 3,260 million and shares closed at $83⁹⁄₁₆ resulting in a market value of $272 billion. (Source: Bloomberg Financial Markets: Historical Price Analysis; GE Annual Report, 1981, 52; Dow Jones Daily Stock Report, Oct/Nov/Dec 1981, 163.)

56. Coca-Cola Annual Report 1997, 42.

57. Bloomberg Financial Markets: Historical Price Analysis, May 14, 1998.

58. Prince, Greg. "Goizueta's Legacies." *Beverage World,* December 1997, 42.

59. Compaq Annual Report 1997, 7.

60. Kaletsky, Anatole. "Wall Street Votes with Its Feet; General Motors." *Financial Times,* December 5, 1986, 26.

61. GM's market share reached a high of 47.7 percent in 1978 and fell to 31 percent by 1997. The total Japanese market share was 12 percent in 1978 and reached 31 percent in 1997. (Source: Standard and Poor's Industry Survey, 1996, A85; *Motor Vehicles Facts & Figures.* (Washington, DC, American Manufacturers Association, 1995), 20;

Sorge, Marjorie. "General Motors 1998 Report Card." *Automotive Industries,* April 1998, 36.)

Chapter 3   Common Sense and Capital:
The Business Thinking Underlying Top-Line
Growth and Bottom-Line Results

1. ITT Corporation Annual Report, 1978, 1.

2. Shares outstanding were taken from ITT Annual Report 1994, 1985 and General Electric Annual Report, 1994, 1979. Stock prices were taken from "The Dow Jones Daily Stock Price Record." October/November/December 1994, 1978.

3. In June of 1995, the "old" ITT (Geneen's ITT) split into three separate companies–ITT Hartford (insurance), ITT Industries (ranging from car parts to defense electronics), and the "new" ITT Corporation (hotels, entertainment, and information services). Araskog continued to preside over the "new" ITT, which came to include such well known businesses as Sheraton Hotels and Caesar's. In January of 1997, Hilton Hotels launched a hostile takeover bid of the "new" ITT. Araskog tried to block the takeover by further splitting his company, but efforts were blocked by a federal court. Hilton, however, did not win the takeover battle; it was outbid by Starwood Lodging. In November of 1997, Starwood swallowed the "new" ITT for a price of $13.7 billion. (Sources: "ITT's Latest Break-Up: Three into Three." *The Economist,* July 19, 1997, 54; Picker, Ida. "Saying Goodbye to ITT." *Institutional Investor,* January 1998, 91.)

4. Economic Value Added is a Registered Trade Mark of Stern Stewart.

5. Coca-Cola Annual Report, 1996, 15.

6. General Electric Annual Report, 1996, 5.

7. General Electric Annual Report, 1997, 2–6, 33.

8. Gilyard, Bill. "Executive of the Year." *Corporate Business Minnesota,* January 1998, 34.

9. For a more detailed discussion, see the article by Eisenhardt, Katherine and Brown, Shona. "Time Pacing: Competing in Markets That Won't Stand Still." *Harvard Business Review,* March/April 1998, 59.

10. United Stated Bureau of Labor Statistics, May 20, 1998.

11. The revenue growth was calculated as an annualized rate. ROE was determined by averaging the year-end ROEs from 1974–1997. (Sources: Wal-Mart Annual Reports, 1997, 22; 1988, 14; 1979, 12.)

12. Calculated over the past six years. (Source: Wal-Mart Annual Report 1997, 22.)

13. McWilliams, Gary. "Whirlwind on the Web." April 7, 1997, 134.

14. McWilliams, 132.

15. *Dow Jones News Wire,* December 11, 1997.

16. Bray, Hiawatha. "Dell Computer Chief Sees No Slack in Demand." *The Boston Globe,* April 10, 1998, C2.

17. McWilliams, 134.

18. Don't confuse building to order with the tricks often euphemistically called accounts receivable management, stretching working capital by delaying payments to suppliers, a begger-thy-neighbor game. With building to order, customers pay sooner—and gladly, because they're getting their orders filled sooner. The benefits flow through the entire chain, ensuring that the supplier too can be paid sooner than he would otherwise.

19. Kirkpatrick, David. "Houston, We Have Some Problems." FORTUNE, June 23, 1997, 102.

20. Dell Annual Report, 1997, 21.

21. Based on total shipments, the standard for the industry, the growth rate was calculated to be 16%. (Source: Taylor, Paul. "The World PC Market." *Financial Times,* March 4, 1998, 4.)

22. Dell Annual Report, 1997, 21.

23. International Data Corporation, May 6, 1998.

24. Serwer, Andy. "Michael Dell Rocks." FORTUNE, May 11, 1998, 51; "Compaq Retains Lead as PC Sales Soar." *New York Times,* July 28, 1997, D2.

25. Silverman, Dwight. "Compaq Reclaims No. 1 Rank in Business Sales." *The Houston Chronicle,* December 9, 1997, 1.

26. Dell Annual Report, 1998, 28.

27. "The FORTUNE 500," FORTUNE, April 27, 1998, F-30.

28. Lear Public Relations Department, May 20, 1998.

29. Lear Corporation Annual Report, 1997, 27; 1986, 6, 32.

30. Lear Corporation Operations Data Table, available at www.lear.com, Investor Information, Financial Documents.

31. American Standard Annual Report, 1997, 3.

32. American Standard Annual Report, 1996, 2; 1991, 14.

33. Tully, Shawn. "Prophet of Zero Working Capital." FORTUNE, June 13, 1994, 113.

34. General Electric Annual Report, 1997, 40.

35. The margin improvement translates into earnings per share of roughly 60 cents pretax ($700 million divided by 1.2 billion shares), which in turn translates into roughly 36 cents per share after tax. If successful, it will create significant value for Ford's stockholders. At Ford's p/e ratio of roughly 10, the improvement would add some $3.60 per share to the price of its stock, currently (April 1998) around $46.

36. Coca-Cola Annual Report, 1996, 48. PepsiCo 10-K, 1996, F-44.

37. Coca-Cola Public Relations Department, May 1, 1998.

38. Return on total capital was 14.5 percent in 1987, and rose only slightly to 18 percent in 1997. (Source: Value Line Investment Survey, February 13, 1998.)

39. Value Line Investment Survey, February 13, 1998.

40. After Fisher was named CEO, the stock increased $5.675 to $62.25 in three days. (Source: Holusha, John. "Kodak Chief Offers a New Vision." *The New York Times,* October 29, 1993, D1.)

41. "Blue-chip Firms Report Profits for 3rd Quarter." *San Diego Union-Tribune,* October 15, 1997, C1.

42. Canedy, Dana. "Sunbeam's Board, in Revolt, Ousts Job-Cutting Chairman." *The New York Times,* June 16, 1998, 1.

Chapter 4   Strategy from the Outside In

1. "The Future That Has Already Happened." *Harvard Business Review,* September/October 1997, 22.

2. From 1987–1995. (Source: "Most Admired Companies." February 1992, 1993, 1994, 1995.)

3. Between 1990 and 1995, sales grew at an annualized rate of 3.5%. (Source: 3M Annual Report, 1997, 46.)

4. (Source: "Taco Bell 1994." Harvard Business School. 9-694-076. Revised July 13, 1995.) Alas, this was the high point. Taco Bell introduced several new initiatives over the next two years, most of which produced mediocre results. Among them was the introduction of the health oriented "Border Lites" line. The line alienated some core customers who weren't after health food, but value. Taco Bell shied away from providing this value its core customer base had come to desire, and upon which it had driven its growth and made its name in the fiercely competitive fast food business. Taco Bell paid the price—sales declined in both 1995 and 1996, and it has been struggling to get back on track ever since. (Source:

Kramer, Louise. "Taco Bell Looks to Boost Sales with Full-Menu Upgrade Plan." *Nation's Restaurant News,* February 10, 1997, 1.)

5. Nike Annual Report, 1987, 16.

6. Low, Kathleen. "Nike Reports Quarter, Annual Profit Plunges." *Footwear News,* July 30, 1984, 2.

7. By 1987, Nike's market share was 18.6 percent. (Source: Schnorbus, Paula. "Running on Air." *Marketing and Media Decisions.* March 1988, 55.)

8. Willigan, Geraldine. "High Performance Marketing: An Interview with Phil Knight." July/August 1992, 96.

9. Willigan, 96.

10. Willigan, 98.

11. Nike Annual Report, 1997, 42.

12. Himelstein, Linda. "The Swoosh Heard 'Round the World." *Business Week,* May 12, 1997, 76.

13. Saporito, Bill. "Can Nike Get Unstuck?" March 30, 1998, 48.

14. The pond is the sum of the total markets: athletic footwear ($18.5 billion), athletic equipment ($40 billion) and athletic apparel ($36 billion). These markets total $94.5 billion. With a conservative estimate of the contract management market and other sports related industries of $6 billion, Nikes' total pond is $100 billion. The Company's current revenues total $9.2 billion, giving them an approximate market share of 9%. Sources: Dow Jones Company Report, July 1997; "Nike Studying Strategies for Long-Term Success ..." *The News Tribune,* August 10, 1997, A12; Nike Annual Report, 1997, 42.

15. Saporito, 48.

16. All quotes by John Trani in this section are taken from an interview with Noel Tichy and Charles Burck, November 1996.

17. General Electric Annual Report, 1997, 33.

18. General Electric Public Relations Department, May 22, 1998.

19. "America's Most Successful Entrepreneur." FORTUNE, October 27, 1986, front cover.

20. Wood also neglected the concept of velocity, which Walton used so effectively (Chapter 3). Again, identifying the need is only part of what it takes to create profitable balanced growth; the business basics must be right, too.

21. In 1997, Target represented 73.4 percent of Dayton-Hudson's revenue. (Source: Dayton-Hudson 10-K 1998.)

22. Dayton-Hudson Annual Report, 1984, 24.

23. Dayton-Hudson 10-K 1998.

24. Value Line Investment Survey, February 13, 1998.

25. "Hitting Up the Internet." *Wall Street Journal,* April 10, 1998, A10; AT&T Annual Report, 1997, 43.

26. Early in 1998, responding to the rising threat from such internet service providers as IDT and Qwest, AT&T was planning to introduce its own internet voice service. "The big carriers are waking up. AT&T, Sprint, DT [Deutsche Telekom], and others—not upstart ISPs—are positioning to capture revenue migration to internet phone service," said Forrester research in a February 13 report. But, added Forrester, "they are in for a profit squeeze as prices cascade downward."

27. Interview with Noel Tichy and Eli Cohen, March 1996.

28. To be more precise, U.S. unit sales in 1986 were 99,134 units and fell to 58,868 by 1991. (Source: "100 Year Almanac: The Sales Statistics." *Automotive News,* April 24, 1996, 120–122.)

29. The radical $18,000 A-class subcompact introduced in 1997 may take its place on the list too, but its initial luster was dimmed by handling problems that required substantial redesign. (Source: Maynard, Micheline. "Benz to Consider Partner Venture to Create Lower-Price Brand." *USA Today,* January 5, 1998, 1B.)

30. Lienert, Anita. "Crowning Touch." *Chicago Tribune,* February 12, 1998, W3.

31. Gramig, Mickey. "Atlanta Based Coca-Cola Falls Shy of Wall Street Forecast." *Atlanta Journal and Constitution,* January 30, 1998, 1.

32. "Earnings; Coca-Cola Profit Rises 8.6%." *Los Angeles Times,* April 16, 1998, D13.

33. Motorola Annual Report, 1997, available at *www.mot.com;* Inside Motorola, Annual Report.

34. Bower, Joseph; Christensen, Clayton. "Disruptive Technologies: Catching the Wave." *Harvard Business Review,* January/February 1995, 48.

35. Bower and Christensen, 48. But here is another success that did not last forever. In 1997, Seagate acquired Conner.

36. *Manufacturing USA 5th Edition,* Volume 1. (New York: Gale Research Publications, 1996), 768.

37. *Business Ranking Annual.* (Brooklyn, New York: Gale Research Publications, 1998), 256.

38. "Praxair Cuts Jobs, Buys Back Stock." *Chemical Week,* December 24, 1997, 3.

39. Interview with Ram Charan and Charles Burck, August 1997.

40. All quotes by Bob Nardelli in this section are taken from an interview with Ram Charan, January 1998.

41. All quotes by Frank Blake in this chapter are taken from an interview with Ram Charan, January 1998.

42. Kirkpatrick, David. "The Revolution at Compaq Computer." FORTUNE, December 14, 1992, 81.

Chapter 5   How John Reed Turned Citibank Outside In

1. "1996 Annual Awards for Excellence." *Euromoney,* July 1996, 54.

2. Fromson, Brett. "For Citicorp's Reed, It's a Dicey Board Game." *Washington Post,* September 13, 1992, H1.

3. Loomis, Carol. "John Reed's Second Act." FORTUNE, April 29, 1996, 88.

4. Bloomberg Financial Markets: Price/Earnings Chart (Citicorp).

5. Bloomberg Financial Markets: Price/Earnings Chart (Standard & Poor's).

6. Hannon, Kerry. "New Bullishness on Bank Stocks." *U.S. News and World Report,* December 19, 1994, 78.

7. All quotes by Ed Holmes in this chapter are taken from an interview with Charles Burck, January 1998.

8. Articulated by Ed Holmes in his interview with Charles Burck.

9. All quotes by Robert McCormack in this chapter were taken from an interview with Ram Charan and Charles Burck, October 1995 and an interview with Charles Burck, April 1998.

10. All company specific information not contained in direct quotes was provided by Citicorp, May 1998.

Chapter 6   Eckhard Pfeiffer: The Methodical Radical of Compaq

1. McWilliams, Gary. "Compaq: All Things to All Networks." *Business Week,* July 31, 1995, 79.

2. Compaq Annual Report, 1995, 24–25.

3. McWilliams, 79.

4. Compaq Annual Report, 1995, 16.

5. Compaq Annual Report, 1997, available at *www.compaq.com*

6. Source: Value Line Investment Survey, January 23, 1998.

7. Hof, Robert. "Power Play." *Business Week,* February 9, 1998, 97.

8. The stock reached its peak on September 22, 1997. All prices and percentages account for stock splits. (Source: Bloomberg Financial Markets: Average Price Line Graph.)

9. Compaq Annual Report, 1996, 15. Other company specific information was provided by Compaq, May 1998.

10. All quotes by Eckhard Pfeiffer in this chapter are taken from an interview with Noel Tichy and Eli Cohen, March 1996 and an interview with Ram Charan, Noel Tichy, Charles Burck and Brian Dumaine, June 1996.

11. Kirkpatrick, David. "Fast Times at Compaq." FORTUNE, April 1, 1996, 120.

12. Value Line Investment Survey, January 23, 1998.

13. Hewlett-Packard Annual Report, 1997, available at *www.hp.com*, March 1998.

14. Akers predicted in 1985 that 1984 revenues of $48 billion would quadruple by the year 2000. Revenues stagnated through the late eighties and fell in the early nineties. IBM is far from its goal; Revenues were only $78.5 billion in 1997. (Sources: "The Worst Could Be Over for IBM." *Business Week*, October 28, 1985, 33. IBM Annual Reports, 1997, 1994, 1991, 1988.)

15. The two acquisitions in 1995 were Networth, Inc., a developer of computing network products and Thomas Conrad Corp., a company specializing in information networks. The combined total value was $241 million. (Sources: "Merger Monday." *The Des Moines Register*, November 7, 1995, 10. "Compaq to Acquire Thomas Conrad." *AFX News*, October 18, 1995. Compaq Annual Report, 1995, 3.)

Chapter 7 John Trani and the New Frontier of Service at GE Medical

1. All company specific information not contained in direct quotes was provided by GE Medical Systems, May 1998.

2. U.S. Department of Commerce, May 26, 1998.

3. All quotes by John Trani in this chapter are taken from an interview with Noel Tichy and Charles Burck, November 1996.

4. All quotes by Tom Dunham in this chapter are taken from an interview with Noel Tichy and Charles Burck, January 1997.

5. General Electric Annual Report, 1997.

6. Stanley Works Annual Report, 1997, 25–26.

7. This and all subsequent quotes are from Stanley Works Annual Report, 1997.

Chapter 8   GE Capital Services: Capitalizing on Change
1. General Electric Annual Report, 1997, 45; 1983, 43.
2. Curran, John. "GE Capital: Jack Welch's Secret Weapon." FORTUNE, November 11, 1997, 116.
3. General Electric Annual Report, 1997, 1995.
4. Curran, 116.
5. Prudential Securities Analyst Report, December 24, 1997, 2.
6. Ashkenas, Ronald; DeMonaco, Lawrence; Francis, Suzanne. "Making the Deal Real: How GE Capital Integrates Acquisitions." *Harvard Business Review,* January/February 1998, 166.
7. Curran, 116.
8. Ashkenas, et al., 166.
9. Prudential Securities Analyst Report, December 24, 1997, 5.
10. All quotes by Gary Wendt in this chapter are taken from an interview with Noel Tichy and Eli Cohen, March 1996 and an interview with Noel Tichy, Ram Charan, and Charles Burck, July 1996.
11. GE Internal Presentation, Crotonville, May 1996.
12. Monroe, Ann. "Delay in Settling Tax Benefits Seen Aiding Leasing Industry." *The Wall Street Journal,* July 7, 1984.
13. Prudential Securities Analyst Report, December 24, 1997, 14.
14. Available at www.penske.com.
15. GE Internal Presentation, Crotonville, May 1996.
16. Prudential Security Analyst Report, December 24, 1997, 2.

Chapter 9   The Genetic Code and How to Change It
1. "Growth: How to Get It." By Gary Wendt, Internal Presentation, 1996.
2. The situation went on for three more years, until pressure from investors finally forced the board to take action. In public humiliation, the CEO was fired. The man they replaced him with was from an entirely different industry and brought in other new genes.
3. Interview with Charles Burck, January 1998.
4. Huey, John. "In Search of Roberto's Secret Formula." FORTUNE, December 29, 1997, 230.
5. Jackson, Tony. "Creating a Common Set of Values." *Financial Times,* June 5, 1997, 16.

6. From Mastering Revolutionary Change, a FORTUNE video series by Noel Tichy and Stratford Sherman, Video Publishing House, 1994.

7. "Wal-Mart Stores' Operations." Harvard Business School Case, 9-387-018, 1986.

8. Interview with Charles Burck, August 1996.

9. GE Internal Presentation, Crotonville, May 1995. All subsequent quotes by Gary Wendt in this chapter are taken from the same presentation.

10. All quotes by Eckhard Pfeiffer in this chapter are taken from interviews with Noel Tichy and Eli Cohen, March 1996 and with Ram Charan, Noel Tichy, Charlie Burck, Brian Dumaine, June 1996.

11. Kirkpatrick, David. "Fast Times at Compaq." FORTUNE, April 1, 1996, 120.

12. Interview with Noel Tichy and Eli Cohen, March 1996.

13. Interview with Noel Tichy and Eli Cohen, March 1996.

Chapter 10   Rewriting the Genetic Code at AlliedSignal

1. All quotes by Dan Burnham in this chapter are from an interview with Charles Burck and Eli Cohen, January 1996, and an interview with Charles Burck, April 1996.

2. AlliedSignal Annual Report, 1993, 24. AlliedSignal 10-K 1997, 1.

3. "FORTUNE's Most Admired Companies." February 1998, 1990.

4. The market value is based upon 1991 sales of aircraft engines and parts to the military and civil sector. (Source: *Aerospace Facts and Figures* [Washington, D.C.: Aerospace Industries Association of America, 1997], 15.)

5. This number is based upon 1996 sales of aircraft engines and parts, as well as products and services related to the aerospace industry and maintenance of commercial airlines. (Sources: *Aerospace Facts and Figures*, 15, 28. *Aviation and Aerospace Almanac* [New York: Aviation Week Group, 1997], 126.)

6. Bloomberg Financial Markets: Historical Price Analysis.

7. AlliedSignal 10-K 1997, 1.

8. Charan, Ram and Tichy, Noel. "CEO as Coach: An Interview with AlliedSignal's Larry Bossidy." *Harvard Business Review,* March/April 1995, 69. All quotes by Larry Bossidy in this chapter are taken from this article.

9. All quotes by Greg Summe in this chapter are taken from an interview with Charles Burck and Eli Cohen, February 1996 and an interview with Charles Burck, April 1996.

10. All quotes by Joe Leonard in this chapter are taken from an interview with Charles Burck, April 1996.

11. Interview with Charles Burck, April 1996.

12. All quotes in this chapter by Haluk Durodogan in this chapter are taken from an interview with Charles Burck, April 1996.

13. New York: Doubleday, 1993, 364.

Chapter 11 Reynolds and Reynolds: Creating Lifelong Customers

1. All quotes by Dave Holmes are taken from interviews with Charles Burck, October 1995 and August 1997.

2. Revenues for 1991 totaled $632 million. Return on equity was 9.9 percent, down from 11.4 percent the previous year. (Source: Reynolds and Reynolds Annual Report, 1992, 19–20).

3. Reynolds and Reynolds Annual Reports, 1997, available at *www.reyrey.com*, 1992, 19.

4. The stock price at year-end 1990 was $2\frac{1}{32}$. It reached its peak in February 1997 and fell to $15\frac{3}{4}$ by the end of June 1997. (Source: Bloomberg Financial Markets: Historical Price Analysis.)

5. All quotes by Tom Momchilov in this chapter are from interviews with Charles Burck, October 1995 and August 1997.

6. All quotes by Rod Hedeen in this chapter are taken from an interview with Charles Burck, August 1997.

7. Interview with Charles Burck, October 1995.

8. All quotes by Mona Yezbak in this chapter are taken from interviews with Charles Burck, October 1995 and August 1997.

9. All quotes by Joe Bausman are taken from an interview with Charles Burck, October 1995.

10. Interview with Charles Burck, October 1995.

11. Interview with Charles Burck, October 1995.

Chapter 12 Can You Pass the Father Cunningham Test?

1. Father William Cunningham, acceptance speech at the University of Michigan Business Leadership Awards, 1992.

2. All information specific to Focus: HOPE not contained in direct quotes or otherwise footnoted was provided by the organization in May 1998.

3. Noel Tichy, Andrew McGill, Lynda St. Clair, editors. *Corporate Global Citizenship*. (San Francisco: The New Lexington Press, 1997), 350.

4. Cunningham, 1992.

Handbook

1. Vladimir Pucik, Noel M. Tichy, and Carole K. Barnett, editors. *Globalizing Management: Creating and Leading the Competitive Organization* (New York: John Wiley & Sons, 1993), 50.

2. Pucik, 52.

3. Pucik, 59.

4. In 1997, ServiceMaster had operating revenues of $3.96 billion, net income of $163.47 million, and over 45,000 employees. It is in a variety of service businesses, including such well-known names as TruGreen-ChemLawn, Terminix, and Merry Maids among a host of others (Source: ServiceMaster Annual Report, 1997).

I N D E X